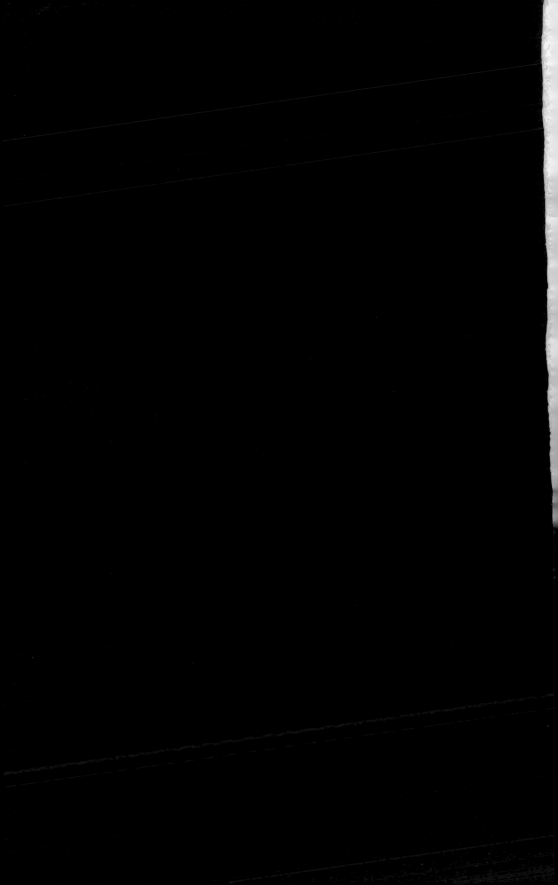

THE
PITS

THE
PITS

The Real World of Formula One

BEVERLEY TURNER

ATLANTIC BOOKS
LONDON

First published in hardback and trade paperback in Great Britain in 2004
by Atlantic Books, an imprint of Grove Atlantic Ltd

1 3 5 7 9 8 6 4 2

A CIP catalogue record for this book is available from the British Library.

Hardback edition 1 84354 237 4
Trade Paperback edition 1 84354 325 7

Printed in Great Britain by MPG Books Ltd, Bodmin, Cornwall

Atlantic Books
An imprint of Grove Atlantic Ltd
Ormond House
26–27 Boswell Street
London
WC1N 3JZ

To my parents for their unconditional support and tireless babysitting, my husband for his love and encouragement, and my baby boy for sleeping in the garden.

Contents

Illustrations

The author and publishers are grateful to the following for permission to reproduce images: 2, LAT Photographic; 1, 3, 4, 8, 11, 12, 13, 14, 15, 16, Sutton Images. All other images are from the author's own collection.

Acknowledgements

I would like to thank Dr Louisa Joyner for her ideas, her friendship and for believing I could write this book. Toby Mundy, I am so grateful for your time, patience, legal brilliance and tolerance of my stationery fetish. Thanks to Bonnie Chiang – the calmest person I know. Thanks to my parents-in-law for hours of faultless childcare and unparalleled Sunday lunches. Louise – my great friend and Croyde's most entertaining aunty. Thanks to Cal for brilliant big sister support. Adrian – bro, you've been an inspiration and an awesome babysitter; now get your own book written. Thanks to everybody who gave me time to work: Kate Charman, Kath Wild, Aunty Nora, Patty Divine, Frankie and Sue Ross, Phil and Eddie, Sarah Hadlow (what would I have done without you?). Natasha Clark – thanks for hanging in there. Tif Loehnis – you're the best; thanks for all your professional wisdom (and mummy advice). Many thanks to the irrepressible Will Buxton. I am also indebted to Brian Barwick, Matt Franey, Kevin Garside, Jim Rosenthal, Nova, Tom Clarkson, Bob McEnzie, Sutton Motorsport, Simon Taylor, Andy Spellman, Mark Cross, Rebecca Hobbs, Scrubber and Professor Richard Mislokci of São Paulo University. A big thank you to Hugh Mantle, OBE, Senior Lecturer at Liverpool John Moore's University. To my girls, for keeping me sane: Lisa Moody, Charlotte Thomas, Sarah Fox, Waveney Thomson, Jane Bristow, Zofia Fielding, Rebecca Healey, Rachel Roome. I would also like to acknowledge Terry Lovell's *Bernie's Game*, Phil Shirley's *Deadly Obsessions*, Professor Sid Watkins's *Beyond the Limit*, Murray Walker's *Unless I'm Very Much Mistaken*, Bruce Jones's *50 Years of Formula One*, and the *Daily Telegraph*'s *The Formula One Years*.

CHAPTER 1

Melbourne

I was willing myself to stay conscious as the world hurtled by, imagining the indignity of removing my helmet to reveal a fireproof balaclava full of vomit.

All morning I'd been told how lucky I was to be taking a trip in a real-life F1 car, driven by a real-life F1 driver. I recalled those words as we mounted the kerb yet again and I concentrated on my breathing like a woman in labour.

In truth, the first lap had been OK – once we had finally left the garage. A crash on the track was being cleared and I had no choice but to wait, buckled in, trapped, picturing bloody limbs strewn across the Donington tarmac.

My pilot for this flight was Damon Hill, though I could not actually see him. The dimensions of a two-seater F1 car restrict your vision to the back of the seat in front and about two inches either side. If you're really brave, you might risk turning your g-force-pressured head sideways to see what the world looks like at 170 mph.

The Minardi team organizing the corporate day had looked after me and their other guests very well. I'd had a medical from a kindly doctor who warned me not to eat and drink too much before my adventure, and I'd been dressed in several layers of seriously unflattering racing attire. But waiting in the car I had time to analyse how the sensory deprivation felt: I was hot, mute, deaf and (not to put too fine a point on it) shit-scared.

The earplugs and helmet gave the garage a nightmarish quality. I couldn't hear a word anyone said and they couldn't hear me. What if they were telling me the back of the car was on fire as I nodded back smiling? And the pressure of the seat belts on my chest was almost unbearable. I'd spent the morning worrying about the eye-popping speed and here I was fighting off the rising panic of claustrophobia. But just as these thoughts raced around my head, the mechanics got word that our time had come and we sped off into the sunlight and the fairground rush of physical acceleration.

Damon ran a smooth lap and I let out an involuntary yelp of excitement. I happily obliged the TV camera awaiting my enthusiastic response, announcing that it had been 'Fantastic! Amazing! Brilliant!' or something similarly insightful. I had hoped that ITV had all the pictures it needed, but unfortunately that was only the demonstration lap.

All the other passengers climbed out, handed over their seats to paying customers and went to watch the race in the grandstand. But not me. I was entered in the main event. Great.

Frankly, it was just nice to be out of the car and regain the use of my lungs. I hadn't paid the requisite £30,000 to have Damon Hill as my driver for the race, so as an excited businessman climbed in with Hill I was introduced to my next high-speed chauffeur.

Belgian David Saelens was a swaggering Minardi test driver whose Zorro-like countenance filled me with dread. This wasn't helped when his protests that the car was badly backfiring were dismissed by the Italian mechanics buckling us in: 'Is OK ... Too late now ... People they pay much money.' Oh God.

My gloved fingertips fumbled about looking for the red emergency button on the end of a black wire – it lit a bulb on the dashboard, which, if it went out, signalled to the driver that I had fainted or died. The mechanics worked out the meaning of my excited gesticulations and shrugged, 'Ah ... thiz car, it appear no have one.'

I felt like a punter waiting for a fairground ride to begin. My seat belt wasn't secure, my helmet was loose and if I expired no one would know until after the race.

I spent ten laps holding on to my chinstrap with one finger, trying to resist the g-force braking, which threw me six inches out of my seat at every turn. And I realized why Saelens is a test driver. He launched at every kerb as if we were in a beach buggy, as car after car left our backfiring, spluttering wreck in its wake.

Eventually I lost count of the laps and gave up smiling for the tiny TV camera attached to the wing. This was no time for theatricals. Every neural synapse was sparking under the pressure to stay conscious. And there was no escape. Round and round we went, the pit lane drawing tantalizingly close, then disappearing again as we sped by. I couldn't believe how long it seemed to be taking. I closed my eyes and began to hum.

Finally, after the longest twenty minutes of my life, I felt the car lurch to the left and begin to slow down. After all that, we still came last. But the nightmare wasn't over yet. I swore under my breath as I spotted the TV camera waiting for my reaction. Now I had to try and articulate my experience to an audience of F1 fans.

I was unbuckled and hoisted out of the tiny seat, struggling with shaky fingers to unfasten my helmet strap. At least it wasn't a live broadcast. This would need some snappy editing. I pulled off my balaclava and the cameraman flinched. My face was ghostly white, eyes ringed with black, mascara smudged on sweat-soaked skin. My mouth was dry and I feared that at any moment I would reveal more than just my deepest thoughts on television. My stomach churned while a camera was pushed in my face, ready to record my joy.

Every cell in my body had been put through a blender. The vibrations and the g-force had given rise to an instant hangover – one in which the world continues to swim around you when you sit still. I tried to look thrilled, but it wasn't very convincing. The other passenger suffering similarly undignified symptoms was the boxer Chris Eubank – and he's used to having his head knocked about.

I made an effort to join in the champagne presentation, but my legs were clearly not up to celebrating. Concerned officials led me to the medical centre and laid me on a couch. I vaguely recall a white-haired lady taking off her silk scarf, running it under the tap and cooling my brow. (Although looking back, that seems far too romantic, so maybe it was a hallucination.) There were some angry, hushed whispers that I'd been in the car too long and the doctors concluded I was dehydrated with low blood sugar.

I wasn't allowed to drive myself home; I had to sip lots of water, endure sympathy from people who were secretly sniggering and Minardi weren't at all interested in my feedback on the technical set-up of the car. The only thing that had been tested was my ability to keep the contents of my stomach to myself.

I gained a whole new respect for F1 drivers. I always knew they must be slightly mad to do what they do, but I had no idea about the physical stresses involved. G-force isn't something any of us can experience on a regular basis and my thumping head confirmed it wasn't something I wanted to grow accustomed to.

In 2003 Formula One racing will be fifty-three years old. It currently comprises ten teams and twenty drivers, attending sixteen races across five continents between March and October. At its most elemental, F1 is a bunch of people spending as much money as possible to make their car go round a track faster than anyone else's. But equally fundamentally, it is an expensive, influential global stage for some very powerful automobile multinationals.

The price of failure is high – financial pain and public humiliation await the losers. But success on the track guarantees global marketing and cohesive brand-building. When Michael Schumacher holds aloft a trophy, he is selling the reliability, speed and precision of a Ferrari. When the Mercedes team engineer a car that drives seventy laps at more than 150 mph without breaking down, the consumer can walk into a showroom on the high street and buy into that dependability. Expensive advertising campaigns boast of Toyota's F1 association; Honda pride themselves on supplying engines to F1 teams and (some might say) BMW drivers act as if they own the road because they think they are Juan Pablo Montoya. The brand cachet of BMW, Mercedes and Ferrari is directly related to their F1 glory, because Formula One is the zenith of motor engine technology.

For some fans, the life of a racing driver has always represented the ultimate wish fulfillment. With the advent of F1 in the fifties, these men were instantly more than just good drivers. They possessed a greater mystique, born of their willingness to face death; their romantic belief in Fate, which seemed then to be an extension of wartime bravery. Alberto Ascari, Juan Manuel Fangio, Giuseppe 'Nino' Farina and Stirling Moss represented post-war extravagance and glamour in refreshing contrast to wartime austerity.

It's true that some critics expressed contempt for the frivolity of these young men, when so many lives had recently been lost in the war, but the world was hungry for new sporting heroes and for the

British fans Stirling Moss in particular took to that role with ease. He won sixteen F1 races between 1951 and 1961, but failed to win a championship. Nevertheless, he is an F1 legend, intrinsic to a glorious age of motor racing and now fills his diary with after-dinner speaking engagements.

But it was in the sixties and seventies that Formula One became synonymous with a distinctive type of wealth and glamour. The arrival of sponsorship money changed the nature of the sport overnight. Cars no longer raced in national colours, but sported the backers' liveries. New teams joined the party as the Ford Cosworth DFV engine became available to anyone with £7,500 to spare. The cars got faster due to bigger engines, down-force enhancing wings and later aerodynamic developments.

But the vehicles were pretty much the same, so this placed all the value on driver skill. They began to be used by sponsors for promotional activities and TV appearances, morphing from motor-sport competitors into famous 'personalities'. Colour photography and TV coverage breathed life into the sport and its drivers began to enjoy lifestyles that were the envy of men worldwide.

Graham Hill – the father of 1996 champion Damon – won the Monaco Grand Prix five times between 1958 and 1975 and epitomized the fast-living, charming Formula One star. With his slicked-back hair, clipped moustache and debonair wit he was the life and soul of any party. In a statement that would be echoed by drivers down the years, he claimed that meeting death during a race would mean 'simply that I have been asked to pay the bill for the happiness of my life'.

And then came James Hunt – for many British fans still the ultimate F1 'character'. An outspoken public schoolboy with indestructible confidence and a fecklessness that manifested itself in heavy drinking, smoking, gambling and womanizing. The photo libraries are full of Hunt striding manfully in his racing suit, an athletic figure with surfer's hair and strong hands. He can often be seen drawing on a cigarette, clutching a beer, surrounded by women smiling coyly under *Charlie's Angels*-style hair. James Hunt lost his wife to the actor Richard Burton in a very public split, but he was philosophical about this intrusion into his life.

'Limelight's a danger and so is wealth,' he said. 'It's like giving a dog a big juicy bone. When he didn't have one he could live without it, but once he's tasted one, he hangs on like grim death.'

In order to cling to that limelight Hunt took a position in the BBC commentary box with Murray Walker. On their first broadcast together, a drunken stunt on a snowboard meant that Hunt had to commentate from the floor with his leg in plaster. As the race – the International Trophy at Silverstone – concluded, Walker turned to Hunt for his reaction to the events.

'What a load of rubbish!' said Hunt, with an honesty that is all too rare in the sport.

On their second attempt, James turned up barefoot, unshaven, wearing frayed jeans and carrying a bottle of wine. He would freely express his thoughts about other drivers, not always restricting himself to their professional abilities (he called mid-grid, seventies' driver Jean-Pierre Jarier 'a French Wally: always has been and always will be'.)

Icons such as James Hunt, along with the later figures of Nelson Piquet, Alain Prost, Nigel Mansell, Damon Hill and Ayrton Senna have played a leading role in expanding the appeal of Formula One. Football teams have eleven players on the pitch and five on the bench during any game. That's thirty-two men to watch during a single match. There are twenty teams in the British Premier League alone. That's a minimum of 320 top-level players to support and identify with in any season. Of course, football fans master this system with relative ease, choosing to align themselves with those who score the most goals, or stop others from scoring the most goals. But in Formula One the selection process is even easier.

At the time of writing, there are just twenty drivers and only ten teams to pledge allegiance to – down from sixteen teams and thirty-two drivers in 1989. Followers of Formula One can therefore choose a favourite driver in a short space of time, after watching only a few races. With so few participants, there is plenty of attention to go round and F1 drivers tend not to shy away from the media glare. Today's drivers might not be the same hedonistic playboys of former decades, but they are still presented to the public as powerful, masculine figures with enormous personal wealth earned by living on adrenalin and risking their lives in the pursuit of sporting glory. They are modern-day knights in shining carbon.

Of course, my own ill-fated ride in an F1 car had been merely a marketing exercise during the off-season. The serious business of tyre-, chassis- and engine-testing had been quietly taking place all over the world. And now, after five months of refining their racing cars, the teams were back on the grid. The F1 circus was about to hit the road once again.

*

Arguably the world's best F1 venue and home to many of its staunchest fans, Melbourne is a fitting location for the first Grand Prix. It launches the season with a fanfare that must bring a glow to Bernie Ecclestone's little cheeks. Australia is arguably the sporting capital of the world; a place where sport is about the brute force of the rugby player, the grace of the lone swimmer, the exertion of the rower and the courage of the surfer, harnessing nature's gifts in search of the perfect wave.

Australian sport seems to possess a simple physicality, a humanity even, that is at odds with the essential characteristics of Formula One: science, technology, engineering, hours spent formulating designs; the ear-melting roar of the engines, the exhaust fumes, garages, petrol and the burning brakes. Australians grow up blessed with the great outdoors, a cricket pitch close to hand, football fields available to the young and keen, athletics tracks at every school and an Olympic pool in almost every town. But it is undeniable: Aussies love their motor sport. Formula One is a religion to many Australians and Melbourne is the ritualistic start to their year of devotion.

From Thursday the 6th to Sunday the 9th of March, Melbourne's Albert Park would encompass everything that is great about Formula One: the unpredictability, the promise of competition and the palpable camaraderie. This was 'back to school', F1-style. Team personnel went about their daily tasks in new uniforms and shiny shoes. The Jaguar team wore black combat trousers and bright white shirts; the Jordan team appeared to be sporting cycling-inspired pumps and shiny black and yellow Lycra (which would have been very unforgiving, if the women weren't all so super-slim). Everything felt new and resplendent under the Australian sun.

The score sheet was blank, untainted by controversial tactics or depressed by one team's domination. The season's fatality rate stood at zero and animosity between the drivers remained a media creation, spun by publicists in exchange for column inches – a game as real as the sport itself.

Throughout the city there was a buzz that extended well beyond the high-pitched, distant wail that emanated eerily from Albert Park. The cars were out on the track to fire up their engines and Melbourne's residents were doing their own preparations. All across town, bars and restaurants boasted F1 SPECIALS, the daily papers devoted heavy slabs of their sports supplements to the imminent Grand Prix and morning TV hosts anchored themselves in the city's biggest park. 'We're coming to you live from the site where this weekend the world will descend on Melbourne,' they beamed proudly as sun rose nonchalantly in the background.

Although it was the start of my third year working in the esoteric world of elite motor racing, it was my first visit to the Australian Grand Prix, and I was keen to know what all the fuss was about.

Adelaide had been the home of Australian Formula One until it was wrested away in 1996. Today the premier of Victoria, Steve Bracks, boasts that his state benefits to the tune of A$130 million (£54.1 million) by hosting the Grand Prix and claims that 30 per cent of the 400,000 spectators expected to attend are from interstate and overseas.

For one weekend Melbourne would be the focus of attention, rather than being Sydney's poor relation. Writing in the official race programme, Ron Walker, Chairman of the Australian Grand Prix Corporation, stresses that 'hundreds of millions of international tele-vision viewers are treated to spectacular pictures of the lakeside circuit and the surrounds.' For Melbourne, the Grand Prix is a four-day inter-national press and TV advertising campaign. Not that the fans bedecked in trainers and rucksacks trudging to the circuit care about that.

No other Formula One host city caters for spectators like Melbourne. Free shuttle trams run every one-to-four minutes from the city to the track. That's one-to-four minutes. For free! Imagine that at Silverstone.

The circuit is located within the impressive surroundings of Albert Park, a 225-hectare recreational ground, home to the Melbourne Aquatic Centre, a five-kilometre lake and an eighteen-hole golf course. The title sponsor ensures that no spectator at the officially named Foster's Grand Prix need walk more than a few steps to the next bottle of beer.

The circuit is flanked by the city on one side and the beach on the other. To the north is the eclectic, vibrant honeycomb of lanes that extend into the suburbs to house the city's three million inhabitants. Less than a quarter of a mile to the south of Albert Park is the beach: the lazy sands of Port Philip dotted with ocean-front cafés and two-storey restaurants offering excellent local wines alongside sophisticated Asian-fusion food, all served with a complimentary sunset.

The location of the Albert Park track is simply unparalleled. Silverstone might offer motor-racing heritage, but the A43 is hardly picturesque. And the local Little Chef would be pushed to gain business on the strength of its sunsets.

Among the lawns and swaying trees of Albert Park it is hard to imagine how any Melburnian could not worship at the altar of Formula One, or at least consider it a jolly day out. The natural backdrop to the race, the convenient infrastructure and – at the very least – the well-founded hope of regular sunshine must surely make for the perfect outdoor sports event.

Not every F1 host city creates such a pleasant spectator experience. And most fans would be outraged at the suggestion that they are only in it for the pretty skylines and friendly banter over a picnic lunch. To the initiated it is blasphemy to compare a Grand Prix weekend to a day at the beach or a trip to the zoo with the kids. And, of course, for most fans the experience is enjoyed at home in front of the TV. Those millions of spectators couldn't care less about transport routes to the venue or the choice of falafel on offer. The Australians in particular have a long tradition of motor racing that goes beyond the televised, fast-living, shiny bonnet of Formula One.

To many Aussie motor-sport fans the Bathurst 1000 is the only event worth watching. A 1000-kilometre race encompassing 161 laps of the spectacular Mount Panorama circuit 130 miles west of Sydney, it lasts for seven hours, during which the drivers' enthusiasm is matched only by the crowd's ability to drink. It is a raucous, day-long event that has legendary status for many Australians. But as much as that day represents a specific element of Australian culture, the F1 Grand Prix signifies the country's European heritage.

Several spectators explained to me that motor racing allowed them to indulge in their loyalty to heartfelt ancestral ties. 'The Italian community here in Melbourne come along dressed in red and shout for Ferrari. They don't get much chance to celebrate their "Italianness" in Australian sport,' said one onlooker. But there is another reason why the sport is currently enjoying a renaissance in Australia and it's a lot more attractive than an abstract theory about European culture. The reason many Aussies are switching on is the 6'2", brown-eyed, square-jawed, James Bond *doppelgänger* Mark Webber.

In the week running up to the Melbourne Grand Prix, Webber was in considerable demand. He drove for Minardi in 2002, but had recently joined the bigger boys by securing a seat at Jaguar for 2003. Jaguar have a reputation for being a friendly, hospitable team, although they've been dogged by internal politics almost from day one of their foray into Formula One in 2000. At the start of 2003 their F1 aspirations were somewhat snagged, and it remained to be seen whether they would cut their losses and return to sepia ad campaigns or whether Webber in a car that could last the distance would keep them in the sport. It seemed that every article written about Webber trumpeted his 'down-to-earth, easy-going' attitude and maintained that his charismatic presence would be good for Jaguar. On the Monday before the Australian Grand Prix, I interviewed him at his parents' home in Queanbeyan, a small town outside Canberra.

Having failed to anticipate the complete absence of traffic jams, we arrived at the Webbers' half an hour early at 7.30 a.m. Mark's mum Diane welcomed us warmly into their suburban family home, serving coffee and toast while telling us that Mark was out on a run and his father Alan had gone to the local tip.

'We had a bit of a barbie yesterday and there were, you know, a few empties to get rid of.'

Their bungalow consisted of an open-plan area with a kitchen behind a breakfast bar and a lounge that opened up onto a terracotta patio. A large wooden dining table formed the centrepiece to the area and I wouldn't have been at all surprised if Madge Bishop had walked in at any moment. This was real-life *Neighbours*. The comfy settee, the flowery curtains, the house-proud mum, the mismatched mugs, it was all so wonderfully normal. The only sign that the Webbers' was slightly different was the pile of magazines on the coffee table: Mark smiled back from the covers of every one.

Soon the man himself appeared in an old T-shirt and running pants, face aglow with his early morning exertions, and started to tell us that he'd just bumped into a friend from school 'building a house down the road!' He seemed a little envious and reminisced about their schooldays. Mark's dad Alan returned.

'You've all met the wife?' he asked. 'She's OK really. She'll make you drinks and things. You all right dear?' Alan then appeared with 'Mark's first car', a small, dusty, red pedal car that had sat in the shed for twenty-five years. 'He still can't drive it,' joked Alan, 'too fast for him.'

We walked from their house to the garden and into glorious Australian sunshine. The peace and tranquillity were such a contrast to Mark's life in Formula One that we set up the camera to take a few shots. The roads were empty, each front lawn neat and lovingly tended; a small girl wearing a chequered uniform, knee-high socks, a straw hat and a rucksack walked past on her way to school. A neighbour attentively mowed his lawn, distinctive birds squawked in the trees above. Then a school bus drove past and a lad opened the window and shattered the moment by yelling: 'Get your tits out, camera-woman!'

'Welcome to Australia!' laughed Mark.

We followed him to his primary school. He hugged the kerb on the straights and swung the car out at corners and didn't once use his indicators. He signed autographs for the kids and chatted to the teachers.

That same weekend, twelve months earlier in 2002, Mark Webber had made his Formula One debut after eleven years of ascending the ranks. He finished an impressive fifth, giving Minardi their first points since 1999. He had jumped at the offer to join Jaguar in 2003 and as we chatted at his aunt's farm, Mark explained that performing at his home Grand Prix was particularly important, although at that stage nobody knew how the cars would compare. But he was realistic about being a 'mid-grid driver'.

Back in Melbourne, Albert Park was coming alive. By 9 a.m. on Friday morning the racing cars were out practising, filling the park with that unmistakable screeching sound. Branches crunched underfoot on dusty grass and the air smelt of autumn, permeated by the occasional waft of burnt rubber. Spectators wearing rucksacks walked purposefully into the heart of the park, the early birds stopping for coffee and a wrap.

Security personnel were positioned at every gate and doorway, a clipboard and a laminated map of the park their only defence against hundreds of disoriented spectators. They wore smart black trousers, red and blue shirts emblazoned with *Event Staff* in white and wide-brimmed blue hats. Some of them looked just as bemused as the punters enquiring about directions to their seats.

Food stalls offered an impressive selection. Everything from Indian to Mexican, with some boasting of superior seafood, hot dogs, waffle cones and gourmet bagels. The organizers had thought of everything. There were ATM machines in Portakabins and plenty of toilets for everyone. Even St John's Ambulance had seized the chance to make a few bucks, selling *Grand Prix Survival Kits* for a very reasonable $3: paracetamol, sunscreen, earplugs, plasters and refresher towels.

And then there were the merchandising stalls without which no Grand Prix is complete. Ferrari, BMW, Foster's, Jaguar and Toyota were all selling branded goods from twenty-metre-wide stands and doing a fine job of turning the crowd into one enormous advertisement. Wooden picnic tables with big green umbrellas were spaced out across luscious lawns, positioned to enable a perfect view of the giant TV screens relaying live track action.

And tucked away in a corner, hidden behind electronic security terminals and grid girls in tight blue Lycra was the Formula One paddock – the concealed refuge for team personnel, media representatives, drivers and their agents, wives, friends and families; as well as the ubiquitous hangers-on that Formula One attracts. The paddock is strictly pass-holders only. At European Grands Prix the teams park their luxurious motorhomes there, side by side in strict formation.

Even F1 teams cannot justify flying these enormous hospitality vehicles to Australia, so temporary offices and kitchens are erected at the back of the garages. But these garages are more NASA than ESSO: machines bleep and blink and rows of computers analyse data that can make a difference between life and death. There isn't a rusty drill, a spanner in a greying rag or a girly calendar in sight. In Melbourne these garages open on to a lawn area with tables and chairs for team personnel and VIP guests.

But access to the paddock does not guarantee a seat at these tables. Not just anyone can rock up and share a sausage sandwich with Michael Schumacher under a ruby sunshade. There is an undefined code of conduct operating in the paddock that is rooted in intimidation and preys on people's unfamiliarity with their surroundings. I've seen grown men wither under the glare of a team employee who spies an uninvited guest making their way to the luncheon buffet.

However, the paddock is not just a place to entertain special guests. The teams are fed there: bleary-eyed engineers and mechanics can be seen quietly slumped over a bowl of risotto; the drivers themselves refuel there, tucking into whatever is on the menu – although some prefer individual catering, such as Jacques Villeneuve, a notoriously fussy eater.

I wandered through the paddock, catching up with people I hadn't seen since the end of the last season. Outside the Jaguar garage, Mark Webber appeared with his manager, walking hurriedly on his way to yet another media appearance.

'Oi!' he yelled. 'Get your tits out, camera-woman!' and was gone.

Conversations were animated; eyes smiled behind Oakley sunglasses; the chat was all about the coming race, the rule changes and how simply fabulous Melbourne was. But for all the anticipation that weekend, there were some people who would not be celebrating. Not everyone is thrilled to have the Grand Prix in their backyard.

Driving in to the circuit with six other people I caught a flash of yellow from the corner of my eye and glimpsed a group of what seemed to be protesters. My travelling companions made no comment and I knew better than to ask about something that was so evidently anti-F1. But I was intrigued. I asked a few casual questions and learned that for 365 days of the year these locals sit in a yellow-roofed tent on the edge of the park, demonstrating their heartfelt desire to see the race banned. I was fascinated.

They sat at the entrance to Gate 1, a thirty-foot-square area cordoned off with a bright orange and green fence, in the centre of which stood the famous yellow tent. It was more like a tall yellow umbrella with a clear tarpaulin wrapped around it so as to keep the occupants on display (and allow outsiders to admire their knitting). Around the edge of the plastic fence were a series of yellow bodies made from MDF, just like those used in shooting galleries, except that they had blown-up newspaper cuttings stapled to their fronts, laminated to withstand the rain.

Within their little compound – which was strangely uninviting for an organization seeking supporters – were several deckchairs and many plastic bags full of sandwiches and flasks. The group members milled around chatting about the weather, brushing rain from their sturdy macs. There was no banner-waving, no chanting and no megaphone. In fact, it was difficult to know what they were protesting about without reading the clippings gallery. I took some pictures from behind a tree and nervously approached for a chat, fully expecting to be sent packing. I introduced myself as a member of the British media and a small man wearing a blue mac and an unfeasibly awful woolly jumper pushed forward to extend a cold hand.

He introduced himself as a 'civil engineer', put down his plastic bag and carefully explained the aims of the group. A common misconception about these protesters is that they are campaigning against the damage to wildlife caused by Formula One. Subtle enquiries within the paddock met with responses that varied from 'Oh, they're worried about swans and shit like that' to 'They're a bunch of cranks who don't like cars and have nothing better to do.' The truth is more complex.

Albert Park is unlike any other racetrack in the world. For 350 days of the year it's a normal public road. It is only a glamorous racetrack for four days in March. Monaco is similarly a 'road' track, but Melbourne's pride and joy is contained within a public park – something of particular concern to the protesters. Their spokesman pointed out that for four months of the year the park is of limited use due to the assembling and dismantling of the race ground and its component parts. But this is not their only grievance.

They argue that the Grand Prix is killing drivers. Not racing drivers, but locals who can't resist the chance of a quick spin on the tarmac that Michael Schumacher belts around. And they have pages and pages of documents to prove it.

There are two roads in question: Lakeside Drive and Aughtie Drive. It turns out that even before the Grand Prix came to town in 1995, these roads were accident black spots; so much so that the Government of Victoria implemented additional road safety measures. A 2.2-metre, rough-surfaced central median strip was built along Lakeside Drive, which resulted in a 50 per cent reduction in crashes and a zero-fatality rate. At Aughtie Drive – where there had been five deaths between 1987 and 1989 – a similar median strip was built; lighting was improved and safety increased.

In 1995 along came the Grand Prix and the bulldozers. Both roads were rebuilt. The meridian strips, kerbs and lighting were removed and the roads were altered to encompass a series of straights, curves and S-bends. According to the protesters these changes were accompanied by an annual Grand Prix marketing campaign 'glamorizing speed'.

To some drivers, they argue, the road will always be a racetrack. Their figures are pretty convincing: before the realignments in 1995, only thirty-nine people were injured and there were no fatalities over a seven-year period. But between 1995 and 2002, eighty-three people were injured and three were killed on the park roads. Consequently, in October 2001, Lakeside Drive was officially declared a 'black spot', receiving A$308,000 (£128,000) of public money for road safety works. However, the campaigners argue that the total cost of casualty crashes on both roads is A$15.2 million (£6.3 million). The cost to the locals is three times higher than it was before 1995. They conclude:

The total gross cost of realignments, including casualty crashes, PDO (non-injury crashes), black spot funding, post-1995 attempts by Parks Victoria park managers to reduce crashes, consultants fees, legal fees, and all management fees on the reserve roads was estimated to be about $23 million (£9.5 million).

Public road safety in Victoria, they claim, is effectively controlled by the international motor-racing organization the Fédération Internationale de l'Automobile (FIA) and its local subsidiary, the Australian Grand Prix Corporation (AGPC). Business tycoon Ron Walker, Chairman of the AGPC, was responsible for convincing Bernie Ecclestone that Melbourne should host the race, but it was Walker's good friend Jeff Kennett, premier of Victoria's Liberal-National government, who eased the way. The Kennett government approved a twenty-one-page report on the economic implications of staging the Grand Prix, without submitting it for the usual Cabinet approval or Treasury evaluation of its cost-benefit analysis.

Kennett confirmed that total payments for the Grand Prix would be underwritten by the taxpayer, but he failed to give full details of the deal to the Treasury or the Auditor-General, arguing that Ecclestone's 'commercial confidentiality' clause prevented it. In July 1994 Victoria's opposition Labour Party attempted to force the government to release contractual information about the Grand Prix, but was unsuccessful. The Grand Prix Act effectively overrides the Freedom of Information Act.

Albert Park soon became the favourite racetrack location of the AGPC and Kennett himself, but at a cost of A$60 million, with a further A$14–16 million annually (to erect and dismantle the temporary venue) to be met by taxpayers, it quickly attracted opponents. The disruption caused by the race extends beyond four days in March. For almost two months, 2,200 people work day and night to install 3,000 four-tonne concrete barriers, 120,000 spectator seats, 40 kilometres of fencing, 65 tonnes of rock for the gravel traps, 35 kilometres of electrical cabling and 50,000 square metres of artificial grass.

Opponents of the Grand Prix accused the government of breaching planning regulations and environmental laws – not least the felling of more than 1,000 trees – but the Kennett government responded swiftly, passing the notorious 'Australian Grands Prix Act 1994', which essentially granted the project immunity from many long-standing rules and regulations, as well as environmental and planning laws protecting native birds and preventing pollution. The Act allows the AGPC to 'cordon or fence off' any 'declared area' within the park for any length of time and for any purpose. The AGPC can also order the felling of any trees.

The Act was also invoked to prevent compensation claims by residents whose homes had been damaged by construction work. A test case brought by one such local was unsuccessful, with costs of A\$120,000 awarded against the plaintiff. This extraordinary use of legislation to block opposition to the Grand Prix caused enormous controversy.

In February 1995 10,000 Melburnians marched in protest against the use of Albert Park as a race venue and attacked the Kennett government for making decisions that were 'profoundly offensive' to democracy. Formula One was not welcome, said Iain Stewart, the governor of the Save Albert Park group, because 'the city is about parks, gardens, culture and traditionalism, not about glitz, fast life, advertising and money that the Grand Prix has come to represent.'

In the twelve months between December 1994 and 1995 more than 200 people were arrested in demonstrations. Most cases were dismissed, however, when magistrates concluded that people could not be charged for protesting on public land. Kennett's government then pushed through legislation prohibiting any unauthorized person from entering the sealed building site – anyone doing so could now be charged with trespassing.

This was all explained to me in the drizzle in Albert Park by a man I wanted to support, but whose argument was seriously hindered by his inability to get to the point. It's hardly surprising they are often dismissed as whingeing troublemakers. These dedicated campaigners have an image problem that starts with their name: SAPS – the Save Albert Park Society. The SAPS believe that accidents on the park roads are merely symptomatic of political dirty dealings. They claim not to be anti-F1, they just don't believe a public park should be used for private profit. They would like to see a purpose-built track, funded by the AGPC, in a less residential location. It's classic David and Goliath:

We are conducting a very serious and difficult campaign, involving the gross misuse of a public park, basic democratic rights and open-ness and honesty in government. We are opposed to both major political parties, the entire mainstream Australian media and powerful local and international business interests, including the tobacco industry.

No wonder they eyed me with suspicion. The Australian media have, in fact, afforded the SAPS considerable press coverage, intrigued by images of middle-class, conservative suburbanites being driven away in police vans. But the press also reported Kennett's unfounded claim that the SAPS were affiliated to an international socialist movement and the protesters seem unable to forgive them.

In February 2003, however, they struck a little gold. Not exactly the kind that F1 team owners line their baths with, but some encouragement at least. A conference was held at Coffs Harbour by the Council of Australian Universities Tourism and Hospitality Educators: a group of academics who expose the misdirection of resources by private enterprise and government in relation to the tourism and hospitality industries. A paper presented by Larry Dwyer and Ray Spurr of the University of New South Wales was entitled the 'Economic Evaluation of Special Events: A Reassessment'.

The introduction stated that 'The economic impacts and benefits [of special events such as the Grand Prix], if rigorously assessed, are very much lower than those invariably claimed.' Dwyer and Spurr concluded that the analyses widely used have 'inherent biases which lead to overstatement of impacts on output and jobs'. Using an 'input-output' method to calculate the benefit of tourism and special events has largely been rejected in most other areas of economic evaluation. Yet this was the means, they pointed out, by which the figures had been reached regarding the benefit of the Melbourne Grand Prix: A$95.6 million in 1996 and A$130.7 million in 2000.

To further illustrate their point, Dwyer and Spurr ran a study of a simulated event 'with size and expenditure pattern of the Formula One Grand Prix'. They concluded that the true net impact on Australia as a whole was just A$9 million and that the benefit to Victoria was very much at the expense of other states. Steve Bracks's claim that his state benefited to the tune of A$130 million thanks to the Grand Prix had been profoundly undermined.

Bernie Ecclestone himself admits that the organizers of new Grands Prix won't make money. 'I tell them up front,' he says in Terry Lovell's *Bernie's Game*. 'You are going to lose money running this event. You will not make money. There is no bullshit. If they don't [know] they come crying to me.'

Nevertheless, when Kennett's government was replaced by the Labour Party in 1999, new premier Steve Bracks announced he would end the 'culture of needless secrecy' by revealing the financial details of government contracts. Seventy-six were available for public view, but the Grand Prix deal with Ecclestone has never seen the light of day.

*

Back in the paddock, Albert Park was packed with 116,700 spectators, many regretting the decision to wear shorts. A chilly, grey drizzle prompted fans to huddle together in transparent-plastic poncho-style macs, drinking beer, smoking cigarettes and looking to the sky.

Unlike some Grands Prix, where the spectators sit in the stand idly fiddling with their spongy earplugs for hours on end, Melbourne works hard to keep the crowd occupied all day. Those with a spring in their step could have started at 9 a.m. with a Stirling Moss autograph-signing. At 9.10 and 10.01 (precisely) they could have watched the sky, open-mouthed for the parachute drops of sponsors' flags. At 10.05 they were invited to saunter over to the golf course to ooh and aah at a freestyle motocross demonstration, before sprinting back for a stunt riders' display at 10.15. Another flag drop at 10.26 filled some time before the 10.37 V8 Supercar Showdown and podium presentation. More stunts followed until the 11 a.m. RAAF Roulettes display, after which the F1 drivers posed for the official photograph before beginning their parade at 11.15. At 11.40 a group of local celebrities embarked on their Mini challenge. This would have been as dull as a dropped flag had it not been abandoned after just one and a half laps, leaving a fashion model nursing a fractured pelvis and the organizers checking the small print of their insurance.

The schedule of events continued in this manner for another two hours (the really big planes came out just before the race: RAAF jets, no less) and finally at 2 p.m. the drivers launched themselves from the grid for a gruelling fifty-eight laps.

If they could find the time, spectators might also take in the acres of naked flesh on display, belonging to the many 'grid girls' or 'pit babes'. These ladies wandered in packs (presumably for safety), handing out leaflets or posing for photographs with men who liked to cop a quick feel or plant a beery kiss on their made-up cheeks.

Some fans headed to join the crowd squashed behind the security barriers by the entrance to the paddock, hoping to catch a glimpse of their favourite driver. Soap stars and some drivers would stop for photographs and autographs. New driver Ralph Firman was almost ejected by stewards who failed to recognize the Englishman, until an official remembered seeing him in the newspaper. But ultimately, despite the non-stop entertainment, multifarious watering holes and colourful diversions, the race was the reason most people had come to Albert Park.

Both red Ferraris were on the front row for the start of the race and talk at the circuit was of another 'predictable' season due to Michael Schumacher's dominance and Ferrari's reliability. It would be hard to overstate the desire within the sport to see them fail. This was a crunch year. Formula One's popularity had waned significantly and rival teams blamed a fall in viewing figures on Ferrari's twenty-first-century supremacy.

Rule changes had been introduced to spice up the show, including single-lap qualifying on a Saturday, in which one driver at a time would perform a 'flying lap' with race fuel on board to determine his grid position. The running order of this session would be decided by 'first qualifying' the day before and, as tracks get warmer and 'faster' with each car, the incentive would be to finish well on Friday, thereby claiming a late run in 'second qualifying'. After this outing, the cars would then be confined to a locked garage – parc ferme – until the following day's race. This posed a new tactical challenge: second-guessing the fuel levels in competitors' cars and calculating the optimum number of pit stops per race.

By Sunday in Melbourne, the F1 camp was pessimistic: Schumacher and team-mate Rubens Barrichello had qualified in first and second places. One Australian newspaper captured the mood with the headline THE YAWN OF A NEW ERA – though no one I spoke to within the sport was yawning. When Schumacher completed his qualifying lap they were chewing pens, gripping table tops and gulping shots of espresso. If cumulative yearning could alter the course of events, Schumacher would be in trouble. As it turned out, he was – though it was less the power of combined psychic will and more the weather that thwarted his first Grand Prix of 2003.

By the start of the race the rain had abated, but the track was not entirely dry. The papers joked the following morning that this inclement weather had made Scotland's David Coulthard feel at home, giving him his first victory in nine months – although Monaco isn't known for its showers. The race was eventful: the safety car came out twice, the lead changed six times and the final victory dais saw Coulthard flanked by McLaren team-mate Kimi Raikkonen in third and a frustrated Juan Pablo Montoya taking second place for BMW Williams. Champagne flowed for the winners, but also for the losers.

Not until Saddam Hussein's statue was unceremoniously toppled from its plinth would I witness again such celebrations. No Michael Schumacher on the podium, no red of Ferrari and no journalists wanting to know why the rule changes hadn't made the sport more exciting. There was a collective sigh of relief.

There was also an audible groan around Albert Park when Mark Webber was forced to retire on lap 16. Removing the steering wheel and climbing out, the Aussie hero stood by his wounded car, leaning to look at the left rear wing; taking just a minute to show the world that his ambition had been thwarted by a mechanical fault – he had not crashed, he had broken down, and now like any baffled motorist on the hard shoulder he was looking for the problem. Mark should, of course, have jumped quickly behind the safety fence, thereby minimizing the risk of denting an oncoming car with his body. But he cared about the judgement of the home crowd fans and wanted to leave them in no doubt that this was not driver error.

The big British story of the weekend involved Jenson Button, whose spat with BAR team-mate Jacques Villeneuve had been well publicized in the run-up to the race. In one interview Villeneuve said he wouldn't 'play games just to get people on my side', while describing Button as a 'smiley person'. He also claimed that as a world champion he did not see why he should respect Button until he had proven himself.

Jenson Button is the type of person who tries to avoid most altercations. He understands the need to perpetuate a nice juicy rivalry for the press, but he never seemed to take it seriously. Until the race. On lap 25 Villeneuve was told to come in for a pit stop through the radio earpiece that all drivers use. According to Villeneuve, the equipment broke at that very moment. Button was due to come in to refuel on the next lap and did so as arranged, only to find that Villeneuve had done the same and was sitting in the pit in front of him. Button was forced to do what an F1 driver should never have to do: queue behind his team-mate for a seven-second pit stop. He looked like a Sunday motorist waiting for the car wash. If the press were to be believed, Villeneuve sped away laughing demonically like the Count in *Sesame Street*.

Afterwards the mood in the BAR camp was subdued. Neither driver was anywhere to be seen. Villeneuve had ultimately finished ninth, Button tenth. Button gave a brief TV interview in which he was asked whether this affected his relationship with Villeneuve.

'It doesn't help,' he said coolly before walking off.

In terms of public image, this was one-nil to Button. Villeneuve was the bad guy, sabotaging his team-mate's race with a feigned mechanical fault. Button: the thwarted British hero, victim of a bitter ex-world champion. Apparently, there had been an almighty row in the garage following the race. The BAR team bosses were annoyed with Villeneuve, but could hardly accuse him of lying about the broken earpiece.

The victorious David Coulthard stayed in the McLaren paddock for several hours, obliging journalists with snippets for race reports and shaking hands with the all-important sponsors. His stunning Brazilian girlfriend Simone Abdelnour shone a bright white smile at all the right people, gracious in the face of gushing congratulations.

That night Jaguar threw a rooftop party in a swanky Melbourne bar and people from different teams drank vodka-*Red Bulls* into the small hours of Monday morning. Sporting celebrities such as tennis champion Pat Rafter, swimmer Michael Klim and numerous soap stars mingled with team personnel and mechanics. Mark Webber made a brief appearance, accompanied by his family and non-F1 friends who sat at a nearby table happily entertaining themselves. Pretty coquettes approached him one by one, kissing him on both cheeks and trying to strike up a conversation, but he always made polite excuses and continued chatting to his mates.

The following morning's hangovers were eased by glowing press reports praising the most thrilling race for several seasons. Those who had initiated rule changes to create an even playing field and bring 'real racing' back to Formula One were clamouring to take the credit. Those who had opposed the alterations kept their heads down. Ironically, McLaren's Ron Dennis had been one of the people most vigorously against such changes and now he was waking up to photos of both his drivers showering in champagne.

But the best news? Schumacher had been toppled from his throne.

Many people inside motor racing seemed to forget that the Red Baron had been leading with 14 laps to go, until he went in for an extra pit stop necessitated by a flapping bargeboard beneath his $2 million car. Despite this setback, he still came fourth, whereas eight of the twenty drivers failed to finish. The German simply described the race as 'interesting'. The rest of his season would prove to be even more so.

The crowds were disappointing: the lowest turn-out in five years, down by 23,000 over the same four-day period in 2002, resulting in a total spectatorship of 348,700. Premier Steve Bracks claimed the figures were 'fantastic' given the looming war in Iraq and weekend rain. The SAPS must have been delighted to read in the *Herald Sun* that the taxpayer had spent an extra $6 million on safety fences. This meant that the eighth Albert Park Grand Prix was, according to the newspaper, 'certain to lose more than the $10.3 million picked up by the taxpayer last year'. Bracks asserted once again that the value of the race to his state's economy was $130 million.

The season was under way. The jury was still out on the rule changes, but Ferrari had not appeared on the winner's podium and that brought smiles to many F1 faces. Australia had once again shown the world how to organize a Grand Prix and made a concerted effort to market their country on the global stage.

The drivers were one race down, with fifteen to go. Some were cautiously optimistic: Jarno Trulli and team-mate Fernando Alonso had finished a promising fifth and seventh for Renault. Others were more despondent: Minardi and Jaguar saw both their cars retire. And some, such as those at BAR, were busy trying to distance themselves from internal squabbles and intrusive journalists.

The following day the members of the F1 circus returned to their homes – although many people working in Formula One seize the chance to take a break somewhere tropical before heading straight to Malaysia. Many drivers flew north to Queensland, with girlfriends and wives in tow; a five-star hotel and the solitude of some underwater coral proving the perfect antidote to race-weekend pressure.

And the Save Albert Park Society? Well, they scoured the Monday papers for some kind of support for their long-cherished cause, but found only damning references to their approach and swipes at their unfortunate acronym. Some of them pursued the girl from the English media who had shown an interest in them, but mostly they took up their knitting and returned to their yellow tent for another year.

2

Brazil

Every Formula One race has its own personality, a particular ambience tied to its location and the nationality of the fans. The circuit in Monza, for instance, is just outside Milan and the vociferous Ferrari fans – known as the *Tifosi* – form a boiling sea of red. Magny-Cours, set deep within the French countryside, is characterized by fresh air and roadside picnics. And Silverstone is a great British summer's day out, as campers with beer crates walk miles to the track and the omnipresent threat of rain seeps into every conversation.

The Brazilian race at the Interlagos track in São Paulo has a similarly distinctive character, although it is by no means the location of choice for those within the sport. To the same extent that Melbourne is adored by the F1 *cognoscenti*, São Paulo is detested. There are many occasions when F1 personnel have warned me: 'You don't want to go to Brazil. It's a shit-hole.'

Nowhere is the juxtaposition of extremes between the haves and the have-nots illustrated as clearly as in São Paulo on a race weekend. A sprawling circuit replete with millions of pounds worth of motor-racing equipment and extravagant corporate hospitality sits beside the pungent *favelas* or shanty towns: overcrowded, violent, and among the very worst examples of poverty in the developing world.

The road to the track winds cruelly past these tumbledown houses, as F1-branded people-carriers glide by, their air-conditioning and tinted windows affording an impenetrable, protective shield against the external horrors. Doors are locked and eyes fixed straight ahead. For some passengers this is the moment for a timely nap. Others scan their papers with renewed interest. If anybody is uncomfortable with this cavalcade of the rich among the poor, they never say so. To harbour a conscience would betray the ethos of Formula One.

Although Brazil has an abundance of natural resources and a mixture of religions, languages and cultures that coexist for the most part peacefully, it suffers from deep social problems that senior presidential advisor Vilmar E. Faria describes simply as 'immoral'.

Two or three million children live on the streets and approximately 500,000 girls – some as young as ten – are believed to be involved in prostitution, forced into it by poverty and inadequate educational provision. There are more than two million child labourers in Brazil, due in part to the unwillingness of the Brazilian authorities to enforce any laws against such practices. At the root of such problems, argues Faria, is the prevailing attitude that poverty and destitution are 'natural phenomena and not historical and social conditions, amendable through human intervention and resolution'.

Nowhere is this attitude more prevalent than in the F1 community on a Brazilian Grand Prix weekend. However, the gaping chasm between the super-rich in the paddock and the wretched poor outside is rarely if ever mentioned. Anyone who does raise the topic is likely to meet with a confused silence or a perfunctory 'Well, that's just the way it is.'

There is a steadfast reluctance among those working in Formula One to consider anything outside the race, beyond the quality of the restaurants or the distance of the track from the hotels. ITV's anchorman Jim Rosenthal is one of the few to have expressed his discomfort at the social issues raised by the Brazilian Grand Prix.

'I find it very problematic,' he told me, 'all that poverty alongside the F1 excess... it's very difficult to reconcile.'

Ferrari's budget for 2003 is $306 million. Michael Schumacher's wages from Ferrari alone are $30 million (a figure he will double through merchandising and sponsorship). Jacques Villeneuve's basic remuneration is $18 million, while local Brazilian boy Rubens Barrichello earns a mere $8 million.

The inhabitants of São Paulo's *favelas* earn approximately $720 a year from begging and selling items in local markets. If a mother can find cleaning work, she might earn up to $1,440 a year.

Back on planet F1, Toyota – the team most frequently described as 'disappointing' since their arrival in 2002 – won just two world championship points in their debut season, which cost them approximately

$70 million each. British team McLaren's 2003 budget is $291 million. Team boss Ron Dennis has admitted they could cut costs, but 'the point is whether you want to make them. We spend a lot of money working on projects nine months ahead that might yield us 0.9 of a second.' He was not assessing the morality of Formula One's gross expenditure, but the implications of cost-cutting for the sport as a whole – the smaller teams, the racing quality and the TV viewing figures. In fact, these are the only areas in which F1's relationship to money is ever discussed by those inside the sport.

Formula One is very much at home in Brazil, a country of great social and economic extremes. Although São Paulo is the richest city in the Third World (but not rich enough for the First), poverty is widespread, educational attainment low, health alarmingly poor and income inequality has reached one of the highest levels in modern urban societies. The city houses some 17 million people, 4 million motor vehicles and 10,000 miles of streets. It's a multiplying mass of unmitigated, chaotic sprawl: a consequence of one of history's largest internal migrations during the late sixties and early seventies, when millions of people from the drought-ridden north-east moved to the industrialized south-east hoping for a better life. The population explosion came in a wave of such ferocity that any attempts at urban planning were washed up onto a crowded shore: it was too little too late. Yet São Paulo also has a lust for wealth, as is evident from its architecture, the Modernist commercial buildings that sprung from the intersection of its two rivers: the Anhangabau and Tamanduatei.

Today, its *Blade Runner* cityscape has giant TV screens alongside neon signs and garish billboards. Investment banks and dot-com start-ups thrive in the gleaming forest of skyscrapers that stand along the banks of the filthy Rio Pinheiros. To many Paulistanos these symbols of capitalist endeavour are viewed with pride and reverence. They are as shiny as an F1 car, as pioneering as its engine technology and as fashionably exclusive as the paddock club. Formula One reaffirms the collective aspirations of Brazilians and they embrace it.

Unemployment in São Paulo hovers around 20 per cent and the crime rate is one of the worst in the world, but it is on the roads that São Paulo's problems manifest themselves with such ugly visibility. The public transport system is woefully outdated; there are frequent violent clashes between unlicensed minicab drivers and the police and commuting is a long, stressful daily grind. (The congested, limping traffic on a race weekend is another reason for the F1 community to resent the Brazilian Grand Prix.) Roberto Mangabeira Unger – a long-standing Brazilian activist and Harvard law professor who ran for mayor in the 2000 election – identified transportation as the most critical factor in repairing São Paulo.

He proposed hefty taxes on car use to enable greater investment in public transport, as well as free car parks around the city limits to facilitate park-and-ride schemes. 'There is no solution without a radical circumvention of the automobile,' he declared. Yet every year the F1 circus drives into town, accompanied by a hard-hitting press campaign and a culture of glamour to promote the very thing that is suffocating São Paulo.

The polls showed that only one or two per cent of Paulistanos supported Unger's candidacy. His plans for a city that had been founded on the deification of the motor car were simply too radical. A previous mayor, Paulo Maluf, claimed that São Paulo's legendary traffic jams were actually a sign of progress, because the desire to own a car represented the desire to better oneself.

To many Brazilians, Europe is the epitome of sophistication and, as in Melbourne, no organization is more evocatively European than Formula One. Football might be the game of the people, but in Brazil Formula One finds a receptive middle-class audience hungry for status symbols. Wealthy Paulistanos have amassed the world's third largest urban fleet of helicopters after New York and Tokyo in an attempt to rise above the squalid roads beneath them. To those Brazilians, the competitive commercialism and conspicuous consumption of Formula One is to be admired. Meanwhile the inhabitants of the *favelas* have to watch the F1 circus swing past each year.

São Paulo University's sociology Professor Richard Miskolci explains that Formula One is now a 'more élitist kind of sport. The masses just watch it when Brazil has a champion like Ayrton Senna. Nowadays it has not the same popular appeal. Today I believe it is much more a middle-class or upper-middle-class interest.' Brazil's poor no longer identify with a sport that once united the nation. Ayrton Senna's death in 1994 resulted in three days of official mourning and an eruption of national grief. It is hard to imagine such a phenomenon today.

South America has a long and passionate relationship with motor racing. From the great Argentinian Juan Manuel Fangio in the fifties, to the Brazilians Nelson Piquet, Emerson Fittipaldi and Ayrton Senna, to a new line-up that includes the Colombian Juan Pablo Montoya and three Brazilians: Rubens Barrichello, Cristiano da Matta and Antonio Pizzonia. Are they boys from the *favelas* who have used their talents to lift themselves from poverty? Or are they – and other F1 drivers – privileged children whose love of fast cars has been indulged by wealthy parents? Did Ayrton Senna grow up kicking a football with other kids in tattered shoes yearning to be the next Pelé? Or did he spend his formative years mingling with the polo-playing set?

The first F1 Grand Prix came to South America in 1953, the championship's third year. This was in part due to the success of Argentinian Juan Manuel Fangio, who won the title five times between 1951 and 1957. But it was the Brazilian Emerson Fittipaldi's success in the seventies that sparked calls for a championship race in Brazil. In 1972 Bernie Ecclestone convinced local politicians and TV network Rede Globo that São Paulo's Interlagos circuit would be the ideal location. Fellow countryman Nelson Piquet later declared that 'Emerson created the sport of motor racing in Brazil,' and inspired a new generation of drivers. But Fittipaldi did not become the youngest ever world champion at twenty-five without some significant parental assistance.

Fittipaldi was the son of a successful motor-racing journalist. His route to sporting success was eased by his familiar surname, the financial security of his family and the enthusiasm of his father. He moved from go-karts to cars and was soon signed to the Lotus Formula Two team – so began his journey to F1 glory.

Five years before Fittipaldi was born, another of Brazil's future sporting heroes came into the world. Footballer Pelé (Edson Arantes do Nascimento) grew up in a household of four brothers and sisters, a devoted mother and a supportive father who loved football. The family moved to the city of São Paulo with the promise of a public sector job (and a place on a local football team) for his father. The job never materialized and persistent injuries forced Pelé senior to focus his aspirations on his skinny little son. Pelé formed a local neighbourhood team with some older boys, calling themselves 'September 7th', after Brazil's Independence Day.

'We couldn't afford a ball,' Pelé recalls, 'so we did what most other kids did: we would stuff the largest man's sock we could find with rags or crumpled-up newspaper, roll it into as close a ball shape as we could manage, and tie it around with string.'

Between the ages of seven and fourteen Pelé worked as a shoe-shine boy, a meat-pie salesman (pestering passengers through train windows), a shoe-factory employee, a dry-cleaning assistant, a market trader and a peanut-seller whose stock comprised any nuts he found on the floor. He made his way consistently through the junior football leagues until he became the most successful footballer in history, scoring 1,283 goals and winning three World Cups. Initially, his mother wasn't keen on her little boy following his injury-prone father into a football career, but in the end she was pragmatic: 'You were never a good student, and I don't want you sewing boots for the rest of your life.' Or, presumably, selling second-hand peanuts.

Ayrton Senna had no such worries. Childhood photos show the smartly dressed, brown-eyed boy sitting outside the gated family home in a mini go-kart. His father, Milton Guirado Theodoro da Silva (Ayrton adopted his mother's maiden name 'Senna' when he began racing, because 'Da Silva' was a common name), owned more than 500,000 hectares of land and several businesses, including distribution companies for car components and drinks.

'Whenever we went to buy shoes he would try on a pair, generally preferring ankle boots,' Senna's sister Viviane Senna Lalli recalled. She also remembered her brother's generosity: 'Whatever he had he gave away' – including, apparently, 'gold chains' to his girlfriends. He is described by childhood friends as 'always having a toy car in his hand' or always being seated 'behind the steering wheel of a car'. Senna freely acknowledged his privileged existence: 'We always had everything we wanted in life. In that respect I am a fortunate guy.'

Senna spoke with the confidence of an educated young man and it seems to me that one of the differences between an average F1 driver and one who excels is intelligence. Senna was famously inquisitive about the workings of his car, always striving to fully understand the complicated technology and interpret the vehicle. He also possessed the eloquence to relay his findings to the engineers and technical experts. After races he could recall in minute detail the subtle sensations created by the car and was admired for his insightful comments.

Most F1 drivers first discovered the thrill of speed while karting. For many of us, our experience of karting is mainly confined to seaside holidays. Remember those small go-kart tracks beside the crazy-golf, trampolines and amusement arcades? Well, competitive karting is very much like that – only faster, fiercer and somewhat more expensive.

Paying for your child to participate in an average karting season of ten races in the UK will set you back between £15,000 and £20,000. A second-hand kart costs about £2,000; other necessary expenses include replacement tyres, fuel, engine maintenance, lessons, entry fees, as well as travel to and from the venues. Yet despite this financial burden, there is a vast subculture devoted to encouraging boys and girls to fly round tarmac bends at up to 70 mph. The importance of karting to motor racing cannot be overestimated. It is here that future world champions are born.

Senna fondly recalled his own excellent karting career: 'I have only good memories for go-karts.' He was only four when his father gave him a kart and a small motor. Young Ayrton would spend every day cleaning and polishing the machine and painstakingly repairing the brakes – when he wasn't shopping for ankle boots or gold chains. By the age of eight he was given a 'proper' go-kart and competed in races until he was twenty-one, winning the Brazilian championship four times.

These tournaments were the preserve of Brazil's middle and upper classes. Archive footage shows well-dressed, healthy-looking fathers pulling up in huge cars, off-loading karts from expensive trailers and sending their sons out to do the family proud. By the time he'd won three world championships for McLaren, Senna had bought a farm in Brazil and built a 1,000-metre go-kart track in his own backyard.

Jacques Villeneuve is another driver who benefited from parental generosity, as well as his father's Formula One success. Raised in Monte

Carlo and educated in Switzerland, Villeneuve was showered with snowmobiles, motocross bikes and, naturally, go-karts.

But the days when Formula One was a self-selecting, middle-class preserve might be coming to an end, albeit slowly. In the championship's early days, F1 drivers were either successful businessmen in their own right by the time they took to the track or else the sons of wealthy parents.

Graham Hill's father was a successful stockbroker, so Damon Hill was the grandson of a stockbroker and the son of a wealthy F1 driver; Britain's first world champion, Mike Hawthorn, was the son of a motorcycle competitor who owned a prosperous garage business in Surrey. Sterling Moss's father Alfred was a dentist, but in the twenties the family was sufficiently wealthy to own racing cars in which both parents competed. Jochen Rindt was born in Germany to wealthy parents – his father owned a spice mill and his mother was a lawyer. Jackie Stewart's father owned a Jaguar garage and was a keen motorcyclist. Niki Lauda was born into a family of affluent Viennese industrialists.

James Hunt's father was also a stockbroker who gave his son a public-school education and young James considered medicine as a career. Unlike most F1 drivers, however, his father had no relationship with cars or bikes and Hunt admitted 'the one thing that never entered my head was becoming a racing driver.' But a friend took him to Silverstone on his eighteenth birthday and his fate was decided: 'I went back to my parents that night and announced that their fears about my fecklessness were over. I was going to become a world champion driver.'

These are just a few examples of the drivers for whom Formula One was almost a birthright. In the last ten years, however, more and more young drivers have made it to F1 with less financial support from their parents.

Mika Hakkinen, for instance, is the son of a Finnish harbour master. Michael and Ralf Schumacher grew up in a comfortable suburb near Cologne, but their family is described in F1 biographies as 'not wealthy'. Fortunately Mr Schumacher, a bricklayer, backed his children in their chosen pursuit. They also lived near a go-kart track at which their mother often worked. Willy Weber, a rich businessman and motor-sport enthusiast approached Michael after watching him drive in Formula Ford and financed his move up to the more expensive Formula Three championship in 1989. Weber continues to manage the Schumacher brothers today.

David Coulthard received enormous support from his parents, who saved on karting expenses by staying in a caravan at competitions nationwide. Similarly, Ulsterman Eddie Irvine's parents preferred a caravan to costly hotels (and they continued to camp at races, even when Irvine was earning many millions a year).

Mark Webber claims he only became a driver because he wasn't as good at cycling, rowing or athletics. He knew he wanted to be a sportsman and chose motor racing through a process of elimination. His father owned a motorcycle garage that provided his family with a comfortable, though by no means extravagant, lifestyle. Webber's father admits there were times when money was so tight his son's career looked in doubt. They even had to borrow £25,000 from local resident, friend and rugby hero David Campese. 'I've since paid him back,' says Webber.

Jenson Button's father John was a second-hand car dealer who stretched himself to the financial limit to help his son pursue go-karting and other minor racing leagues. Although he grew up in Frome, Somerset, Button now has a home in Monaco and a white mansion on Surrey's private golf-club estate, St George's Hill. When he isn't supporting Jens at races, John now lives in St Tropez. But the racing driver who truly signals the start of a new, more inclusive era is Justin Wilson.

This Sheffield lad is racing in his first F1 season for Minardi – but still works as a driving instructor in his spare time. He had to bring a sponsorship package of £1.2 million to Minardi to secure his seat. In a first for Formula One, Wilson sold shares in himself to raise the revenue, the idea being that backers would profit from his success in years to come. Despite driving for the minnows of the sport in a car that will never match the big guns, Wilson is always smiling, chatting to mechanics and enjoying every minute of his F1 experience. On race weekends, he still walks over to the more modest Formula 3000 championship to greet his old sparring partners.

Significantly, these new drivers who seem to break the traditional mould, through sheer determination and talent, are from developed nations where meritocracy is more common. But would sheer talent and enthusiasm help today's Brazilian boys step out of poverty and into success? Are they more like Pelé, enjoying the fruits of social mobility through a combination of graft and talent? The answer is no. Publicizing Antonio Pizzonia as 'the jungle boy' is good PR for Jaguar, but the truth about their new driver is slightly more predictable.

Although he was raised in the Amazonian town of Manaus, situated on the banks of the Rio Negro, the twenty-two-year-old's family is by no means poor. Their large urban apartment is a far cry from São Paulo's *favelas*. Although not enormously wealthy, the Pizzonias are certainly comfortable by Brazilian standards. Antonio's father runs a plastic recycling business and benefits from Amazonia's tax-free status, but he had no interest in motor racing and never expected his son to become a professional driver. It was the gift of a go-kart from a friend on his eighth birthday that inspired Antonio to take up the sport. He soon spent every weekend racing in São Paulo's karting league and was signed by a professional team, moving to England in 1997 to begin a five-year climb to Formula One.

Cristiano da Matta was born in Brazil's affluent Belo Horizonte. His father was a sports-car driver, winning fourteen Brazilian championships. He cut his professional teeth in America and now drives for the struggling Toyota team. Rubens Barrichello, the longest-standing Brazilian on the grid, grew up close to São Paulo's Interlagos track, but like Pizzonia, his family was sufficiently wealthy to buy him a go-kart when he was nine. Their financial support paid off, earning him the Brazilian championship five times. There is no doubt that 'Rubinio' is popular in his native country, lifting the hopes of fans at every Brazilian Grand Prix.

But, it is ironic that a sport so riven by internal politics should produce such apolitical sportsmen. It is rare to hear a driver publicly – or even privately – offer an opinion on anything other than Formula One. They have access to an enormous audience of loyal followers, yet there are surprisingly few examples of any attempts to 'make a difference'. It's unfair to put the blame squarely on them, however. Drivers exist in an environment that hardly fosters altruism. After all, they compete in a sport in which your greatest rival is your team-mate and trust is rare. Today's drivers have been conditioned from a relatively young age by powerful team bosses and forceful agents and it is possible that if no one has suggested that they start a personal charity, they are unlikely to think it up on their own. When Pelé scored his thousandth goal in 1969 – a penalty for Santos against Vasco da Gama at the Maracana – he didn't dedicate it to God or his family, but used it as a chance to ask the world to remember the poor children of Brazil. It is hard to imagine an F1 driver holding aloft the championship trophy and making a similar plea.

Ayrton Senna was, by all accounts, a generous anonymous benefactor of several charities, but his sister established the Senna Foundation after his death. The charity aims to develop the potential of underprivileged, marginalized children who view education as unnecessary. It cleverly 'bribes' them to attend school in exchange for daily sports training. But this is one of the few charities established by a racing driver, past or present.

The American NBA basketball league is made up of very tall men, the most successful of whom enjoy incomes similar to those of F1 drivers. They own big cars, wear blinging diamonds and live in houses Justin Wilson can only dream of. Just like F1 drivers, they all have sponsorship deals and they all have their own websites. But unlike F1 drivers, each website features a clearly signposted charity established by the player (or their management). Together these players raise hundreds of millions of dollars a year. Most of them take this commitment very seriously and they are always coming up with new ways to raise cash.

The impetus for these schemes, however, comes from the NBA itself, which has links with official on-line charities and organizes nationwide schemes to encourage children to participate in NBA-sponsored reading programmes. Any player or team unwilling to participate in money-raising schemes would be frowned upon by the super-powers running the league. Every team has its own foundation, a charitable arm that funds youth programmes and sports initiatives. The Toronto Raptors alone aim to earn $1 million a year for Ontario's children and have amassed $11 million to date. They hold golf tournaments, rap events, dinners, bowling competitions and sell raffle tickets at games. Their star player

Vince Carter held his own charity game, pulling in 19,000 spectators. This is just one team – there are thirty in the league and fifteen players on each team. That's a lot of people doing a lot for charity.

Their season runs for nine months of the year. They play 82 games and if they make it to the play-offs, they may participate in another 28, making a total of 110 nationwide matches. Formula One drivers have sixteen races a year.

Michael Schumacher is an ambassador for UNESCO and all of his biographies describe him as a generous but discreet benefactor. On his website, Schumacher's charitable connections are limited to his sportswear sponsor, for whom he has signed some merchandise for auction, and his participation in charity football matches. Michael's love of football is well known and before this year's Brazilian Grand Prix he took a helicopter from São Paulo to Santos in order to play in a benefit game with national champions Santos FC in front of 15,000 fans. The instigator of this event? Pelé, of course.

Afterwards in the conference room of the Transamerica hotel, Schumacher told a press conference that it is 'always good to do things for charity, as it is important to do things for those who need it and to help make their life enjoyable'. The problem is that within Formula One it's hard to find evidence of deeds that support these words.

The F1 drivers' websites contain details of their results, a little personal history and a lot of flattering photos. You can also find 'grid-girl contests' and message boards, but there are no opportunities to read about their favourite charities. On Kimi Raikkonen's site you can join his fan club. There are three tiers of membership and for £30 you will receive a welcome letter, membership card and a magazine. Plus, of course, there are plenty of links to personal and team sponsor's websites. Obviously, we can never know how much the drivers contribute to charities anonymously, but in a sport predicated on PR and self-promotion my guess is that it is unlikely to be of great significance. The teams are even less likely than the drivers to hide their charitable work under a bushel.

However, there is one driver promoting his own charity. Jacques Villeneuve set up Formula Charity in 1998 to help various children's organizations, including Cystic Fibrosis in Children, the Down

Syndrome Association and a school for autistic and blind children in Lausanne. Because Villeneuve is the presiding spirit, there are no tombolas or auctions, but instead a twenty-four-hour ski relay-race in Switzerland, in which the teams aim to clock up as many miles as possible in a weekend. Perhaps this is a glimpse of Formula One's future.

All of this is not to say that drivers are selfish – but they are products of their environment. In 2000 a fire marshal, Mr Ghislimberto, was killed by debris from a race accident in Monza. Afterwards, Ralf and Michael Schumacher personally sought out chief medical officer Professor Sid Watkins to find out the address of Ghislimberto's widow who, they discovered, was in the first year of marriage and pregnant with their first baby. The Schumachers wanted to make a financial donation to her. Later that week, Bernie Ecclestone started a fund for Mrs Ghislimberto with $40,000 and asked each of the eleven teams to donate $10,000, following the initiative taken by the German brothers.

It is surely only a matter of time before F1 drivers follow the lead set by America's top sportsmen. But if Brazil doesn't prick the collective conscience of Formula One, it's hard to imagine what could. In a moment of rare insight, Eddie Irvine admitted: 'In F1 everyone just disappears. It's like you're raping a country. You go in, do the race and get out before you get caught.'

The Brazilian Grand Prix highlights the inertia of a sport that could do a great deal more to help the people who welcome it so noisily and enthusiastically. Not only does the Formula One party display little sign of action, it hasn't even reached the thinking stage.

One former F1 hostess, Kim Norbury, was shocked by the extravagance she had witnessed: 'The waste at meal times was unbelievable. In São Paulo, where people live in shanties on the edge of the F1 circuit, we were offloading roast dinners and platters of salad into the garbage, sometimes just an hour or so after preparation.'

On one occasion, a fellow hostess was ordered to replace hundreds of pieces of perfectly good china after the Jordan team changed its logo from a bee to a shark. 'The hostess bragged she had spent A$30,000 on odds and ends,' says Kim. 'There seemed to be money to burn.'

She recalls how Ferrari had their flower arrangements freighted in for every race and once a colleague was flown by Benetton (now Renault) 'from England to Australia, with a car part in an A4 jiffy bag and flown back twenty-four hours later. Oh, and the car part wasn't used.'

Perhaps the drivers born into privilege and cocooned in the cosy world of Formula One have simply never witnessed enough misery to spur them on to humanitarian acts. Pelé knew first-hand about disadvantage and it has remained with him all of his life.

If the weather spoke for Brazil's disenfranchised poor on the afternoon of the race, it was very angry indeed. A monsoon roared from the heavens shortly before the start of the seventy-one-lap battle, creating a skid-pan made even more treacherous by an ill-thought-out tyre decision.

In a cost-cutting move, the two manufacturers Bridgestone and Michelin had agreed with the teams to bring just one type of rubber to deal with damp conditions. No one had imagined the track would become traversed with streams. The race started under the safety car, which peeled off after eight laps leaving the drivers to a race that saw the wrecking of ten cars, including Michael Schumacher's (a joyous cry went up from within the paddock, celebrating his defeat yet again).

Giancarlo Fisichella's yellow Jordan was leading when the race was stopped due to two big smashes – the first involving Mark Webber and a safety barrier, the second involving Fernando Alonso and the strewn remains of Webber's car. In the ensuing confusion, Kimi Raikkonen was crowned the winner, while Fisichella cut a despondent and damp figure as he collected second place.

Local boy Rubens Barrichello sent the 70,000-strong crowd into a cacophonous frenzy when he overtook David Coulthard, only for his red Ferrari to splutter to a halt. Journalists later suggested to embarrassed-looking team bosses that he had, in fact, run out of petrol. They were reluctant to confirm this – and hastily called him a helicopter.

3

Imola

Imola in April was the first European Grand Prix of the year. It began with the memory of Brazil's almighty smashes still fresh in everyone's minds. Some were earnestly discussing the FIA's decision to subsequently overturn 'Iceman' Kimi Raikkonen's victory and give it to a grateful Giancarlo Fisichella. But many F1 personnel and, of course, fans, were still recalling the crashes.

'Did you see that photo of Mark Webber with no legs? Amazing! And the one of Alonso sticking his thumb up at the camera as he was stretchered into the ambulance? Ha ha!'

In racing terms, many insiders considered the Interlagos weekend a farce: right weather, wrong tyres. To the international viewing public however, it had been a reminder that Formula One could be as much fun as a log flume on a hot day, and just as wet. Crashes are the crack cocaine of Formula One and this race gave ITV its highest-ever F1 viewing figures at just over ten million. Watching great drivers get picked off one by one in the pouring rain combined the tragic with the comic – rather like watching Sarah Ferguson in *It's A Royal Knockout!*

Webber's horrendous accident on lap 54 provided us with one of the most memorable images of the season: he sat in the middle of the track, his yellow helmet peeping nervously above the cockpit, with the front and back of the car completely chopped off. It seemed impossible that his 6'2" body could still be inside the remaining shell of the car, like the magic trick in which a magician cuts a smiling lady in half. Mark probably wasn't smiling, but it seemed absurd that he climbed out of the vehicle unscathed.

Images of Fernando Alonso crouching by a low concrete wall were the most unsettling to watch. Television pictures showed that Spain's newest super-hero was conscious; his big brown eyes darting anxiously from medic to medic, his clammy hair pressed against his forehead after 54 laps. The young Spaniard had been badly shaken and a neck brace had been fitted as a precautionary measure, but the look in his eyes was beseeching, as though he was asking the medics to just sit him back in the car and let him finish the race. As he was stretchered into the back of an ambulance, he waved to the camera and put two thumbs up to the crowd. He later admitted he was desperate to let his family know that he was OK.

Arriving in Imola after the carnage of São Paulo was portentous. Imola lies near a mountainous area to the south-east of Bologna in Italy. It is the one place in which the F1 community prefers not to be reminded of the risks involved in motor racing. More than any other venue, Imola forces us to question the sanity of Formula One. It makes us ponder the psychology of fear. What on earth motivates people to drive over tarmac in a carbon-fibre shell at 200 mph? Is it a belief in themselves or faith in the strength of the car or simply that the thrill of driving at such suicidal speeds negates the fear of death?

These questions hang heavy in the Italian air. Because Imola is where Ayrton Senna died during the infamous 1994 Grand Prix, described by Niki Lauda as 'the weekend God took his hands off motor racing'.

On Friday 29 April 1994 Rubens Barrichello miraculously survived an atrocious smash during race practice. His Sasol-Jordan team car left the track and crashed at 160 mph. It was the kind of accident that other drivers take note of, and it sent a collective shiver through the paddock. But there was worse to come.

The next day, the affable Austrian driver Roland Ratzenberger took to the circuit for Saturday qualifying in his Simtek car and failed to return. He had crashed at Imola's Tosa curve at 200 mph. He was thirty-one. It was the first death in Formula One for twelve years. He would have been remembered for that grizzly statistic, had the following day not claimed the life of a more significant hero.

Senna had planned to wave an Austrian flag as a tribute to Ratzenberger in the event of victory. But the thirty-three year old never made it to the podium. Approaching Tamburello corner at 186 mph, he failed to negotiate the bend in his Williams-Renault FW16 and flew off the circuit into a concrete retaining wall.

Just under two minutes later, paramedics were cutting through Senna's chinstrap to remove his helmet, while intravenous infusions were intubated into his unresponsive body.

Professor Sid Watkins, F1's on-track surgeon for sixteen years, was one of the first on the scene. Senna was a close friend and Watkins knew as he lifted the Brazilian's eyelids that he had suffered a massive brain injury. An inquest later recorded that Senna's death had been caused by the impact of the right front wheel and right front suspension arm piercing his helmet at the edge of the visor opening.

This was the great Ayrton Senna, a national hero in Brazil, a dashing, articulate, charismatic ambassador for the sport, a driver who took the car to the very limit and a man who was considered untouchable and invincible. At that time, he was probably the most famous sportsman in the world, his unswerving faith in God matched only by his faith in his own ability.

Officially Senna died in hospital. Unofficially, Watkins knew he had lost his friend before they left the circuit. He recalled how Senna was laid on the ground, ten metres from the fatal point of collision, and here, his life ebbing away, he 'sighed, and though I am totally agnostic, I felt his soul departed at that moment.'

In that same fateful year J. J. Lehto and Jean Alesi suffered neck fractures in private testing; Andrea Montermini along with Barrichello received severe head injuries with mild concussion; during official practice in Monaco, Karl Wendlinger had an accident that left him in a coma and Pedro Lamy received multiple injuries in private testing, including two broken legs. In total there were eight serious accidents in 1994, but nothing shook the sport like Senna's death.

Max Mosley, the President of the FIA, launched a zero-option policy, stating that 'zero mortality' was the aim in Formula One. Circuit design, safety-barrier development and personal protection for the driver within the cockpit took on unprecedented importance. Research into the prevention of injury through studying the biophysics of accidents was stepped up and Mosley established an Advisory Expert Group who would conduct research and development to effect greater safety. Its chairman was Professor Watkins.

'Each test session,' he recalls, 'cost several thousand pounds, but Max Mosley had given us *carte blanche* intellectually and financially.'

In 1996 all teams were ordered to fit the new, obligatory Confor head-and-neck protection collar – a 75mm-thick, horseshoe-shaped foam structure that significantly reduces the strain placed on the head and neck in high-speed impacts. Watkins revealed that one team boss complained it had cost him £1 million to redesign the car chassis to fit the Confor collar. The Professor told him to subtract it from his driver's salary, which was seven times that amount.

By 2003 Formula One was undoubtedly safer than it had ever been before. Between the first Grand Prix at Le Mans in 1906 and the 1998 F1 season, 300 lives had been lost among drivers, officials and spectators. Between 1963 and 2000 there were 17 driver deaths and more than 100 serious injuries. In 1994 Senna was the last driver to die behind the wheel of an F1 car. However, the fact remains that there is always unpredictability in Formula One and with it comes danger. No human being can be propelled at up to 200 mph without some risk. So why do it, and how do drivers – many of whom have wives and children – reconcile their chosen vocation with the risk of injury or death?

*

The name Gilles Villeneuve is synonymous with a certain kind of F1 mentality. Competing in the late seventies and early eighties, the French-Canadian displayed bravado in everything he undertook. His day-to-day road driving was so petrifying that his uncomplaining wife would cower on the floor behind the seats – even on short journeys. Villeneuve would often take off in his helicopter with the fuel gauge on zero, and enjoyed flying in and out of power cables and pylons. His love of speed began with snowmobile racing in Quebec – a sport that regularly throws its competitors out onto the ice at 100 mph. He possessed a supreme confidence in his own skill and judgement. In retrospect, the most surprising thing about his death is that it didn't come sooner.

Gilles Villeneuve was living on borrowed time. After a crash at Monte Carlo, the then twenty-eight year old declared: 'I was not frightened at all. My only fear was for the car.' And when asked by a Quebec newspaper which was more likely to kill him, Formula One or the snowmobiles, he replied: 'Neither. I'm more afraid of dying of old age.'

Fortunately then, for Villeneuve at least (but not for his young widow and eleven-year-old son), he died aged thirty-two, while qualifying at Zolder, Belgium, in 1982. He was embroiled in a bitter feud with rival Ferrari team-mate Didier Pironi. Twelve days earlier, the Frenchman Pironi had, according to Villeneuve, reneged on an unspoken agreement and 'stolen' victory from him at the Imola Grand Prix. Villeneuve went out to qualify at Zolder, despising Pironi and desperate for revenge.

As the qualifying session drew to a close it became apparent that Villeneuve was not going to beat the time set by Didier. Ferrari issued team orders for Villeneuve to come in at the end of the next lap, but he refused. He never returned.

Germany's Jochen Mass was coasting back to the pits after qualifying for his 100th Grand Prix, when he saw Villeneuve appear as a red flash in his rear-view mirror. He kept his car to the right, the usual manoeuvre that would allow Villeneuve to pass on the left and give him a better line for the upcoming turn. Inexplicably, Villeneuve selected a non-existent space to the right of Mass's car.

Misjudging the space, Villeneuve's left front tyre touched the right rear tyre of Mass's March car and was propelled into the air. It remained airborne for several seconds, before nose-diving with shocking force and flipping over and over across the track. On impact, the front of the car snapped away and Villeneuve's helmet came off, but he was still strapped in the seat belts connected to the chassis. The car flew into the wire-mesh fencing at the side of the track. Villeneuve died from a broken neck.

It was not only Gilles Villeneuve's career that ended that day. Mass was haunted by the memory of Villeneuve's car somersaulting past him.

'In the end, it made me stop racing,' he later admitted, 'even though I know I did nothing wrong. It made me question my own mortality, because when you live life at the limit sooner or later you must face up to the possibility of serious injury or death. One day I woke up and looked at my wife and children and thought, "Enough is enough, no more risks."'

But in the world of Formula One Gilles Villeneuve is hailed as a hero. He only won six races from sixty-seven Grand Prix starts. In his first race, with McLaren, he took one spin after another; in his second, for Ferrari in Japan, he ran into Ronnie Peterson's Tyrrell and flipped his car into the spectator area, killing two onlookers and injuring several others. His first full season didn't start much better and he was involved in a series of accidents. But motor racing adores Gilles Villeneuve.

F1 books describe him as an 'inspired genius' or 'a megastar. Not just in the sense of being super quick...his commitment, verve and sheer abandon were breathtaking.' Eighties' driver Keke Rosberg called him 'the hardest bastard I ever knew'. Formula One is a sport that reveres hard bastards, a fact not lost on Villeneuve's son, Jacques.

'I really enjoyed that,' said Jacques after a big crash in 1998 at Eau Rouge, in which he utterly destroyed the car. And in 1999, after a similarly spectacular collision, he said: 'That's the best accident I've ever had.' He speaks with all the insouciance of an RAF fighter pilot.

The 1997 world champion has carried the weight of his father's name ever since he started racing in Formula Three at the age of eighteen and he has clearly inherited his father's love of speed and danger; but Jacques Villeneuve is often asked whether he is also carrying the weight of his father's expectations. Is he, like Hamlet, forever chasing his father's ghost?

Jacques was an impressionable eleven year old when his father died and he wrote poems about him as the family travelled home for the funeral.

'I can't remember too much,' he says, his eyes never betraying any emotion. 'I don't have a lot of memories of my father. He was never at home – he was always racing, testing, playing with his boat or whatever.' But Jacques always won at his boyhood passion, Scalextric: 'I always won...because I always played by myself.'

His mother Joann raised him almost single-handedly: 'Gilles was very demanding – he wanted his son to be more than perfect. I didn't have any problems with Jacques. He would sit calmly at the table and not drop his glass of milk. But when Gilles was there he would drop his glass of milk. He would get very nervous just trying so hard to please his father.'

Jacques is not a man who in my opinion exudes confidence. He is known for his dry wit and almost childlike mischievousness, but there are other sides to his character that are only comprehensible to people who worship at the altar of Formula One.

During my first season in the sport I was asked by Villeneuve's personal assistant, Jules Kuplinski, to join the driver for lunch in the BAR motorhome. Two years earlier – before I was working in Formula One – I had met Villeneuve at a BAR press event in Barcelona. The team wanted to burst onto the scene with maximum publicity and Villeneuve had apparently hand-picked celebrities to be flown in to Spain – all expenses paid – for a weekend of partying in the capital. At least I could recall that event if conversation dried up over lunch, I thought.

It seemed odd that although we had frequently passed one another in the paddock, he had sent someone else to make the arrangement on his behalf. But I turned up at the agreed time, was met at the motorhome by a hostess who was expecting me and was shown to a table near the back of the room where Jacques was sitting. He was already eating. We exchanged continental kisses and I sat down. He carried on eating.

'How's it going?' I asked.

'Fine. You?'

'Yeah, good thanks. Still getting my head round the new job and F1 itself. It's a pretty unusual place, eh?'

'I guess.'

Silence.

'Well, obviously you're pretty used to it,' I continued, 'but, er, for an outsider it's all very different.'

Silence.

'Sooo . . .' I said, wondering what the hell I was doing there. 'Are you staying nearby this weekend?'

'Yeah. My campervan. It's very convenient,' he said between mouthfuls of pasta.

Eventually a waitress came over and asked if I wanted lunch. I went straight for the main course. Then I asked Villeneuve if it was OK for me to have some of the water on the table.

He shrugged. 'Sure.'

I poured myself a drink. 'So,' I went on, 'the last time I saw you was in Barcelona on that publicity weekend.'

'Yeah. I remember.'

'That was some party.'

'Yeah, it was fun.'

So that was Barcelona covered. Jacques looked at me through thin-framed angular glasses, a half-smile never left his face and occasionally it seemed as if he was about to ask a question, but he never did.

'I don't know a lot about F1 yet,' I said, assuming this was safe enough territory. 'How did you get into driving?'

'I grew up with snowmobiles, bikes and stuff, it was kind of inevitable.' He didn't mention his father.

'Oh, I see...I've, er, been working on the NBA. You know, the American Basketball League and, er, now I'm doing F1 instead.'

'Right.'

He didn't make any attempt at conversation as I worked like mad to find any common ground. Guessing that maybe this was purely a networking opportunity, I moved on to the topic of work. 'So, I'm filming some pieces with drivers away from the track, doing things that are not related to F1 and if you're up for it, we'd love to do something with you.'

There was a long, painful pause.

'We'll see.'

'Obviously we'll work around your schedule...'

He shrugged. 'Maybe.'

'OK,' I said. 'Get Jules to tell me if you have the time.'

Lunch dragged on as Villeneuve blocked innocent questions and showed no interest in anything I had to say. It was so disappointing that the driver most often described as opinionated had, when I met him, no opinions and seemed unaware that he should make any conversational effort. It seemed to me that the spoilt boy had become an indulged adult.

I was still eating when Villeneuve decided it was time to leave.

'OK,' he said smiling, 'I've gotta go. Nice to see you.'

I finished my lunch alone, under the hostile glare of the others in the motorhome.

It was easy to see how the animosity had arisen between the ex-world champion Villeneuve and his team-mate, up-and-coming Jenson Button. Button is self-confidence personified and Villeneuve must have hated sharing his F1 toys with him. The thirty-two-year-old Villeneuve is rarely photographed without his baseball cap. Button often appears on lists of the 100 Sexiest Men (which very few colleagues can boast about). But for their many differences, one similarity remains: they both choose to risk life and limb in pursuit of their sport.

With Button it is perhaps easier to explain than with Villeneuve. Button has a supportive father who used every last penny to get his boy to the top. Villeneuve saw his father die behind the wheel of a car, which he then stepped into. Sports psychologist Hugh Mantle suspects that Villeneuve is under the illusion that 'It won't happen to me...plus of course,' he adds, 'there is often the motivation to prove you can do better than your parents.'

The one characteristic that most F1 drivers share is an ambition since childhood to become a world-class racing driver. Through go-karting they hone their judgement and skill to control the dangers – like a gymnast learning to negotiate the parallel bars above a foam pit.

Hugh Mantle has worked with professional sportspeople for nearly twenty years, including golfers, Olympic athletes and F1 racers, and he believes this experience of driving from a young age is the key to a motor-racing mentality.

'It's the relationship between their competence, their knowledge and the task they see ahead of them. If you believe you have the ability to do something, you go out and do it.' He likens it to an eye surgeon who conducts a two-hour operation during which there is a risk of blinding the patient. They do it because they know they are capable of carrying it out successfully. 'Most of what we find if we look at drivers is that none of them believe they are not competent. It's that critical combination of confidence and competence.' Belief in themselves negates the fear of death or injury.

Research into the attraction of dangerous sports has found that this 'perception of risk' is subjective. Each individual develops what is termed a 'protective frame' around their chosen sport. For instance, a few weeks after his crash in Brazil, Fernando Alonso seemed entirely untroubled by the event, shrugging it off as 'one of those things'. After a period of convalescence at his parents' home, he was soon back in the cockpit. However, on the day I spent with him he displayed quite bizarre levels of concern about his personal safety.

Alonso will rarely allow himself to be driven by anybody else. He was anxious about climbing into a rowing-boat for our interview and even paused to allow me to go first on the wooden jetty.

'That doesn't look too safe,' he said. 'After you.'

He was due to fly to Canada later that week and looked gravely concerned about the prospect. 'I'm going to wear a mask,' he insisted, 'because of SARS.'

I explained that although Canada had indeed been at the centre of the SARS outbreak in North America, the respiratory disease was no longer considered a threat to travellers. He remained unconvinced. Alonso's 'perception of risk' differed so wildly from mine that he regarded sitting in a stationary rowing-boat as considerably more perilous than a 200-mph spin through torrential rain. However, this perfectly demonstrated the classic personality type of someone who has built a 'protective frame' around motor racing.

'F1 is, er, normal,' he said. 'It doesn't mean anything special to me. It's my job, like waiting in a restaurant or working as a bank clerk.'

This psychological tactic is nicely described by the psychologist J. M. Apter: 'A protective frame gives the individual a feeling of safety, even when the dangers and threats are part of the phenomenal field, and this produces the paradox of danger-which-is-not-danger.'

The truth is that most of us want to go on living. We are motivated by a desire to be safe and to avoid situations in which our lives are threatened. We all have individual boundaries for self-preservation, lengths we will go to in order to avoid death: quitting smoking, driving with care, bypassing dark alleyways in the small hours of the morning. So the question is: do F1 drivers have a set of parameters that differ wildly from the rest of us?

Psychologists often use the example of 'skating on thin ice'. If the ice on a frozen pond is thick near the bank and thinner in the middle, with a strip of unfrozen water at the centre, where would you skate? Some people choose not to skate at all, sipping hot chocolate in what is termed the 'detachment zone'. Others might venture cautiously onto the edge, remaining within the 'safety zone'. But a minority will be drawn to the thin ice, precisely because of the risk and the possibility of hearing it crack underfoot. These people perceive less danger than the others (though that doesn't mean they are right). Their 'protective frame' extends much farther out from the bank than those who stay in the 'safety zone'. The risk-takers who explore the 'trauma zone' enjoy the state of arousal induced by courting danger.

It may be no coincidence that several ex-F1 drivers went on to lose their lives in spectacular fashions. Didier Pironi suffered a massive career-ending crash at the 1982 German Grand Prix, but he retained his love of speed and took up powerboat racing instead. While competing in the 1987 Needles Trophy event off the Isle of Wight he flipped his boat at 100 mph and died. (A few months later, his girlfriend gave birth to twin boys, naming them Gilles and Didier.) Britain's first world champion in 1958, Mike Hawthorn, died when his Jaguar collided with a lorry, and the inaugural world champion Giuseppe Farina's Lotus-Cortina skidded into a telephone pole in the French Alps. Hugh Mantle believes that although F1 drivers take safety very seriously, there is some evidence to suggest that as boys they tend to do 'more "crazy" things' than ordinary children. 'There is,' he says, 'an element of the "adventurer" in them.'

Ayrton Senna worked hard to ensure he remained somewhat childlike. 'The difference between a man and the children is only the toys,' he claimed (echoing generations of women the world over). He believed we should learn from children.

'They don't think about tomorrow, they don't think about next year, next month, they just see a game and they try to play that game right now. They enjoy completely life to its full potential.'

For most people, the intoxicating thrill of living in the moment normally gives way to adult responsibilities and commitments. With maturity comes the ability to choose between thinking about others and thinking about oneself. So where does that leave racing drivers? Must a man be selfish and immature to choose life in the F1 fast lane?

Time and time again I have heard it said that Formula One drivers must be devoid of emotion. Racing legend James Hunt once described what it takes: 'You do everything in your power to control your fate. Instinct plays a part, but emotion . . . well, that's unreliable, dangerous.'

According to seventies' driver Ronnie Peterson, most racing drivers confronted with a crash think '"Oh shit, this is it" and face it in a rather unemotional kind of way. It's the way we are; very analytical, clinical and pragmatic.'

It seems racing drivers can block out any guilt they might feel at forcing their loved ones to watch them risk life and limb behind the wheel of a car. According to one unnamed driver who asked Hugh Mantle for assistance, it wasn't really a consideration: 'He [the driver] simply said that when you get behind the wheel of a car your love of the sport overrides the implications for your family.'

Alberto Ascari, an Italian driver in the fifties, once confided to a friend: 'I never want my children to become too fond of me...because one of these days I may not come back and they will suffer less if I keep them at arm's length.'

Nowadays drivers are more likely to be heard saying they want their family with them on race weekends.

'Connie brings me news from the outside world,' says Juan Pablo Montoya of his wife, 'it relaxes me.'

Giancarlo Fisichella admits that having his wife Luna with him at a race is a positive influence: 'I feel calmer when she is around.'

In my experience, the wives and girlfriends of racing drivers accept the responsibilities – and the risks – with very little questioning. They are usually motor-racing fans themselves or grew up with relatives who drove competitively, so they have faith in the skill of their partner and the safety of the car. Connie Montoya, for instance, admits that she was once a fan of Montoya's who eventually grew to love the man rather than the celebrity. She was well aware of the risks.

Similarly, the fathers of drivers have watched their sons progress through the racing ranks and therefore have a more realistic under-standing of the risks. On the other hand, they also develop a 'protective frame' in relation to their son's career. It is often much harder for the mothers.

Mark Webber's mother Diane hates the danger of her son's profession and she really struggles to get through a race weekend. If she is at home in Australia and the race is in Europe, the time difference means the action takes place at night. She stays up, pacing the house and 'drinking tea, just trying to keep my mind off it'.

When Mark had the horrendous crash in Brazil, Diane and Alan were in Australia. She was watching the time-delayed broadcast on TV, while Alan followed the action live on the Internet. He saw each crash come up on screen, as described by the webmaster in Brazil.

Then came the words Alan had been dreading: 'Webber – crash. MASSIVE.' They had watched the previous eight crashes during the race and each one had looked pretty 'MASSIVE' to them, but only Mark's was described in those terms.

Shaken, Alan told Diane to turn off the TV. He didn't want her to witness the accident until he knew Mark's condition. Eventually, the call came from Mark's manager Anne Neal to say their son was unhurt, but the memory of waiting for that news will stay with them for ever.

Mark is a typical twenty-first-century driver in his phlegmatic attitude to the sport. For him, as for his peer Fernando Alonso, it is just a job like any other. But this down-to-earth attitude (in perhaps two future world champions) is a fairly recent phenomenon. Earlier in the history of motor racing the drivers would talk excitedly about being addicted to the adrenalin high.

'You really do go through hell for a couple of hours,' said 1992 world champion Nigel Mansell, 'but it's worth it for the buzz. It overrides everything, even the danger of death.'

Two years before his death, Gilles Villeneuve said: 'I'll die a happy man, because doing what I do makes me feel alive.'

For Didier Pironi the exhilaration of racing was 'Better than sex.'

In 1992, the psychologist J. Farmer conducted a survey into another hazardous sport – surfing. Fifty surfers were asked to rank in order of importance six varied motivations for engaging in this pursuit, along social, aesthetic, competitive or health-and-fitness lines. Overwhelmingly, 79 per cent of them assigned their love of surfing to the 'pursuit of vertigo'. In this instance, vertigo is defined as a 'confusion of balance and perception' characterized by speed, acceleration, rapid change of direction and overcoming the body's limitations.

The parallels with racing are uncanny, though vertigo is usually pursued purely for pleasure, as a form of excitement-seeking. One surfer alluded to the feeling of 'spinning crazily in a world that is neither land nor sea nor air'.

Echoing such sentiments, Didier Pironi claimed he experienced an implosion of boundaries in the world inside his car: 'My heart, mind, body and car fused into one force. An out-of-body experience of sorts.' Ayrton Senna described this spiritual experience as 'violent but beautiful . . . so mortal, but living life to the full. This sport can break the body, crush the soul, but make the spirit soar.'

Although few F1 drivers could describe it with Senna's lucidity, they are all motivated by the sheer intensity of driving at very high speeds. It goes beyond money or fame – for some it is their very *raison d'être*. Senna spoke of his occasional desire to walk away from this dangerous occupation, but found that he could not because 'It's in my blood.'

He was perhaps closer to the truth than he realized. A significant body of evidence suggests that people who participate in dangerous sports endeavour to spend more time in a 'paratelic' state, as opposed to a 'telic' state.

The paratelic individual's behaviour is impulsive, sensation-orientated and spontaneous, with a marked preference for high levels of arousal (due to excitement, nervous adrenalin or being 'psyched up'). In this state a person will try to prolong the activity for as long as possible.

A 'telic' personality, on the other hand, feels this sort of extreme arousal as 'fear' and tries to avoid it. They are more goal-oriented rather than sensation-seeking, more given to planning than spontaneity and are more likely to be 'serious' rather than 'playful'. Everybody shares these characteristics, but those with more 'paratelic protective frames' (such as F1 drivers) seek out these sensations, experiencing them as pleasant rather than fearful.

However, it seems to me that an F1 driver's relationship to speed and physical arousal has another dimension: the thrill of competition can sometimes compensate for a deep-rooted insecurity. The sense of power that comes from being a racing driver can bolster fragile egos. Former British F1 driver Jonathan Palmer has spoken of the 'belief that in the fullness of time you will be appreciated and rewarded'. This external validation comes from applauding team-mates, the crowd and loved ones. It is manifested in standing on the podium, the playing of the national anthem, the pop of the champagne cork, the TV interview beamed across the globe and financial rewards beyond one's wildest dreams.

Adulation is addictive, but so is competitiveness: the sensation of being first past the chequered flag; knowing that you have outclassed your peers. 'The power and speed make us feel good, give us a thrill and a sense of being extraordinary,' observed the God-fearing Scottish driver Jim Clark. 'It's simply an extension of what most men become when they get behind the wheel of an ordinary car.' Clark should know: he was twice world champion. He struck a tree and died in Hockenheim in 1968, during a minor F2 race.

Six months before his own death, Roland Ratzenberger said: 'Motor racing is everything to me. Life would be empty without it.'

Other drivers have similarly explained their commitment to danger as a fundamental factor in their emotional and psychological well-being. Without it, they say, they would be unbearable to live with. Hugh Mantle recalls one driver explaining: 'When you're doing well, the self-fulfilment and self-esteem are such that you will do that sport irrespective of the effect on your family.'

This theory is supported by the case of Alison Hargreaves who became the first woman to climb Everest without oxygen, but famously died attempting a subsequent journey to K2. The newspapers ran front-page photographs of her widower and two children aged four and six, expressing outrage that not only a woman but a *mother* should undertake such a selfish act. Yet her husband calmly explained that without such personal ambition, Alison would not have been the woman he loved. Climbing was central to her self-belief and was the best use of her talents.

Nevertheless, the one theme that comes up again and again in interviews with racing drivers is their strong belief that they can control their fate: they can stare death in the face and still elude it. It's a theory commonly applied to extreme sports fanatics: the notion that those who base-jump off buildings or climb rock faces with their bare hands are in fact deeply afraid of death – more so than the rest of us.

Taunting death makes racing drivers feel immortal – at least for a moment or two. Paradoxically, crashing can give them greater confidence and less fear. It actually reinforces their faith in their cars.

'I think they see that their safety equipment works,' says Hugh Mantle. 'They think, "Well, OK, it was all right." Crashes are really a trial of their equipment.'

Ronnie Peterson agreed that crashing can make a driver feel more confident: 'It's a strange phenomenon, but true…especially if you escape from a bad accident without getting seriously hurt. It makes you feel invincible and gives you a greater desire to go out there and do it again. It's pretty rare that an accident has a negative effect on a driver. It's usually just the opposite.'

Fernando Alonso couldn't control the treacherous rowing-boat or the SARS virus, but he did believe he could control his F1 car – even after an almighty crash that suggested he wasn't completely infallible.

Alain Prost sums up this universal feeling among F1 drivers: 'The best risk is the one you control yourself. The one I hate and would never take is the risk you can't control.' But in Formula One, of course, there are always factors left to chance – the mistakes of other drivers and the omnipresent threat of mechanical faults.

The reason for Senna's crash has never been formally established, and ten years later, the Italian legal system is still investigating it.

Senna was a self-confessed control freak. As a child he lost the first kart race that he ran in the rain. He was devastated and following that defeat would take his kart out and practise in the rain until nightfall. His theory: you must control the rain, you cannot let it control you. But there are two types of control critical to Formula One: the tangible – controlling the car, the immediate environment, split-second decisions made on the track – and the intangible: the ability to control fear; a skill most F1 drivers strive to perfect.

'I don't think there is a driver alive that doesn't think about being hurt,' says Jacques Villeneuve, 'but if you let that fear control your actions, then you don't belong in this sport.'

Similarly, his father spoke of his ability, while chasing for pole position, to 'squeeze the fear'. We cannot know how many racing drivers have psychologists to help them deal with their fear, but I suspect many do. However, most psychologists agree that inside all professional sportsmen there is one fear that overrides all others: the fear of losing – that is, coming second rather than first.

'Ultimately the driver's will to win is greater than their fear of failure,' says Hugh Mantle. 'They are committed to anything that will give them an edge.'

Although most F1 drivers start each race knowing that their inferior car will not allow them to win, their years of competing in lower formulae have compounded a competitive desire that keeps them aiming for a better team, a better car and better results. The will to win is so fierce that it must be born of a deep and natural instinct. Driver Jim Clark certainly thought so: 'If cars didn't exist, men would race horse and cart, and if the wheel had never been invented, man would just race horses and each other. It's a natural instinct, only technology has transformed this need for speed into a potentially deadly pursuit.' And into potentially gripping TV.

In *Deadly Obsessions* the respected F1 writer Phil Shirley admits that 'the danger of death or serious injury makes for great entertainment.' Trends in F1 popularity and TV viewing figures would certainly seem to support this macabre fact. Formula One experienced a huge surge in global viewing figures with Ayrton Senna's death. But the sport is now facing a new dilemma: after years of working tirelessly to increase the chances of drivers walking away from 'spectacular' crashes, has motor racing become too soft?

The new 'head-and-neck support' (an improvement on the Confor device) is just one of many measures that some say have removed the element of danger and given way to a 'safer' and therefore less exciting sport. In the early days, racing cars had their engines in the front, there were no safety belts, no barriers between cars and the spectators, no gravel traps, minimal medical facilities and the drivers wore cotton trousers, short sleeved T-shirts and linen helmets! In the immediate post-war climate there was little sympathy for men who chose to dice with death in this way. But today, serious injuries are few and the last driver to die was Senna in 1994.

Jacques Villeneuve is in no doubt about the implications of this change: 'The harsh reality is that if Formula One was totally predictable, in that accidents or near misses didn't happen, then the sport would not be so popular.'

A mechanic from one of the top teams once sat me down before the Brazilian Grand Prix and attempted to explain the ways in which my role on ITV was part of the general shift towards castrating the sport and making it 'fluffier'.

'Less dangerous, you know,' he said. 'Drivers just don't die any more and the sport does need that.' His attitude was indicative of the anxiety some in the sport feel about a danger-free Formula One. In the near future we are less likely to hear people talk about death in Formula One than about the death of Formula One.

The story of Tazio Nuvolari perfectly illustrates how much has changed in terms of safety. Nuvolari is a legend in motor racing, although he began his career on motorbikes, racing in Italy in 1920 at the age of twenty-eight. At the Monza motorcycling Grand Prix he crashed while qualifying, breaking both legs.

He was told that walking was out of the question for at least a month, but the very next day he was back in the race, with both legs in plaster. He had to be tied to his bike and needed mechanics to hold him up at the start and catch him at the end. Nevertheless, he won the Grand Prix – and thereby entered the sport's hall of fame.

Today, of course, there are questions of insurance and litigation that make such behaviour unthinkable. But perhaps lawyers aren't solely to blame for this shift in attitudes. Today, more than at any other time in history, we believe there must be a good reason to die.

The lives of Western consumers are viewed as more 'valuable' than ever before. We live in a culture of safety in which seat belts are mandatory, harmful products carry health warnings and governments spend millions warning us about heart disease, sexually transmitted infections and crime prevention. Some of us drew a collective breath when we learned that coalition troops would engage in hand-to-hand combat in the Iraq war. But if war isn't considered a good enough reason to die, how can sport be?

On the other hand, millions of people still want to watch dangerous sports. Some motor-sport fans are already looking elsewhere for their kicks, seizing on rally driving as the new death-threat of choice (a fact that has not gone unnoticed by those who monitor TV viewing figures). But if people do turn their backs on Formula One because it is too safe, what can the organizers do to stop them? Introduce changes to increase the danger? Ban certain safety measures? Bring back linen helmets?

*

Fortunately the 2003 season was turning out to be a lot more exciting than had been anticipated. Fears about Formula One's waning popularity proved to be unfounded – at least in the short term. Many people in the sport were rejoicing in the fact that Michael Schumacher had yet to win a race and the championship remained wide open. Coulthard and McLaren had won in Australia, 'Iceman' Kimi Raikkonen had seized victory in Malaysia and Jordan now had their first top spot, thanks to a lot of rain and Giancarlo Fisichella in Brazil. But now we were back in Europe and Ferrari were on the attack.

By Sunday morning in Imola a sombre mood had fallen over the paddock. Michael and Ralf's mother Elisabeth had died barely twelve hours earlier. The ill-will continually directed at Michael was swiftly replaced by a mixture of guilt and sympathy as the ashen-faced driver climbed into his red Ferrari.

Many commentators questioned the wisdom of the Schumachers taking to the track after having just left their mother's deathbed, but Michael replied through a written statement: 'My mother and father had always supported us. They made it possible to do what we do and she would have wanted that we did this race today, I am sure.'

The brothers were side by side on the front row of the grid. Michael drove a near-perfect race, both physically and strategically, to take Ferrari's first victory in the forty-two days and nights of the season thus far. Ralf came home fourth and retreated to the Williams motorhome, away from the TV cameras. Michael took to the podium wearing a black armband, fighting back tears and biting his lip. There was no champagne celebration.

Afterwards the Schumachers were praised by McLaren boss Ron Dennis: 'You must have passion to compete in Formula One, but at the same time, we all have families and there are times when our responsibilities towards both can conflict. Michael and Ralf conducted themselves perfectly on this occasion. They were able to admirably balance their commitment to their sport and to their family.'

4

Barcelona

Many teams flew out of Imola feeling pensive. Reality checks are extremely rare in the world of Formula One. Ferrari's first win of the season in their new car would have brought inevitable despondency and resentment from the other teams and the media (which was braced once again for a 'red' season), but how could anyone begrudge Michael his success?

For some insiders this made it even more frustrating: Ferrari had won under circumstances that didn't allow them to gripe and moan. But to more reasonable people within the sport, it was simply a sad day. Everybody knew that the Schumacher brothers had been very close to their mother.

The following morning's newspapers ran front-page photographs of Michael on the podium looking pale and gaunt. Some journalists took this opportunity to speculate about Schumacher's psychology: how could a man leave his mother's deathbed to go and compete in a sport? How cold and calculated must he be to race so calmly under circumstances that should have been far too distressing? How much pressure did the team exert on him to drive? Was it really his choice to take to the track?

I think the truth is that Michael and Ralf would have had few reservations about climbing into their cars to race at Imola. Formula One is much more than just a job – not only for the drivers, but for the people who work within it. The boundaries between life and work become blurred. The allure of the F1 'lifestyle' attracts acolytes to its doors but the truth about daily life for most people inside the sport is somewhat less glamorous.

*

Barcelona was the next city to welcome the championship. Above all others this is the circuit the teams know best. Throughout the winter cars are tested in preparation for the coming season here at the Circuit de Catalunya. It's a home from home for many F1 workers. It is a tough track that tests every component of the car and allows thousands upon thousands of kilometres to be driven in changeable conditions: temperature, wind speed and direction, rain and humidity, even sand blowing across the track, all have a bearing on the efficiency, speed and reliability of a car.

Spending so much time at Spain's premier racing venue tests not only the cars, but also the resolve of the employees – and the strength of their relationships back home. More than any other location, Barcelona symbolizes a commitment to life in Formula One.

I flew into Barcelona on an easyJet flight (accompanied by several stag parties competing in their own championship: who could break wind most vigorously). More and more racing teams use low-cost airlines nowadays. Luxury travel in Formula One is reserved strictly for the highest echelons of the sport. All the behind-the-scenes people who make the championship possible are crammed into economy class, wearing their distinctive team uniforms. They are dedicated to a job that takes them away from home for much of the year and forces them to live out of a suitcase.

In the departure lounges of Heathrow, Gatwick, Stansted and Luton on the Tuesday or Wednesday before a race, you can see the same faces with the same bored expressions as they embark on the same crowded planes to visit the same tracks. It's the F1 commute and these airports are the motor-racing equivalent of the platform at Paddington station.

Only these journeys start earlier and last longer: a trip around the M25, a slow check-in, a cramped flight, a scrum for taxis and a long drive to the hotel. And that's just the lucky ones. On landing most people head straight for the circuit to begin their various duties, finishing late before starting early the next morning. Many F1 recruits were initially attracted to the sport for the travelling. Now it's the thing they most loathe.

One such team member describes himself as 'the technical person for the motorhome'. In his thirties, he's been working in Formula One since

1999 and could be relied upon for a friendly smile and a cordial chat. I asked if he'd give an interview about his experiences of life on the road.

'Aw...go on then,' he said bashfully, unaccustomed to being the centre of attention.

I could normally find him behind his team motorhome fiddling with wires, running inside pressing buttons on hundreds of remote controls or helping guests who'd wandered into the motorhome and were having trouble accessing their favourite website on the complimentary computers. But he was also responsible for making sure that all the on-site computers used by the engineers and team bosses operated in precisely the same way as they did in the UK-based factories.

'So they can just plug in and go!' he said, as if he were talking about a kettle or a hairdryer. When not at a race, he works at the team factory, which must seem like leisure time compared to a race weekend.

'From Thursday to Sunday I'm at the track from 6.30 a.m. to eight or nine o'clock at night, sometimes ten if something goes wrong.' He was smiling, but often rubbed his forehead, pressing his temples from time to time. 'It's always exciting when you're over this side in the paddock, and it's the start of qualifying so you go across to the garage and you get a bit of a buzz, your heart gets going and it is exciting.' He wasn't convincing.

Did he think a love of Formula One was a necessary prerequisite for working in the business?

'Definitely not. I had no idea about Formula One. Before this I had no involvement with motor sport whatsoever...erm...I enjoy it now though!'

He was the first person I'd met in Formula One who didn't consider themselves a devoted fan.

'I think the majority of people who work in it, love it,' he agreed. 'I think you have to, because you wouldn't work the hours if you didn't have some sort of excitement, some sort of passion.'

In the four-month off-season, this team member, like other F1 personnel, works hard at the team headquarters or factories. 'During the off-season we do an enormous amount of work on the motorhomes. I have to go to the office when we aren't at a race, but some people go to testing; some people work on a roster system where they have some time off every second or third week and others go into the office and only have every second weekend off.'

But what about the glamour? Formula One is considered to be the most glamorous sport in the world.

'You know, if you're in Monaco or Monza or Melbourne, the sun is shining...you're sunbathing...' he trailed off. 'Some of the European races can be boring,' he admitted, 'and one of the problems is that everyone arrives at once – and some places, like Austria, it's a small, little town and you've got to drive an hour to find your hotel and because so many people have arrived in one spot, well, you can't always find a nice hotel, let's say.'

I turned off my tape-recorder.

The power structures at work in Formula One are very real. Team members are terrified of saying anything about their employers or the sport that could be misconstrued or reflect badly on their bosses.

'The truth is,' he said when the machine was off, 'I'm getting out of this shit. I've had enough. I almost walked out on this job last year, but I've stuck it out and I'm going at the end of this season. Sod it.'

Jane Stewart is a new addition to the Jaguar Racing team and was recently promoted to head of PR. At twenty-five, the Scottish redhead now has the task of liaising between the media and Jaguar, issuing press releases and organizing the drivers. She fizzes with efficiency and energy, always ready with a smile or a polite refusal. When I talked to her she was still delighted with her promotion and she remains one of the most thoughtful, well-mannered and engaging people in Formula One.

We had dinner in the Jaguar 'atrium' motorhome as the sun was setting, eating three exquisite courses from the team kitchen, with as much wine as we could drink. MTV played above us on the plasma screens usually reserved for race footage. It was an extremely rare scenario – there were no team bosses to be wary of and no sponsors, journalists or photographers constantly coming in and out of the atrium.

This glass-fronted mobile structure was divided into two levels. Entering through the sliding doors, there was a small coffee bar-cum-reception area to the right and computer workstations to the left, behind which was a curved padded green sofa for the queue. In the centre of this first floor were three metal steps to the next level, which was used for dining guests. Inside the metallic motorhome were eight round black tables, each seating about seven diners. On either side of this space there were entrances to private offices and the drivers' areas.

The result was a slick black and dark-green nerve centre with smooth interior walls, tinted windows and discreet doors that opened with a sigh at the push of a silver button. There was always the welcoming aroma of coffee and the temperature was controlled to counter the extremes outside: an oasis of cool in the heat of Budapest; a warm, dry refuge from Silverstone's gales.

Throughout the day jars of dried fruit, plates of muesli bars and silver dispensers of fresh orange juice or cold milk were placed on the counter at the back of the room. Beneath was a row of low fridges, full of soft drinks, plastic bottles of water and some excellent white wine, reserved for the sudden arrival of the head of a multinational corporation or an A-list Hollywood star (although it was usually gulped down by thirsty photographers or the drivers' relatives). Sitting in this impressive structure, with fans rotating overhead, it was hard to believe it could – and would – all be packed away and driven hundreds of miles to the next location.

Jane admitted that she hesitated before accepting her new position. She desperately wanted the opportunity, but had to consider its impact on her relationship with her boyfriend.

'It is hard being away so much, but we can manage it. For instance, a couple of weeks ago I was home for one night, then I went again. When I returned my boyfriend had already left on a business trip, so when we were both finally at home together it had been about three weeks in total.'

The racing season is eight months long. At any moment there are dozens of people walking around the F1 paddock either in the middle of a separation, recovering from a recent divorce or wondering if they will ever meet someone special while working in such a demanding industry.

'There are so many break-ups!' said Jane. 'So many people come up and want to talk about the problems they're having with their partners back home. Most of them don't survive the periods of separation. Now more and more people within the sport seem to be getting together.'

Jane was sitting next to a pretty young woman who had been listening intently. She had a senior position with one team's major sponsor.

'Well,' she said, joining our discussion, 'I'm divorced. My husband couldn't handle me travelling so much. Also, if you are not here, you think it's all parties and drivers coming on to you. He made me choose between him and Formula One...I chose Formula One. Plus, of course' – she took the hand of a handsome man beside her with a brilliant white smile – 'now I have him.'

I nearly choked on my olive bread. Jane was right: relationships within the sport are the only way for some people to stave off the loneliness. But they, too, had their perils.

'An awful lot of cheating goes on,' Jane revealed. 'Before I met my boyfriend I'd struck up a friendship with a guy from another team and, you know, I thought he was really nice. Anyway, we all went out one evening and there was a chance that our friendship might evolve into something else. Part way through the evening he takes a mobile call and his friend tells me "Oh yeah, he's got loads of hassles to deal with at the moment...with the wedding and everything. That'll be his fiancée on the phone again." And I was like, "What?!" Not even a girlfriend – a fiancée!'

She confronted him about it, only to be told, '"Oh look, I'm sorry, but you know how it is." There is definitely a sense of what happens away stays away,' she added. 'I think lots of men use it as an excuse. It's like, "Oh, I'm away from home so there's no other option for me." The lifestyle gives them that excuse.'

One thing is certain: people are queuing up to work in Formula One. After Jane's promotion a new position for press officer was available. 'We haven't even advertised yet and we've had loads and loads of applications, because word just gets around.'

Seduced by the idea that Formula One is synonymous with a luxury lifestyle, people are clamouring to get inside. Usually they are fans of the sport, which might be a disadvantage. 'Really, we don't want an F1 geek,' Jane explained. 'We had one girl working for us for a while who actually asked a driver for an autograph and that is strictly a no-no.'

Some people in F1 are afraid of losing the kudos their position gives them out in the real world. Many a date has been sealed by the promise of tickets to the British Grand Prix, the chance to meet Montoya or an invitation to a party on Eddie Irvine's yacht. When they leave the sport, they worry they are no longer cool by association. This anxiety and the fanaticism that Formula One inspires allow it to make demands on its workforce that would barely be tolerated elsewhere.

The teams' 'truckies', for instance, have a particularly unenviable job. One such grafter was Neil Dickey, a slight man in his forties who drove the Jaguar set-up truck to each race, built the garage and was responsible for Mark Webber's tyres over the course of the race weekend. Neil leaves the Jag factory at 6 a.m. on the Sunday preceding a race, arriving on Monday afternoon. If the garage floor has been painted white ('by the catering staff') it means he can start building the garage early the next morning. During a race weekend he must be at the track by about 6 a.m., leaving 'Whenever we get finished in the evening – anytime from seven till midnight.'

After a long weekend and the attendant pressure of the race, Neil drives the truck back to the factory, arriving home on the Tuesday. 'Depending what time we drop the trucks off, we unload and then usually go home. We might have a day off during the week and if I'm really lucky I might get the Saturday off before departing again on the Sunday.'

He relates all of this quite calmly, while wrapping a tyre in thick black padding. Neil seemed to assume that everybody works such torturous hours. 'I'm recently married,' he said. 'We see each other roughly one or two days every fortnight. It's very hard, but we've known each other a long time and we're both doing what we've always wanted to do. I was in desktop publishing and took the decision to make a career change ten or twelve years ago. We're not actually putting any pressure on each other to stop.'

He loves motor sport, but knew little about the lifestyle when he originally joined in 1997. 'I think you have to love the sport to be able to do it. I love travel, I love going to new places. I enjoy my job, I enjoy doing the tyres. But it is difficult to have relationships at home, yes.' Most people, he says, assume he drives an enormous number of miles a year, but he shrugs, it's not that much. 'It's roughly about 35,000 kilometres per year.' (That's 21,749 miles.)

For Neil, like most other team members, the job's costs are outweighed by the moments of success on the track. Every team has its own character and sense of common purpose, but watch any award ceremony and it is plain to see that the mass of people crammed against the fencing below are usually wearing the same colours as the men on the podium above. When Michael Schumacher won in 2002, he stood up in his car and pointed with both hands to his support team, acknowledging their contribution.

'The last two races we got two sixth places,' says Neil; 'to other teams that may not mean anything, but it feels like a job done. It makes it worthwhile. Gives you a bit of a lump in the throat.'

Drivers differ wildly in their appreciation of the team around them. Some can be rather economical with their gratitude. Others are revered by their teams.

'Mark Webber,' recalled Neil, 'well, he's such a team player. He's very conscious of moving the team forward.'

Ayrton Senna also appreciated the contribution of his entire team: 'When I win a race I try to pass to them the feelings I am going through,' he said, 'because the hours that the mechanics and engineers put behind to prepare a racing machine for us – many times going through the night with no holidays through twelve months a year – can only be justified if they get some of the thrill that I get.'

I left Neil Dickey to his tyres. At the end of our chat he had confided that today was his wife's birthday. 'And I can't be there . . .' he said ruefully.

How long did he expect to continue in his job? 'I'd like to do another three years, to see Jaguar get to a position where we are challenging. I'm not sure if I can go longer than that . . . it depends on the wife!'

It seems that most people living in Formula One fall into two camps: those who last a maximum of three to four years, deciding that the rewards are not worth the costs; and those who stay for fifteen years or more – the 'visitors' and the 'lifers'.

The financial rewards are not always great, although the consensus seems to be that the more successful the team, the more generous the payment structures at every level. However, there is no such thing as overtime in Formula One and most employees earn a set amount each month. Teams such as Minardi, where funds are considerably smaller, depend heavily on a person's willingness to work in Formula One – regardless of the personal costs.

Once on the road, the teams meet most personal expenses, as Nick Haworth, Operations Director for MSL Locations, explains: 'Our truck driver gets his meals paid for, his hotels, his laundry, everything. So the second you leave the UK, as long as you're not a raving alcoholic or you can't stop talking on the phone, it just doesn't cost you anything.'

Nick is an F1 'lifer' and has been in the job for fifteen years. He's a stocky, straight-talking southerner who runs the paddock catering and hospitality for Jaguar Racing and admits it can be a challenge.

'I get here on a Tuesday before a race, the trucks have been set up in the last three days, and basically hospitality starts Thursday lunchtime and runs till Sunday night.'

He has to provide about seventy-five team members with breakfast, lunch and dinner – all from a small, temporary kitchen. The workforce leave their hotels at 5.30 a.m. and breakfast starts at 7 a.m. 'But if we were in Austria say, they'd probably have to leave at 4.45 ... As long as there are no special guests for dinner, we should all be finished round about 9 a.m., something like that.'

The Jaguar atrium motorhome also accommodates sponsors, senior executives, media representatives and drivers' guests. Nick might be co-ordinating menus for a hundred people one minute, then pouring cappuccinos the next. He attends every race, leaving his wife and three young children at home. 'I miss the kids growing up,' he said, showing me a photograph of them on his website, 'but as I've gone a bit higher in the company I tend not to stay out so much. It used to be that I was away more than I was home.'

Nevertheless, Nick's job remains all-consuming. Relationship pressures are inevitable, but he is one of the few who has managed it successfully, partly, he believes, because his wife knew what she was marrying into.

'I was doing this for five years before I met my wife. First of all, she got very bored so I bought her a cat, then I give her some kids. I've only been home three times,' he jokes, 'and I've got three kids!'

Until the extended break between Hockenheim and Hungary was introduced in 2003, Nick had not had a summer holiday with his children for nine years. 'I get a week now, which is nice. Before that it was only a couple of weeks at the end of the season when the kids had gone back to school.'

So why did he make so many personal sacrifices?

'I don't know really. I do like the travelling. It's something that's in my blood now, I think. I've done it for so long, I know so many people.'

That sense of being surrounded by friends and feeling part of a community is a recurring theme in the sport. Murray Walker has spoken of the magical 'Camaraderie of Formula One, the non-stop buzz...being an integral part of the Grand Prix scene...and generally being in the thick of it all'. For many, Formula One is their entire life, their identity, their family.

Yet there is loneliness, too, predicated on the sport's ruthlessness, which undermines any sense of security. Team owners perpetuate an unsettling system of power politics – managers are routinely sacked, technical directors are poached, and the youngest, prettiest PR girls rise through the ranks. Everybody is judged on their immediate success and there are few second chances. And on that Barcelona weekend, the cool blade of the axe was edging ever closer to one person in particular. One driver was about to discover that friends could quickly become enemies.

The Brazilian Antonio Pizzonia was having a bad season by F1 standards. The twenty-two year old had come through the lower ranks of motor sport with an impressive track record, and as a Williams test driver in 2002 his times were as quick as Montoya and Ralf Schumacher. Hopes were high, but by the time of the Spanish Grand Prix, Pizzonia was failing to make the grade and his Jaguar team were doing little to disguise their dissatisfaction.

At that time he had raced in only four Formula One Grands Prix: finishing thirteenth in Melbourne; spinning out of the next two races and managing fourteenth in Imola, after a systems failure at the start. His career had changed overnight, particularly with all the PR commitments expected by a team like Jaguar. The piranhas in the paddock could smell blood. Pedro de La Rosa had been ousted by Jaguar the previous year and on national TV he went in for the kill: 'They made a mistake getting Pizzonia there. He's too young, he doesn't know the tracks and the new format doesn't suit him. I told Niki Lauda when he was going to replace me with Pizzonia it was a mistake. He could replace me with Michael

Schumacher or Fisichella, but not Pizzonia!...The poor guy was not responsible for the wrong decisions they have taken there.'

In the meantime, Pizzonia was preparing for Saturday qualifying, trying to block out the distractions that were clearly getting to him. The vitality that normally filled his dark eyes was gone as he moved self-consciously about the paddock. There is no other sport in the world that would treat a rookie with such impatience and lack of understanding. Which brings us to a key feature of the F1 lifestyle: the sport has more than its fair share of unpleasant characters. And many of them hold positions of power.

One skill that people have to learn pretty quickly upon entering Formula One is the ability to hold their tongue. It can be frustrating to work in a place where common sense is often in short supply and egos are perpetually pampered. Add outside commercial pressures and internal power politics to the equation and it can be one of the unfriendliest, most unsettling and dissatisfying places to work. Comparing motorbike events to Formula One, even Murray Walker admits 'The bike crowd are still a lot more friendly than those in Formula One.'

One woman became so fed up with the conditions at one top team that she left after two demoralizing years. 'The politics between the backers and the team were unbelievable!' she said. 'It was very frustrating to be trying to do a job well amongst all of that.'

'I'm just sick of all these sleazy men,' said another young woman who resigned from her post as a team PR manager. 'I've got to get out.' Another former employee described working 'for two weeks, seven until midnight, living on Red Bull.' She saw one male colleague 'reduced to tears a couple of times' because of the 'hostility within the team. Senior employees would talk to us like dirt. They would try to make us fail so that they would look good.' She eventually resigned, prepared to work her one month notice, but was told to leave after three days. 'They then cancelled my pay because I'd left early!' she said. After seeking legal advice, she was told that her former bosses had broken four employment laws, 'breach of contract, bullying, personal victimisation and harassment'. The dispute is ongoing.

The hours, the travelling and the unpleasant people take a terrible toll. At a candlelit dinner in one team's motorhome – with their drivers, the team boss and several other influential figures – I noticed that one of the waitresses looked especially tired and on the verge of tears. I asked if she was OK, only to be told that she'd had a miscarriage at the previous race.

'But I told her,' said the team boss when the waitress had returned to the kitchen, 'there's a reason for these things. I believe it's the body's mechanism of getting rid of a child that's not right.'

It didn't look as though his words of consolation had hit quite the right note as she laid our desserts before us with tears in her eyes.

Even more archaic attitudes were about to surface. It was rumoured that two of the team's mechanics were gay. Hardly a sackable offence, but apparently cause for considerable controversy in Formula One.

'It's not right,' said the boss.

One of his associates laughed nervously. 'Ahem, You can't say that today.'

The boss's wife simply sipped her wine as though she had heard it all before.

I asked if it was causing a problem among the mechanics.

'No, no. It isn't, not really,' said another associate, but as in many walks of life, people frequently alter their opinions to suit the views of those in power.

After another, very different dinner, Eddie Jordan invited me to come upstairs to see a video of his band. I was tired and had another long day ahead of me, but he was very insistent. His beautiful wife Marie came along too, slumping into the cream leather settee in Jordan's plush, walnut-lined office. A huge plasma screen lit up before us showing footage of Eddie's band, the V10s, playing on a big stage.

After forty minutes of saying how great it was and how cool his drumming was, I was ready to leave. But he kept diving for another DVD saying, 'Oh, wait till you see this bit. You'll love this bit!'

I kept looking to Marie to save me, but could see no hint of embarrassment on her face. It was to me a bizarre act of narcissism – even by the standards of Formula One.

Eddie Jordan started life in Dublin as a bank clerk and after trying his hand at go-karting, gradually worked his way through the lower formulae until he got a test in an F1 car. But his own driving ambitions ended there and he set up Eddie Jordan Racing in 1979, competing in Formula Three and F3000 with drivers such as Jean Alesi, who would go on to greater things.

Jordan not only employed his drivers, he also managed them, thereby entitling him to a percentage of their earnings for years to come. In 1991 he entered Formula One, partly financed by such driver agreements and by sponsorship from backers enchanted by Eddie's ebullience and seduced by his marketing savvy. Formula One had led to meeting rock stars and eventually wanting to be one, which is why I was sitting in his motorhome watching videos.

I eventually made my excuses and left, walking alone through the paddock to the car park wondering what it must be like to work for a man with an ego like Jordan's (and Eddie Jordan is undoubtedly one of the most popular team bosses in the sport). Some powerful men – lacking Eddie Jordan's confidence – had attained such a position of power that nobody dared tell them the truth any more, like those movie stars who fire agents and discard old friends because they don't kowtow enough.

Back in Barcelona, Pizzonia was not troubled by sycophants. He was on the receiving end of more than his fair share of straight talking from Jaguar bosses and pushy journalists, as his position in the team grew doubtful. Managing only sixteenth position in Saturday qualifying, he had to endure twenty-four hours of increasing speculation about his impending dismissal.

Team-mate Mark Webber had out-qualified Pizzonia once again, and in Formula One that is the benchmark by which each driver is judged.

Ex-driver and Jaguar executive Niki Lauda pondered Pizzonia's dilemma on ITV: 'He's a very skilled and talented young driver with an immense amount of natural ability. The problem is when you're under pressure, particularly in qualifying with only one lap; even the most experienced Grand Prix drivers are having difficulty with that. And he hasn't been able to do it in qualifying; the rest of his driving skills are pretty high.'

The Jaguar team accepted that pressure was Pizzonia's problem – then proceeded to heap even more of it on him.

'I think it will be finished soon, one way or the other,' said Lauda. 'If he's good or not no one really can tell, because he needs a couple of races to really understand him. So to sack him early, I think it's not the right thing to do. I would wait a little further and see if he makes it. Sometimes people make it, sometimes they don't, but to decide today I would think is a little early for him, because you don't really know.'

Williams test driver Marc Gene was in the studio to discuss the weekend's events and his views about Pizzonia were typical. 'The word "patience" is not in the vocabulary of Formula One. It's true that his pace has not been what everybody – including himself – expected, so it must be very tough to feel that, but I know that is Formula One, and if you don't perform people get very nervous.'

Pizzonia was not the only one feeling a few nerves by race day. Ferrari were launching their new car, the F2003-GA, and not since 1998 had one of their debutantes failed to win on its first Grand Prix outing. Schumacher and Barrichello were starting up front, having qualified in P1 and P2 respectively, and the Italian team had very high hopes. It was a scorching hot, dry day and the Circuit de Catalunya was crammed with bare-chested fans in shorts.

The race was imminent. Baseball caps were the uniform of choice – a wise decision as the sun drilled down overhead. The tarmac floor was grey and dusty, spotted with fag ends and pimples of grey gum. Thumping dance music played across the whole area and huge green dustbins spewed their contents onto the floor. Most people were sucking drinks through straws from large red Coca-Cola paper cups, strolling very slowly, their eyes distracted by colourful merchandising stalls. Bridgestone displayed its gigantic inflated silver tyre, which formed a canopied roof under which people could wander to marvel at tyres. Inside the air was heavy with tobacco smoke and warm breath.

At the permanent Circuit de Catalunya gift shop, fans could buy T-shirts emblazoned with a drawing of the track or queue to take part in a mock pit stop on the elevated Michelin stand. The outside rim of the grandstand resembled British sports stadiums such as Twickenham, with thick concrete walls promising excitement and action behind their sturdy grey exterior. Running through these walls was a long, cool tunnel that dipped beneath the track and led out into the paddock on the other side. To emerge from this subterranean walkway into the pre-race Spanish air was to be assaulted by a riot of noise and colour.

Fernando Alonso was rapidly becoming a household name in Spain and his compatriots were out in force. Formula One has never ranked among the country's most popular sports. Motorbikes are more likely to stir the passions of those inclined to motor sport. But the Renault rookie with the swarthy looks had captured the nation's imagination – and his Brazilian smash the headlines – and here at his home race he had qualified third fastest behind the two red barons. Alonso had suffered a week of intense media attention in the run-up to the big day, including a drive through the streets of Madrid, which had attracted a crowd of 100,000 people. I wondered how the boy who considered Formula One to be 'just a job' was coping with the attention.

Championship leader Kimi Raikkonen had disappointed his McLaren team by making a schoolboy error in turn seven of qualifying, causing the Finn to start at the back of the grid. In front of the 'Iceman' was the Briton Justin Wilson, with Antonio Pizzonia next in line. He climbed into his Jaguar looking like Ann Boleyn on her way to the chopping block.

Heat haze rose from the track as the starting lights lit one by one. Two red cars sat in front of the two blue Renaults. All eyes were on the new Ferraris and the quick-footed Alonso behind them. He set off with total confidence, easing past Rubens Barrichello and sitting casually on Schumacher's bumper on the long run down to turn 1. As the German swerved to take the inside line, Alonso sat in his slipstream, daring the greatest driver in the world to loose his cool. But Schumacher's Ferrari hugged the rumble strip, flowing into turn 2 and setting up position for the long right-hand turn 3. However, the feuding pair had not reckoned on Barrichello, who took turn 1 wide, then had to jump on the brakes and run briefly off the track to avoid collecting team-mate Schumacher on turn 2. Barrichello then slotted in behind him, edging Alonso back into his grid position of third. The crowd loved it. But Alonso had more manoeuvres up his sleeve.

Ferrari and Renault were both on three-stop refuelling strategies and after Alonso's first stop on lap 17 he moved into second place when Barrichello refuelled on lap 20. Alonso kept the pressure on Schumacher, the race leader, albeit from a respectful distance. However, it was Michael's younger brother Ralf who was causing Alonso problems.

After Renault called in Alonso for another pit stop on lap 37, he re-entered the race to be repeatedly blocked by Ralf.

Finally, on lap 41 Ralf bent under the pressure, slipping off-line and into the dirt as Alonso's blue Renault responded and took up position behind Michael Schumacher yet again. He would hang in there for the remainder of the race, coming home just under six seconds behind the Ferrari. Barrichello crossed the finish line third, thirteen seconds later. McLaren, Ferrari and Renault (thanks to Alonso), now sat at the top of the constructors' standings. Raikkonen, Schumacher and Alonso headed up the drivers' championship.

The drivers spoke with more emotion than usual in the post-race interviews. 'This is the best day of my life and I feel I am dreaming!' said Alonso. Schumacher, hand on heart, eyes lifted heavenwards, said: 'I really love this new car!'

Mark Webber was not quite so in love with his car, but after qualifying down in twelfth, he was able to climb to seventh, grabbing his first points for Jaguar. 'To take two championship points back to the workforce is a just reward for all their hard work,' he said afterwards, which must have heartened Neil Dickey on his long drive back to Milton Keynes.

Antonio Pizzonia didn't get off to a great start. He barely had time to draw breath before the cars shot off the grid and Kimi Raikkonen leapt into his gearbox. Pizzonia's launch control had failed for the second consecutive race. Justin Wilson had somehow managed to swerve round the Brazilian, but Raikkonen was less agile. Both men were instant retirements.

Pizzonia slouched back to the paddock to face the press vultures. With TV cameras in his face, tears welled up in his eyes and he was lost for words. Pizzonia had desperately needed a little luck. His former employer, BMW Williams, said that Pizzonia had been impressive while he was with them and drivers don't just become slower overnight. The problem, they implied, must lie with Jaguar.

Later that day Pizzonia was spotted going into Bernie Ecclestone's motorhome with his personal manager. No one outside that meeting can know for sure what was said behind those tinted windows, but Pizzonia emerged into the sunlight looking much happier. His manager even patted him on the back.

Paddock whispers suggested that Ecclestone, who has been known to protect drivers from harsh treatment by their corporate employers, had called Ron Dennis at McLaren to say that they were not allowed to sell their test driver Alex Wurz to Jaguar (the handsome Austrian had been repeatedly linked with the team over the previous few weeks). It seems Bernie may have advised Jaguar to allow Pizzonia one more chance to prove himself. But the clock was still ticking for the Brazilian and for him, at that moment, life in Formula One really was the pits.

5

Monaco

The Formula One commuters arrived at Heathrow airport for their flights to Monaco, wondering if they would be going anywhere. The previous day's travel had been blighted by French air traffic control strikes and several teams had been forced to fly to Italy, then drive to Monaco.

Check-in was a procession of long faces and even longer queues. All the usual characters were there, varnished by rusty tans that couldn't disguise their lack of sleep. An exchange of silent nods was the most effusive greeting anyone could muster.

Luckily most flights were running as normal. Shoulders in white shirts were crammed into the budget seats and a gloomy silence fell upon the passengers, many of whom had been up since dawn. You'd be hard pushed to identify them as a bunch of people on their way to one of the most glamorous cities in the world.

Two hours later, bleary-eyed and dry-mouthed, we stepped into the white, startling vibrancy of Nice airport and the unmistakable confusion of Wednesday morning in Monaco before the Grand Prix. Pan-European voices reverberated around the concourse; sweating men gesticulated wildly while talking into mobile phones and apathetic F1 workers in team uniform held up signs saying VODAFONE, JAGUAR, MERCEDES or HSBC. Out in the hazy sunshine, the taxi drivers could barely disguise their excitement at the prospect of a Formula One weekend: all those captive passengers with money to burn.

Driving north along the Côte d'Azur to the principality of Monaco, the hillsides are bedecked with white rocky outcrops and lush green trees. The road sweeps gracefully round the coast and the ocean appears as a silver expanse falling to swirls of white upon the rocks far below the roadside. But most visitors to Monaco on an F1 weekend have not come to see the sea. Many of them aren't there to see the racing, either. More than any other date on the motor-racing calendar, this weekend is about much more than sport. It's about branding, status, kudos and the looks on the faces in the office when you announce casually that you're off to Monaco to watch the Grand Prix.

Monaco is about excess and indulgence. It symbolizes glamour and Formula One decadence. The mere mention of its name conjures up images of million-pound yachts bobbing in the harbour and bronzed playboys drinking $500 bottles of champagne or whizzing around on jet-skis, before easing themselves effortlessly out of swimming trunks and into tuxedos in time to take a limo to the annual Grand Prix ball. The women all look like supermodels and have breasts designed to point skywards while reclining on deck.

The first Monaco World Championship Grand Prix in 1950 was a purely financial venture. The principality was suffering from the hangover of the Second World War and racing was a means of generating interest in the region and, of course, money. But nobody could have foreseen the impact that Monaco's success as a motor-racing venue would have on its global identity.

Today it is defined first and foremost as a host town for Formula One – and that has little to do with its qualities as a racetrack. Without Formula One Monaco would be a pretty town where rich people live in the hillsides enjoying zero-rated income tax and reading about their royal family in *Hello!* magazine. Never before has a place become so cool by association. Although the Grand Prix only comes to town for four days, Monaco lives off its Formula One status all year round.

The heir to the Monegasque throne, Prince Albert, rates the importance of the race to his domain as 'fifteen out of ten'. He was, however, writing in Bernie Ecclestone's official magazine and it looks rather like a grovelling affirmation of his allegiance to Formula One: 'Our level of commitment to the future of the Grand Prix goes far beyond just supporting the event by allowing it to happen and turning up to watch it – we are also investing £10 million into changes to the track and pit areas.'

Prince Albert is one of the wealthiest men in the world and is responsible for one of its most prosperous communities, but he seems to me to be unnerved by the prospect of having the Grand Prix taken away from him. It's unlikely to happen, of course, but be in no doubt that Monaco needs Formula One and fully exploits the sport to sustain its image. The charming Monte Carlo country club might currently be hosting the opening tournament of the tennis clay-court season, but that gets small billing in Monaco's official tourism guides. The Principality is, quite rightly, chuffed to bits about its Grand Prix heritage and if you're an F1 driver, that makes it a jolly nice place to live.

People assume that multi-millionaire drivers live in Monaco because of the favourable income-tax situation. After three years observing the sport, I'm not so sure. Living without paying tax is certainly a major bonus, but when the zeros in the bank account reach a certain number, they become almost irrelevant.

The truth is that Monaco has virtually no crime, no traffic jams (except on race weekends), a large expanse of the Mediterranean Sea to satisfy any nautical passions and the clean air of the Alps just a short ride away. It's a brief flight to most European cities and there's always somewhere to park your yacht. Giancarlo Fisichella, Juan Pablo Montoya, Jenson Button and David Coulthard are among the current drivers who live there.

'A lot of people say we move to Monaco for one reason only,' says Button, 'but I certainly didn't – I love it here.' These are men who enjoy their toys – jet-skis, boats, bikes, skis, helicopters and cars – so for them, Monaco is a giant adventure playground.

Racing drivers are revered here (which helps when booking a restaurant or finding a plumber), but their fellow residents are sufficiently unimpressed not to bother them. With a population of only 32,000 and an area of just under two square kilometres, Monaco has all the benefits of a small community and few of the problems.

'Like a lot of people I looked around at places where I could minimize my tax obligation,' admitted David Coulthard. 'I come from a small town in Scotland and Fontvieille [the next harbour along from Monaco] has the same small village atmosphere.'

Coulthard has opened a successful hotel, the Columbus, and he and his girlfriend Simone now spend much of their time there – and after ten years travelling as an F1 driver, he knows what makes a good hotel.

I arrived at the Columbus for an informal dinner with other members of the press on Wednesday night, along with half the F1 paddock. There were no intimidating doormen and no queue. The simple entrance leads immediately to a wide staircase that curves up to the first floor – the bar to the right, restaurant to the left, reception hidden away in front. There are 181 bedrooms, including 28 suites, but the Columbus is designed to feel more like an exclusive, private member's club than a large hotel – a vital selling point to the Monacan clientele.

The interior is the work of Amanda Rosa, the wife of Coulthard's fellow Scot and hotel co-owner Ken McCulloch. But everyone agrees the style is 'very Coulthard' and 'very McLaren' – precise, understated, smart and neat. The guests get a little bit of F1 chic along with their sparkling mineral water and marinated olives.

The bar room across the mezzanine was dark with low-hanging lamps obscuring a clear view of the area. The Champions League football final was playing on a plasma screen, but the F1 crowd showed little interest until the instant gratification of the penalty shoot-out.

The assembled drinkers were young, but blessed with the confidence of money. I was introduced to Jamie Edmiston, a quintessential Englishman wearing jeans and a blazer, whose father owned a boat chartering company. He told me he was there to sell a yacht.

'You may have seen it in the harbour – the one with the *se vende* sign? It's very futuristic. It costs $68 million . . . We've brought it here to sell to passing trade.'

Now in almost any other setting this would be hollow bravado, but not in Monaco on Grand Prix weekend.

'Passing trade?' I asked. 'You make it sound like a car boot sale.'

He shrugged. 'This is exactly the place where there will be that passing trade.' He invited me to go on board for a look around. 'It's moored next to the *Princess Tanya* – that's the boat for the diamond party . . . Look out for us.'

There are normally only a few major parties at the Monaco Grand Prix. This year they were being hosted by a collaboration of the world's most elite diamond companies, Formula One Publishing and Jaguar Racing. If this lot couldn't pull off the party of the year, no one could.

In my bag were dinner-plate size invitations cleverly laminated with a mirrored coating, to allow guests a quick lipstick-check on arrival. The whole event had been more than five months in the planning and had first been mentioned to me at the Melbourne Grand Prix as a possible TV feature, though it had been hard to decipher what was true and what was spin.

Initially I had been told that Tom Cruise, Sharon Stone, Jack Nicholson and Naomi Campbell and other A-list stars would be popping in from the Cannes Film Festival. As the date grew nearer, however, the guest list had been whittled down to a little-known Canadian model who had once met Tom Cruise and action-comedy hero Wesley Snipes. But as the organizers kept telling us, there were many, many more celebrities who simply could not confirm until the very last minute.

Formula One has difficulty attracting A-list stars because most of them are American and therefore aren't interested. Brad Pitt, Justin Timberlake and Jack Nicholson attend basketball games because they enjoy the sport and Scotsman Ewan McGregor is often seen at motorbike world championships. But Formula One's celebrity guests are usually promoting their latest project, rather than enjoying the race. If they have nothing to plug, they don't show.

At the party the diamond company Steinmetz unveiled an extra-special stone, billed as The World's Rarest Flawless Diamond. A second gathering would take place the following evening aboard a boat moored in the harbour: a 'Diamonds-at-Sea' party, described on the invitation as the perfect place to 'sip Sundowners and flirt with facets and fashion'. But these evenings were not about fun, fashion or facets (whatever that meant). They were about business. This was an expensive weekend of marketing opportunities and everyone involved had much to lose.

My taxi wound its way through the streets of Monte Carlo to the Mirabeau Hotel, where I was staying. Wire fencing stood ten-feet high along the pavement and the black plastic TV cameras on every corner resembled gargantuan crows. Time had stood still at the Mirabeau. The tired cream leather sofas, low, glass-topped coffee tables and bamboo-framed chairs must once have seemed so decadent, but like so much of Monaco today, any description of its elegance had to be prefixed by 'shabby'.

Monaco's 'classic' architecture is better summed up as 'a bit knackered', but the Principality does play with your sense of time: recline on a sun lounger at the Monte Carlo Beach Hotel and there are ivory pillars and sloping terracotta roofs straight out of the thirties. (Look over into the harbour, however, and you see powerboats nipping between the waves.) On the streets, delicate parasols and quaint canopies speckle the pavements, sheltering the emphatic logos of contemporary fashion: Gucci, Armani, Chloe. The collision of old and new, classic and modern, original and fake is starker in Monaco than in any other city on earth.

We had decided to shoot some footage at the diamond party, but our main concern was that a lack of famous faces would undermine its appeal to the TV audience back home. I went to talk to the organizers and found them in a back room at the Hotel de Paris in Casino Square. Sitting among piles of papers, mobile phones and plastic bags full of VIP tickets, the two women in charge of the evening were doing an impressive job fielding enquiries from special guests, guests who thought they were special and guests who were acting special on someone else's behalf.

'Any confirmed celebrities?' I asked.

'The Jaguar drivers are coming, probably Coulthard, Jenson too...We're just waiting to hear if Helena Christensen will wear the diamond for us...Oh! and Wesley Snipes...'

My producer Andy and I qualified as special guests because our British terrestrial TV channel had more viewers than a satellite station. Magazines were similarly ranked in order of importance, with *Hello!* in the top spot, while the local French newspapers received far fewer privileges.

That evening I walked back to the Hotel de Paris along pavements lined with trees pruned to sculptural perfection. The old brick walls of the Principality were adorned with lush dark ivy garnished with purple flowers. Palm trees grew in the public gardens and through the concrete pavements.

Casino Square is perhaps the most iconic landmark in Monte Carlo. Built in 1878, the casino itself has always welcomed Grand Prix guests through its revolving doors. Formula One was the first sport to realize the currency value of celebrity spectators. The Beatles, Peter Sellers, David Niven – all turned up to lend Formula One some additional glamour (and press coverage) over forty years ago.

'It is something to be seen at,' said Jackie Stewart of Formula One, 'so it's more than just a great opportunity for them to come and watch a race.'

The sunny day had blown into a grey, drizzly evening and Casino Square had temporarily lost some of its shine. Outside the Hotel de Paris a replica Jaguar F1 car was hidden beneath a black tarpaulin waiting to be photographed. Two men in Village People police uniforms kept a watchful eye over it. Photographers and camera crews gradually arrived, standing around gawping at everyone else, then their watches, then the sky.

The first people to turn up were old women with weary-looking husbands, their *coiffured* hair blowing in the wind. Monegasque women over the age of fifty all seem to favour the same bleached, backcombed hairdo. The dresses were long and slinky, displaying skinny arms and too much cleavage. The old men wore cummerbunds, while the younger ones took sartorial risks with long cuffed shirts and boot-cut trousers. The whole scene was framed by the majestic mountains against a dark grey sky. The swirling wind made even the most dignified cocktail dresses dance at its mercy.

Cars cruised slowly round the fountain in the centre of the square – Mercedes, BMWs, Ferraris, Porsches, all taking their time to assess the scene and be noticed. Some drivers circled several times before pulling up outside the hotel and tossing their keys to the valets. One out of every three guests tripped on the red-carpeted steps. It was sod's law at its entertaining best. The last thing they wanted was to fall over in front of everyone, so that's exactly what they did.

An immaculately dressed woman from one of the diamond companies was co-ordinating the evening by the front door. Then came the all-important phone call: Mark Webber, Antonio Pizzonia and the supermodel Helena Christensen, plus special diamond, would be arriving any minute now. When a mercury-coloured Jag pulled up with our three celebrities in the back, there was a brief undignified scramble as photographers jostled for the best shot. A few passers-by stopped on their evening stroll, curious to see what all the fuss was about.

The two racing drivers climbed out first, followed by the model, adjusting her low-cut black dress. They had all been given the drill and stood around by the car. The leaping jaguar logo, normally white, had been painted a vivid pink for the occasion. The photographers snapped away as if their lives depended on it. Pizzonia looked especially embarrassed by all the attention. The constant gossip about his imminent dismissal can't have made this kind of public exposure any easier.

Conducting interviews in these situations is always difficult, because the illusion surrounding the event is that the celebrities are there simply to enjoy themselves. But in reality Webber and Pizzonia were there because such appearances are part of their contractual obligations to their team. Jaguar Racing provided the drivers so that their brand would feature prominently in an event that guaranteed widespread publicity and the use of Hollywood celebrity Wesley Snipes for the weekend. The diamond companies needed an F1 presence at their Grand Prix party.

Webber was relaxed after a decent ninth position in first qualifying and a quick practice time, but Pizzonia had finished a lowly fifteenth that morning and looked as if he'd rather be tucked up in bed. Helena Christensen was modelling the diamond because Steinmetz and De Beers had lent her expensive jewellery on previous occasions and she was paying them back. Of course, the combination of a 59-carat pink diamond and the Monaco Grand Prix made this *the* glamour story of the weekend and Helena's face appeared all over the world.

After five minutes of posing for the cameras and answering a few inane questions such as 'What do you think of the diamond?' and 'Why do you like Monaco?' the threesome made their way indoors.

There was one other celebrity yet to arrive: Hollywood star Wesley Snipes. Eventually a flashy black car pulled up and four people climbed out. One of them was a smartly dressed, powerfully built black man. The photographers pounced and a German TV crew jumped in with a microphone and a question: 'Welcome, are you looking forward to tonight?'

'Er, well, yes…very much so, thanks,' replied the man and kept on walking, his three companions looking a little confused. He made his way up the steps and waited politely while photographers jumped ahead, shouting for him to stop. They even bundled into the revolving doors with him, grabbing a few more snaps in the reception hall. Then he was gone.

They all sauntered back outside, scrutinizing the digital images on their cameras, clearly underwhelmed by this big Hollywood star. After a few minutes somebody asked: 'Er, that was him, wasn't it? Snipes?'

Of course it wasn't, but this being Formula One it was assumed that the first black man to arrive had to be Wesley Snipes. I never did find out who the poor man was, though his dinner dates looked impressed.

The real Wesley Snipes arrived standing on the back seat of an open-topped car, waving for the cameras and smiling his trademark grin. He stopped for a photo-call by the racing car, answered a few quick questions and disappeared indoors.

Inside the party room was awash with pink flowers and champagne. Lights flickered on black-veined marble pillars and enormous windows opened out onto a balcony. Jenson Button arrived with girlfriend Louise Griffiths, but as this was a Jaguar-sponsored event the BAR driver was anxious not to do too much publicity. Louise had been chosen by sponsors Moussaieff to wear a piece of their jewellery for the evening and was almost buckling under the weight of the £5 million diamond monstrosity around her neck.

'God!' she whispered as she smiled for the photographers. 'I'm not sure about this necklace.' It had originally been meant for Naomi Campbell, but she was late.

A nervous raven-haired woman in her sixties from Moussaieff kept a beady eye on Louise, coming up to her at the table and saying: 'Don't move. Don't dance. Just sit there.' Louise even had to take a bodyguard to the toilet with her. The photograph of her with Button was immediately beamed back to the offices of *Hello!* magazine in London.

Once we were all seated at circular tables around the dance floor, the lights dimmed and the evening's entertainment began. Through a side door tiptoed an unsmiling young girl wearing a tight pink leotard and carrying a pink rubber ball. She stepped purposefully into the middle of the dance floor, pointing her bare toes.

The compactness of the room gave her performance an uncomfortable intimacy. It seemed to me her act had been chosen for its dubious combination of gracefulness and titillation, although the sight of her bending her legs behind her head was enough to put the guests right off their foie-gras tortellini.

Then she dropped her rubber ball and it went bouncing off in the direction of Wesley Snipes. She had still not managed a smile when she bowed and strode off through the back door. There was an embarrassed ripple of applause before everyone busied themselves with topping up wine glasses and breaking bread.

It was one of those events at which people are always glancing over shoulders to see if anybody more important or famous has walked in. Niki Lauda brought a bit of irreverence to the proceedings by turning up in his trademark jeans and baseball cap.

'Nice of you to make an effort, Niki,' said Button when the ex-driver entered half-way through the first course. I later learned that Lauda attends these events because he likes being seated next to beautiful women. On this occasion he was, but she was also a feisty business-woman and soon after arriving, he left.

The lights were dimmed again and the room took on the atmosphere of a ballroom on a cruise liner. We were asked to welcome our host for the evening, but nobody caught his name and whispers of 'Who?' 'Who is he?' rippled around the room. A middle-aged gentleman thanked the audience for coming, then introduced another silver-haired chap described as the head of Jaguar Cars. Our new host announced that very soon we would all be treated to a glimpse of the 'flawless diamond'.

'And how better to view it than on a beautiful woman like Helena Christensen?' he smarmed.

Helena shrugged and a lady from Steinmetz hurried to put the solitary diamond on its simple chain around her neck. It wouldn't fasten.

Our compère filled the dead time with some waffle about beautiful settings, beautiful people, beautiful cars and beautiful diamonds, finally wishing the drivers success over the weekend: 'The pink jaguar on the cars has brought us luck already, with Mark going quickest in this morning's practice session, so if you win we'll give you this.' He indicated a pink plastic jaguar and the audience laughed politely. It was like a holiday camp show.

Helena was now ready to be paraded. The Jag guy took her by the hand and led her around the tables. She somehow retained her dignity – no mean feat when a man twice your age is displaying you like a prize heifer at an auction.

'My, my,' said our host into his microphone, 'you're much taller than me.'

'Yes,' replied Helena sweetly, 'and younger.' It got the only real laugh of the evening. Perhaps this crowd was less oblivious to irony than one might have supposed. Then again, maybe they just enjoyed his humiliation.

It was explained that we were looking at a 59-carat flawless pink diamond – the largest 'vivid pink' ever seen. This one was about the size of a boiled sweet.

'But,' our host announced, 'it is priced at £52 million!'

The room applauded and I felt as if I had stepped back in time. I turned to my fellow diner, a photographer.

'Is it just me,' I said, 'or is there something slightly anachronistic about all this?'

'Oh my god,' he said shaking his head, 'I'm so glad you said that . . . I've just come back from a UNICEF job, working on a photo-story in Africa about the spread of AIDS. Do these people have any idea what you could do with £52 million?'

Another of my table companions was a pompous German businessman in his fifties. A young representative of Formula One sat next to him, nodding politely at the older man's drunken drivel and rolling his eyes at us.

'Then one time,' began the businessman in a loud voice, 'just after September eleventh, I carried millions of pounds' worth of diamonds from there to America . . . in . . . in . . . my . . . er . . .'

'Arse?' suggested the younger man.

'My baggage – and not one, I tell you, not one person checked . . . Amazing!' He turned from Alex to Jenson Button and peered at the driver's Rolex watch. 'Is that real?'

'Does it matter?' asked Button, maintaining steely eye contact.

'No, no,' said the man. 'It's just that I have one, but with a white face. Very nice. I know you can't normally get them.'

'Is yours real?' Button asked.

'Oh, I don't know. I don't know.'

'Well, where did you get it?'

'The Rolex dealership.'

'I guess it's real, then,' said Button, turning away from the man, whose crude competitiveness had rubbed the driver up the wrong way. That and the fact that he had been staring down the front of Louise's dress. She had glared back at the wrinkly old drunkard, then headed for the toilet with her bodyguard.

After dinner the party quickly divided into those who had to work the next day and those who didn't. The dance floor soon filled with old men and young women. Helena made a swift exit, while Wesley Snipes drank with friends in a corner. Some of the younger party-goers were complaining that it had been a very 'corporate' evening – a surprise only to those unfamiliar with the F1 social scene.

Big businesses use the theatre of Formula One to display their wares, and Formula One takes their money and basks in reflected glory to perpetuate its image as the most glamorous sport. There was a gift at each place setting, although there were murmurs of discontent when guests discovered it was not a diamond. Each small black box contained a tiny magnifying glass – just the thing with which to examine one's diamonds.

The whole evening left a bad taste – and it wasn't just the pea cappuccino starter. It confirmed for me that Formula One is stuck in a time warp. Its insensitive machismo and slavish attachment to fashion belongs in a seventies' *Playboy* fantasy, yet its emphasis on conspicuous consumption and decadent materialism is very eighties. Sitting among the diamond-encrusted perma-tans of the Hotel de Paris, I wouldn't have been at all surprised to hear that J. R. Ewing or Crystal Carrington had taken over ownership of Ferrari. But there was more to come.

The following evening the 'Diamonds-at-Sea' party boarded the *Princess Tanya* yacht, which was moored in Monaco's harbour. We were hoping for a few more celebrity interviews and had been tempted aboard by the promise of some well-known faces. I was about to hop on when I turned to see somebody waving from the boat next door. It was Jamie Edmiston on his $68 million yacht, still waiting for some 'passing trade'.

I slipped off my shoes on the harbour wall and stepped aboard the *Katana*, a magnificent 250-foot long, space-age, five-storey, white and glass dream of a boat. Underfoot was the softest wood I had ever felt. The first deck was an open-air basketball court, at the baseline of which was a gym encased behind full-length windows – just the ticket for sitting on your exercise bike and looking out to sea.

'We have to be discreet,' Jamie told me. 'Mohamed al-Fayed's brother is looking around at the moment.'

We moved from room to room, gazing at the opulence that $68 million buys: handmade wooden furniture; state-of-the-art TV and music systems in every room; walls of curved glass allowing uninterrupted views of the ocean; electronic blinds operated by remote control; comfortable day beds on every level; a hot tub that rises out of the deck on demand, its dark-blue water bubbling invitingly... It was pure James Bond.

I left the *Katana* in a sort of inspired haze. I loved that yacht – and I hated myself for loving it so much. The gratuitous excess of Formula One in Monaco had started to work its way under my skin.

The diamond party was in full swing on the *Princess Tanya*. I was immediately met by an overexcited PR girl.

'Hi!' she said. 'We've got Wesley Snipes!'

The boat was covered in Steinmetz hoardings and decked out with pink roses. The eight-seater jacuzzi had been filled with ice and hundreds of bottles of Veuve Clicquot champagne. Along its polished wooden sides were ashtrays filled with cigarette butts and half-emptied glasses imprinted with oily lipstick. The spicy hors d'oeuvres left an unfortunate pong on everybody's breath.

Like almost every large boat in the harbour, the *Princess Tanya* had been decorated inexplicably in the style of an English baronial hall: heavy bookcases, velveteen burgundy wallpaper, prints of shooting scenes and stag heads on the walls. Three female and four male models had been hired to walk around, silently acting out an odd tableaux for guests and photographers – a sort of catwalk show, without the catwalk. The women wore gigantic diamond necklaces and evening gowns, while the men sported sharp suits and earnest frowns. Helena sat chatting on a sun-lounger at the back of the boat, wearing her flawless pink diamond. We were seriously short of celebrity interviewees, but another bubbly PR girl approached with a clipboard.

'Don't worry,' she said. 'We've got Wesley Snipes!'

I restrained myself from throwing her overboard and decided my only option was to get a quick word from him about the evening. I found Snipes surrounded by an audience of corporate-types who were laughing at his jokes.

'Excuse me, sorry,' I interrupted. 'I wonder if we could grab one last question with you?'

'No,' he replied 'I am done. I been pimping myself all weekend and I am done.'

Snipes was the publicity pawn of the Grand Prix (although we can hardly feel sorry for him – and he might have stretched to just one more interview). In fact, for some F1 teams celebrities like Snipes are far more important trophies than the one up for grabs on race day. The corporate and media piranhas all wanted a piece of Snipes. And it was still only Friday.

In the morning the cleaners began sweeping the decks and people all over Monaco awoke in other people's beds to the roar of racing cars practising outside. On race weekend people pay astronomical rates for hotel rooms, but they are unlikely to get any sleep.

From Thursday to Sunday a lie-in is impossible. It isn't only the F1 cars, but also the support races: Porsche Supercup, Renault Sport Clio and F3000 all take to the streets of Monaco for practice sessions, qualifying and racing with little consideration for those sleeping off champagne hangovers in expensive hotels.

You pay extra for a balcony, only to find that it's impossible to use between the hours of 8 a.m. and 6 p.m. without industrial-strength ear defenders. Street circuits have their own peculiar charm and it has to be said that the incongruous sight of a car travelling at 160 mph along a high street is enthralling. Street circuits also pose a special challenge to the drivers, but they can be a headache for residents and spectators.

Every parking space is taken and special marshals man each corner, directing the shuffling visitors along the pavements (generally known as 'the long way round') and when the famous race tunnel is closed, the only means of getting down to the harbour is on foot along the back roads – a walk that took me one and a half hours from my hotel. In thirty-eight degrees, that can really put a dampener on your day.

Nevertheless, by Saturday morning the crowds were anticipating a gripping qualifying battle. Many were in their seats by 9 a.m. for the practice session and were watching as Jenson Button emerged from the darkness of the tunnel, braked for the Harbour chicane, hit the outside guard rail on his right and spun sideways into the inside guard rail at 170 mph. The scene was relayed across the giant screens all along the race route.

It is so rare these days for a driver to stay in his car after a crash that an anxious silence fell upon the crowds when it became clear that Button's Union Jack helmet wasn't moving. His parents and girlfriend Louise were watching the screen at the BAR motorhome. The car's rear wings had peeled away and both rear tyres were reduced to crumpled rubber.

Soon the ambulance arrived and Sid Watkins crouched at Button's side. The impact had a force of more than 20gs and Jenson wasn't going anywhere without the aid of a stretcher. He spent the night at the Princess Grace Hospital, with Louise by his side, and by dinner time he had revived sufficiently to make jokes about the quality of the soup.

There is nothing like a crash to bring out Formula One's bravado. The old-school racers joked about him being a wimp.

'Give him a couple of aspirins!' said former driver J. J. Lehto.

Button wanted to drive the next day, but was suffering from concussion, so Watkins ruled it out. Another crash could have resulted in serious long-term damage. Instead Button watched the race on TV with his friends and family aboard his own boat. It was a timely reminder that perhaps Button and his fellow drivers earn the financial rewards of their death-defying occupation.

Sunday morning was seriously hot as the temperature climbed to thirty-four degrees. The Principality pulsed with anticipation. The paparazzi swarmed among the yachts, snapping sunbathing celebrities – the ones who wanted to be seen at the Grand Prix without appearing to court any attention. There were some familiar faces such as U2's Bono, boy-band Blue and the footballers Ronaldo and Pavel Nedved ventured into the paddock as guests of various teams.

I interviewed Blue on the steps of McLaren's motorhome. The team got airtime and Blue got some easy publicity. Renault recruited the services of Liberty X. The band were dressed in designer gowns and posed for photographs with an awkward-looking Fernando Alonso and an amused Jarno Trulli. Bono was a guest of Eddie Jordan but by Sunday lunchtime was refusing to talk to the media, leaving Eddie Jordan rubbing his brow as journalists waited in vain for the interviews they had been promised by Eddie's PR team.

BMW Williams had not won in Monaco for twenty years, but today they were P1 and P3, with McLaren's Kimi Raikkonen sandwiched between Montoya and Ralf Schumacher in front. Qualifying positions are of paramount importance in Monaco because of the lack of overtaking opportunities, which can make the Grand Prix less of a race and more of a parade. Michael Schumacher started in fifth place, with an eye on equalling Senna's record of six victories in Monaco.

Ralf Schumacher got off to a blistering start and Montoya overtook Kimi, but their lead was rendered academic when the safety car was deployed on lap two. Heinz Harold Frentzen's Sauber had dive-bombed into the safety barrier at the 'swimming pool' and the field didn't go green again until the start of lap 5. The Ferraris had opted for a relatively higher fuel-load and thus a longer first sector. This strategy, combined with their under-performing Bridgestone tyres, meant Senna's record looked intact.

Ralf stayed out in the lead for the first twenty-one laps, until his earlier refuelling stop handed the lead to Montoya. Williams's pit stops were good; their strategy near perfect. Michael Schumacher crept up to third place, but by now Ralf was struggling with oversteer and understeer. The closing laps saw Montoya under enormous pressure from Raikkonen, the young Finn in grey, with Michael Schumacher breathing down his ice-cool neck.

All three finished in that order, Montoya jubilant with his first Grand Prix victory since Monza 2001. Raikkonen was 'disappointed' and blamed the 'traffic' for his defeat. Michael Schumacher was unhappy with his Bridgestone tyres.

'However you turn it,' he concluded, 'it's what we had, and I think that third is reasonable.'

The Jaguar lads with their pink livery and enormous pre-race publicity had a less successful day. Pizzonia retired on lap 10 with an electrical problem and Webber lasted only until 17, when his engine lost its pneumatics. Later that day I bumped into one of the senior organizers of the diamond-Jaguar collaboration. She was waiting for a taxi outside David Coulthard's Columbus Hotel and grimaced at the performance of the Jags.

'However,' she smiled, arching an eyebrow, 'luckily we didn't just align ourselves with one team. We're giving a diamond-encrusted pedal to Juan Pablo!'

Then she flitted off to make the presentation.

6

Nürburgring

It may be reasonable to assume that while our Roman ancestors probably worked just as hard as an F1 truckie, they took a lot more days off. In the reign of Claudius, 159 days of the year were public holidays and on 93 of these the Romans could put their sandals up and watch a show. In the middle of the fifth century AD there were 200 official holidays a year, 175 of which were used for public games.

Originally these games had religious significance, but more secular activities were introduced under the republic, supposedly to celebrate notable events. There were two types: the *ludi scaenici* or theatrical occasions, attended by small gatherings in seated theatres; and the *ludi circenses*, which were staged in purpose-built amphitheatres or race-tracks.

The latter were incredibly popular and were described by the playwright who signed his works 'Terence'. In 160BC Terence described how an audience assembled to watch his latest production 'The Mother-in-Law'. During the first act it was announced that a gladiator show was about to start in the venue next door. There followed a stampede as theatre-goers abandoned 'The Mother-in-Law' in favour of gladiatorial combat, leaving Terence to reconsider the mass appeal of his play.

It may well be that 'The Mother-in-Law' was as dull as Roman ditch-water, but the playwright's story points to a universal truth: watching men pitted against each other in battle was as popular a way to spend a bank holiday in ancient Rome as it is today. This kind of 'sport' taps into a primordial desire to witness human beings in competition.

There are echoes of Formula One in this depiction of Roman chariot racing from historian Antony Kamm:

The public adulated the most successful drivers and there was heavy on-course and off-course betting. The drivers were slaves, but they were also professional sportsmen who could earn vast sums from winning. The chariots themselves were constructed to be as light as possible and were drawn by two, four or even more horses; the higher the number the greater the skill required by the driver and the more sensational were the crashes and pile-ups. A race was usually seven laps of the track – a total of about 4,000 metres in the Circus Maximus in Rome – with a hair-raising 180 degrees turn at each end of the *spina*, the narrow wall that divided the arena.

Things haven't changed much. Our taste for watching men and machines at full-throttle horsepower remains, as does our thirst for high-speed crashes. The chariot races had a 'staggered' start, with no lanes and apparently no rules, but just like today's motor racing it seems some drivers dominated the field.

During the first and second centuries AD, several star charioteers notched up more than a thousand wins each. One outstanding competitor, Gaius Appuleius Diocles, had driven four-horse chariots for twenty-four years by the time he died aged forty-two, and clocked up 1,462 wins in 4,257 starts. At Nürburgring, round nine of the 2003 championship, Michael Schumacher was going for his fiftieth win and topping the 999-points mark – certainly impressive, but rather modest compared to Diocles.

There are similar parallels between the Formula One circuits of today and the amphitheatres of ancient Rome. Roman expert John Wacher describes them as 'large, elliptical structures, built so that the maximum number of people could view the entertainment. The seating in most British amphitheatres was raised in tiers on earth banks, retained by wooden or masonry walls and surrounding a central arena.' And, of course, it wouldn't be the same without the VIPs: 'There appears to have been provision made, in the form of special boxes, for eminent people.'

But it wasn't only chariot racing that dragged the Romans from their brothels and distracted them from their watered-down wine. Gladiators hacking each other to pieces with a variety of weapons offered a grizzly diversion that is largely responsible for the Romans' reputation as a bloodthirsty lot. At least today's F1 management keep that sort of thing behind closed doors.

However, unearthed relics suggest that Roman Britons had slightly more refined tastes. Chariot racing was much more popular than hand-to-hand combat. The number of gladiator cups discovered by archaeologists are few compared to those showing chariot-racing scenes – the early equivalent of today's Formula One merchandising.

Fragments of a beaker found in St Albans depict a charioteer besides the word *celer* (Latin for 'speedy'), in an early example of marketing image rights. At Chedworth Villa in the Cotswolds, the word *prasina* was inscribed on stone, an abbreviation of *Prasina Factio* ('the Green Company') – one of four chariot team names in the Roman circus. The inscription is no doubt the work of a local fan, like scrawling *Ferrari* on a wall.

No remains of race arenas have yet been found in Britain, but any stretch of flat ground would probably have served the purpose, provided there was a slope on one side where the spectators could sit. Mosaic floors uncovered at Rudston and Horkstow in Humberside show action-scenes of chariot races in which worried-looking drivers suffer the indignity of a lost wheel or a wild swerve as their horse stumbles.

It is indisputable: we have had a long-term love affair with men in the pursuit of speed. They are admired for their skill and bravery. We invest in their desire to win and marvel at their competitive drive as we urge our chosen racer to victory. The Greek sporting ethos was founded in a realization of the power of the human body. To them, physical training and 'games' were a form of knowledge, intended to toughen up the body and temper the soul. Cheating in order to gain an unfair advantage was ignoble.

In the words of American sports commissioner A. Bartlett Giamatti, these ancient sportsmen were 'pure in themselves [and] obedient to the rules so that winning would be sweeter still'. But if we look for such 'sport' in today's Formula One, it isn't easy to find.

After Monaco and Canada (where Michael Schumacher brought home a much-needed victory) the teams moved to Germany for the 'European' Grand Prix. Several Grands Prix could qualify as 'European', but this is Formula One's way of hoping that nobody will notice that

Germany hosts two races: Nürburgring and Hockenheim. Similarly, the 'San Marino' Grand Prix takes place 100 kilometres away in the Italian town of Imola, but Monza is officially the 'Italian' race.

The Nürburgring circuit in the North Rhine region of Germany near Cologne is one of the drivers' least favourite tracks. It is typical of many F1 stadium venues in that it was built for the spectators rather than the drivers: a reverse of the priorities governing most other sports. Nürburgring was one of the circuits used in the inaugural 1950 season and was an enormous twenty-eight kilometres long. But after Niki Lauda's horrific accident in 1976 it was closed down and modified.

Despite hosting three Grands Prix in the mid 1980s, the Nürburgring didn't regain a regular place on the calendar until 1995. Today it is considered a 'gentle' track that places too few demands on the drivers. Renault's Jarno Trulli summed up the feelings of most of the competitors when he said: 'It's pretty uninspiring, really.'

In contrast, the Belgian Spa-Francorchamps race might not be the most exciting venue for visitors, but it's a classic driver's track – and the favoured choice for those who enjoy a challenge and want to push themselves to their physical and psychological limits. For TV viewers it also makes for some great races.

F1 Racing magazine polled drivers past and present, as well as technical directors and team bosses, to establish their favourite F1 track. Spa-Francorchamps topped the list. Michael Schumacher rated it his favourite track, explaining that it gives 'the best sensation and the most satisfaction you can feel as a driver'. But early in 2003 the track was dropped from the calendar.

Formula One has been addicted to cigarettes for thirty-five years and half the teams on the grid have leading tobacco companies as sponsors. Ferrari's principal backer is Marlboro, which donated $86 million to the team this season alone. British American Tobacco plough $55 million into their BAR team and another $48 million from their Lucky Strike brand. They also generously provide packs of cigarettes for motorhome visitors.

McLaren's 'West' logo was bought for $50 million by tobacco company Reemtsma, while Jordan's yellow livery is dominated by the logos of Benson & Hedges (for a mere $6 million). However, marketing opportunities for tobacco companies are increasingly limited as governments all over the world finally wake up to the unacceptability of pushing a product that, were it invented today, would surely be banned.

Australia was one of the first countries to restrict tobacco advertising and sponsorship with its 1992 Tobacco Advertising Prohibition Act. However, there is a clause that exempts four events of 'national significance', all of which are motor racing competitions, including Formula One. This clause will no longer exist from 1 October 2006, after which even the Grand Prix will have to run without tobacco money. The European Union banned tobacco advertising on television and posters from the start of 2003. The ban was originally extended to include F1 events in Europe from the end of 2006, but this has since been brought forward by a year.

EU countries have also set their own individual parameters for tobacco-sponsorship bans. The Belgian government acted more swiftly, leaving the 2003 race a no-smoking-logo area. So Bernie and the team owners felt they had no option but to drop Spa-Francorchamps from the calendar as the season began. David Richards, head of BAR (owned by tobacco giant BAT) remarked in an interview with BBC Sport that no exception could be made for Belgium: 'We have to stand firm on this issue when so many other governments and circuits have gone out of their way to accommodate us.' Silverstone and Magny-Cours both restricted cigarette branding and at the Nürburgring the cars carried tobacco logos, but curiously team staff were not allowed to wear them.

At the Nürburgring the team uniforms were imaginatively rebranded. Jordan's *Benson & Hedges* livery became *Be On Edge*; McLaren's prominent *West* branding became *Team* and BAR transformed *Lucky Strike* into *Look Alike*. This was cute, but hardly in the spirit of the ban. One thing that does seem certain is that F1 does not care a great deal about the damaging effects of promoting tobacco. For F1, the calculations are purely economic.

Yet the World Health Organization (WHO) estimates that more than ten million people will be killed by tobacco between 2002 and 2025. That's the same as more than four Boeing 747 aeroplanes filled with passengers falling out of the sky every single day of the year between now and then.

Only Williams BMW have handled the change with one eye on the health issue. They brought on board GlaxoSmithKline's NiQuitin stop-smoking brand, thereby guaranteeing them pages of press comment and allowing them to take the moral high ground. But the figures paid by NiQuitin were relatively small, and therein lies the rub.

The issue of tobacco advertising is complex, not least because of the competing aims of the FIA, F1, the EU and the WHO. In 1998, the EU issued a directive banning tobacco sponsorship from 1 October 2006. In 2001, the EU changed this date to 31 July 2005. FIA president Max Mosley wrote to David Byrne, the EU commissioner for health and consumer protection, warning 'the FIA cannot force teams to break their obligations to sponsors'. F1 would now have to 'seek events outside the EU during part of 2005 and all of 2006.'

The issue of Formula One and tobacco leapt into the public arena in November 1997, when Blair's six-month-old Labour government was accused by the Press of accepting £1 million from Bernie Ecclestone in return for a slackening of tobacco advertising restrictions.

In 1995 Max Mosley had visited Blair at his Islington home in order to promote the FIA's road safety and environmental work. Blair's advisers knew that Mosley's contacts included Ecclestone, who had just been named Britain's highest-paid businessman with an annual salary of £54.9 million. With the general election just eighteen months away, the Labour Party was under pressure to raise campaign funds. During the meeting, Mosley invited Blair to the British Grand Prix and in 1996 the MP attended the race.

In fact, Blair and Ecclestone got on so well that in a letter to *The Times* Bernie later described Blair – who was then Prime Minister – as 'a person of exceptional ability who... would do an outstanding job for our country'.

In Autumn 1996, with the election less than seven months away, Mosley raised the matter of donations with Ecclestone, pointing out that Blair's business-friendly strategy and his intention to freeze top-level income tax at 40 per cent would save him money. Bernie agreed and sent £1 million to the Labour Party. Mosley, Ecclestone and Blair insist that together they never discussed the issue of tobacco advertising.

Soon after being elected, the Labour Party began talking about the tobacco restrictions they had promised, but rather than use domestic legislation they passed the matter to the European Union. Many F1 figures – including Frank Williams and Ron Dennis – began lobbying the Government to reverse the proposal. They argued that by racing outside Europe, tobacco branding would be seen on television anyway.

By October 1997 the Government had decided that Formula One needed a transitional period in which to replace its tobacco sponsors. But this apparent U-turn – and leaked information about Ecclestone's donation – gave ammunition to the press, which had watched Labour fight the election with an 'anti-sleaze' campaign.

The Party was advised by Sir Patrick Neill QC, Chairman of the Independent Commitee on Standards in Public Life, to return the donation in the interest of 'openness and transparency'. The 'cash-for-ash' scenario was embarrassing for Blair and Ecclestone, with each insisting it was an innocent transaction that had been misinterpreted by outsiders.

Formula One is a global stage, accessing an estimated 300 million television viewers per race. Its association with masculine bravado appeals to tobacco companies.

'What we wanted was to promote a particular image of adventure, courage, of virility,' admitted Marlboro's Aleardo Buzzi.

Barrie Gill, chief executive of Championship Sports Specialist Ltd, explains why Formula One and tobacco is such a good marketing fit: 'It's the ideal sport for sponsorship. It's got glamour and worldwide television coverage. It's macho, it's excitement, it's colour, it's international... They're there to get visibility. They're there to sell cigarettes.'

Buying advertising space in this substantial market is not cheap and there are few truly global brands with cash to spare. Corporations such as Coca-Cola and McDonald's have already sunk their promotional funds into football and the Olympics. But in the face of the tobacco-advertising ban, Formula One has had plenty of time to seek new backers.

It had seemed that the future lay with worldwide mobile phone companies, although Orange's experience of Formula One is hardly encouraging. The telecommunications company gave their name to the

Arrows team for £70 million and watched the drivers underperform, the cars break down and the team go bankrupt at the start of 2003.

I interviewed pop band Hear'say in the Arrows motorhome at Silverstone as the Orange representatives stood nearby, delighted at their publicity coup. The band had been flown in by helicopter and were lined up eagerly – wearing branded racing suits – to fulfil their media obligations. They showed enthusiasm at all the right moments and then came the final question: who did they want to win?

'David Coulthard!' they all chorused. 'C'mon David! Yeah!'

The Orange PR people shook their heads as McLaren stole some free publicity. The Orange Arrows drivers were Enrique Bernoldi and Jos Verstappen – but Hear'say had never heard of them. Orange realized that £70 million does not go a long way in Formula One, nor will it teach your hired help to say the right things.

Vodafone were only too aware of this when they announced their investment in Ferrari during Monaco 2001. Fortunately for them, their sponsorship coincided with the Italian team's unrivalled domination of 2001 and 2002, so it was money well spent. Every time Ferrari or the drivers appeared in the global media, there was the Vodafone brand name, basking in reflected glory. In 2003 they contributed $41 million and capitalized on their association with a number of high-profile adverts using Schumacher and Barrichello.

So far, the Ferrari-Vodafone relationship is one of the strongest in motor racing and it is rumoured that Vodafone will cover Ferrari's losses when tobacco sponsorship ceases. However, the Italian team's 2002 record of fifteen victories, including nine one-two finishes, was always going to encourage generous backers. So much so that Ferrari were able to turn away sponsors such as Federal Express.

Ironically, it was partly Ferrari's domination of the sport that caused a downturn in the 2002 audience figures, much reducing the appeal of Formula One as an advertising platform. By Nürburgring 2003, however, Vodafone was in fact benefiting from a downturn in Ferrari's fortunes. The tightest contest in years had viewers switching back on – for the time being, at least.

So if tobacco advertising is phased out, who is waiting in the wings to cash in on this vast, predominantly male consumer base? The main contender is alcohol. This keeps Formula One firmly on the same side of the ethical fence, not least with regard to drink-driving. There was outrage when Foster's started sponsoring the Melbourne Grand Prix.

'Even the most passionate high-octane fan would acknowledge alcohol should have no role in spectator sports,' said David Crosbie, a member of Australia's national alcohol policy body. 'Australia needs to catch up with France and other countries where they have put in place measures to reduce alcohol sponsorship.'

The French have banned all alcohol and tobacco brands on TV. In Magny-Cours, for instance, Jaguar has to sidestep the law by using only the colours of the German *Becks* beer logo, without the name.

But F1 won't give up the tobacco habit so easily and have sought a way to get round the law. They found the solution in developing markets. It's classic playground tactics: if you don't want to play my game, I'll take my ball elsewhere.

The new venues of choice are therefore outside Europe: Shanghai, Dubai and India... Countries with less stringent public health policies, where cigarettes are flogged through any possible medium, and with governments eager for development, accept the request of F1, for the prestige it brings.

Formula One's European audience will still be able to absorb at least five hours of tobacco imagery every other weekend, making the EU ban about as useful as an ashtray in an F1 car. But fans will have to go much further to see F1 *in situ*. What is the cost to the 'sport' of these new venues? More long-haul flights in an already exhausting calendar does nothing for team or driver morale. The increase in travel costs will hit the smaller teams hardest. And there is always the risk that those developing countries with no racing heritage will soon grow tired of the events, benefiting from the international exposure, but failing to support them at ground level. Since Sepang joined the championship in 1999, for instance, Malaysian crowds have been falling steadily. It seems the 'sport' is losing out in favour of big business.

In 2001 Justin Wilson became the most successful Formula 3000 champion of all time. Excelling in this feeder league ought to have guaranteed him at least a test driver position in Formula One. But the cheerful Sheffield-born lad with the 6'3" frame spent a year looking around for a welcoming team and found none. They all dismissed him as too tall to fit into their cars. By the middle of 2003, after racing competently for Minardi, it became obvious this was just an excuse. Wilson didn't have enough money.

He was eventually hired by Minardi's Paul Stoddart at the start of the season, but only after he had taken the drastic step of turning himself into a limited company to raise a cheque for £1.2 million, payable to Minardi. More than a thousand investors bought shares in Wilson's talent and will watch anxiously to see if he can make it. He earns £40,000 a year at Minardi and continues to work as a driving instructor on the side.

Wilson's story reminds us that the drivers in the world's most elite motor-racing event are not necessarily the best in the world. These days, drivers have to buy their seat on the team, often at the expense of much better rivals and the quality of the sport itself. This aspect of Formula One is rapidly becoming the norm.

Jos Verstappen returned to Minardi to partner Wilson and few would question the Dutchman's experience. But he brought more than that to the table. In fact, he arrived with a £5 million package from Dutch backers keen to see a fellow countryman in the championship. Previously, Minardi had welcomed Alex Yoong to the fold because the good-looking Malaysian would cause a whole nation to switch on and thereby encourage Asian backers. Inevitably his record was dire and he was dropped in 2002 after failing to qualify within 107 per cent of the pole-sitter's time.

Back in 1995, a Japanese driver named Taki Inoue joined the Footwork Hart team at an estimated personal cost of $4.5 million. By Monaco his season was going pretty badly with his qualifying pace consistently ten seconds behind that of his team-mate Gianni Morbidelli. In Saturday's free practice he saw Heinz-Harold Frentzen in his mirrors and scurried up the escape road where he stalled, sat in the car and waited for the practice to end. He asked for a tow back to the pits after the session, but as he sat without a helmet in his on-tow Footwork, the safety car hit him, throwing the vehicle upside down. Incredibly, he had nothing more serious than concussion and a reputation as the unluckiest man in Formula One.

Five races later, having crashed with compatriot Ukyo Katayama at Silverstone, Inoue found himself at the Hungarian Grand Prix. As usual he started the race in twentieth position, lolloping round the track until lap 14, when he broke down yet again. Noticing smoke from the engine, he ran for a fire extinguisher, but in his excitement failed to notice the marshal's car hurtling to the scene. Seconds later he was on the ground with a broken leg. Although he returned for the Belgian Grand Prix, Taki Inoue's time in Formula One was up.

Takuma Sato also soon found himself out of his league. In 2002 his parents watched excitedly from the paddock as the twenty-five year old took to the track in Australia – and became the first rookie to crash. Soon afterwards, he ran into his team-mate Giancarlo Fisichella. Takuma had yet another accident in Austria, only this time he was stretchered off to hospital. He may have brought Jordan several millions to keep the team ticking over, but he almost paid the ultimate price.

Briton Jonny Kane had seven motor-racing championships to his name in 1998, including Formula Three – placing him among past winners Ayrton Senna and Mika Hakkinen. But Kane was never able to generate the vast quantities of cash needed to launch himself on a bigger stage.

'It's frustrating from a driver's point of view,' he says without a trace of bitterness, 'but you have to understand that motor racing is a business.'

Others might consider it a sport, but for the 213 sponsors involved in Formula One it is definitely a business. As Sir Frank Williams is fond of saying: 'Between the hours of two o'clock and four o'clock most Sunday afternoons at Grand Prix races, it is a sport ... The rest of the time it is a business.' But when business considerations affect every detail of the sport, from the car to the driver, this sentiment rings rather hollow.

In 2003 the top five contributors to Formula One are car manufacturers. Honda is the most generous benefactor, paying $210 million to the BAR team. Then follow Toyota, Renault, Mercedes and BMW, each offloading between $180 million and $125 million to their teams. The tyre supply in 2003 is split evenly – five teams with Bridgestone, five with Michelin. They each pay $22.5 million and $22.4 million respectively for the privilege of supplying tyres to the world's fastest cars.

Completing this list of sponsors to the motor-racing business are the petrol companies: Esso provide $32 million to Toyota, Shell fill up Ferrari to the tune of $30 million and Mobil provide McLaren with $29 million. But there are other sponsors whose connection with Formula One is rather more tenuous.

Wella, for instance, are the forty-ninth most bountiful sponsor of Formula One, giving Toyota $4 million (and presumably lots of hairspray). These sponsors take their investment very seriously and have little patience when it comes to poor results. In fact, backers are increasingly making more and more demands on teams, even down to choosing the drivers: a clear case of putting business before sporting excellence.

This season's treatment of Antonio Pizzonia is a classic example and bodes ill for the future of the sport. After his tears at the end of the Barcelona race, Pizzonia's progress was still dogged as he notched up a ninth, a tenth and a retirement. But it seems to me that the demand to remove him from his seat must have come from Ford, which after all had invested $85 million in Jaguar. Despite numerous mechanical and technical problems with the car itself, Pizzonia was an easy scapegoat.

'That's Formula One,' said Williams's test driver Marc Gene. 'The word "patience" is not in the vocabulary of Formula One. It's a shame, because it's true what they all said, Antonio was very quick in testing... but his pace has not been what everybody, including himself, expected... I know that is Formula One, and if you don't perform people get very nervous.'

That means the investors and the teams desperate for a return on their investment. The Greek ethos of realizing the power of the human body has been replaced in Formula One by the capitalist ethos of realizing the power of money. The unreliability of the human competitor has become a nuisance. The chariot itself has taken on an even greater importance.

Most sportspeople take to the field relying primarily on their own powers and their hours of preparation. In pursuit of individual excellence or team glory, they push the boundaries of their physical abilities: the Olympic principle of *citius, altius, fortius*: faster, higher, stronger.

But Formula One drivers can never experience such freedom: they are always at the mercy of their car and those who have assembled it. They might drive a perfect race, taking the ideal racing line at every turn, overtaking skilfully and calmly, defending their position well, choosing the right strategy on the day. They take the final bend, tasting imminent victory, the crowd rise to applaud them – and their rear tyre falls off and they spin into the hoardings as the chasers overtake.

That is the real danger of Formula One. Even the very best drivers are only as good as their car: they will never know the autonomy of the long-distance runner or the self-reliance of the footballer sprinting for the goal. Of course, most sportspeople today place a certain reliance on their equipment – trainers that cushion the foot, Lycra that keeps them cool, tennis racquets that won't break or swimming goggles that stay on – but few athletes know the fear of being utterly reliant on their equipment.

Formula One is considered a sport, yet ultimately the humans behind the wheel have little influence over the result. And within the 'sport' itself the debate continues to rage about the extent to which success can be attributed to the driver or the car.

In 1997 the Canadian baseball player Larry Walker was beaten to the prize of Canadian Athlete of the Year by Jacques Villeneuve. Walker responded by saying he had been 'beaten by a machine and not a man'.

When Bridgestone ran an advertisement boasting of their association with the five-times world champion Michael Schumacher, they applauded his achievement, but also reminded us that *Schumacher relies most for both his success and safety on just four rubber rings – his Bridgestone Potenza tyres. For no matter how hard he works . . . Schumacher still needs the grip and staying power of his tyres to keep his car firmly pinned to the track.* And if you were still under any illusion that the driver mattered, they hammer home the message: *Bridgestone has a track record even better than Schumacher's. This year Michael is chasing his sixth Formula One championship in nine seasons, and Bridgestone is after its sixth too – but in a row.* Only in Formula One would a backer compete with its star attraction.

When Fernando Alonso spoke to the press after his brilliant third place in Malaysia, the Spaniard innocently remarked, 'I had a problem and had to change gears manually. I didn't think I'd finish the race.' People exchanged confused glances: did one of the world's best drivers really just complain about having to change gears himself? Everybody knows racing cars have automatic transmission; it was just a shock to hear a driver admit to being fallible without it.

Formula One finds the whole debate of 'man versus machine' or 'technology versus sport' rather troublesome. Ferrari's supremacy in 2001–2 divided the community and caused the FIA to review the technology of the cars in order to avoid one team's outright supremacy. The organization's president Max Mosley had banned some high-tech gizmos back in 1993, fearing they signalled the end of racing and the start of computer-controlled exhibitions.

'It is important,' he said, 'that racing drivers should be seen to be in charge of their machinery. There is a very real danger that cars could be conducted around a track without needing a driver.'

The telling phrase is 'seen to be in charge' – the emphasis in Formula One is always on presentation (and thereby sponsorship investment). The computer gizmos made a return part-way through 2001, when it was decided policing things such as traction-control use was impossible. Formula One technology means that drivers should never have to change gear; should never spin the car and should never stall at the start. The computers control all of these functions.

In 1996 Chrysler first used robots in endurance tests as vehicles lapped a track via a system of inductive coils and a guide wire. They were cheaper and had more stamina than real drivers. Max Mosley responded to the development by saying that drivers could become obsolete.

'If development continues at its present rate,' he said, 'F1 cars could simply become high-speed computer gizmos.' The issue divides the sport into two camps.

There are those who believe technological advancement is at the heart of Formula One and should be pursued at all costs. Heading up this group are McLaren boss Ron Dennis and Sir Frank Williams. In a joint letter to the FIA they expressed concern that changes designed to remove technical differentiation were 'against the spirit of Formula One, its restless drive for automotive excellence and its need to live on the technological cutting edge'.

That sentiment is true – if Formula One's relationship with the motor industry is more important than the sport, and the sponsors are more important than the drivers. They went on to claim that the FIA changes 'seek to distance important stakeholders from the sport'.

Ferrari's director of engine technology Paolo Martinelli agrees with Dennis and Williams: 'One of the most attractive aspects of Formula One is that it represents a unique combination of sport and technology...But it's their combination – not exclusivity – that creates the Formula One spirit.' He also emphasized the importance of using Formula One to develop technology that is then passed on to ordinary car drivers.

Similarly, Hewlett Packard, which spends almost $40 million a year on Formula One sponsorship, stresses that the association with elite technology is the major attraction. 'The glamour is not important,' admits sponsorship manager Andrew Collis. 'The things that matter to us are the popularity, the excitement and the interest, but the technological image is really most important.'

On the opposing side are team principals Flavio Briatore at Renault, John Hogan of Jaguar and BAR boss David Richards. They want the 'sport' to be prioritized over business and technology.

'The engineers believe it is a technology challenge at the highest level,' says Richards, 'but the truth is that there is a very small amount of people interested in that finesse. Most just want to turn on the TV and see a race.'

Flavio Briatore may be best known for his playboy lifestyle, but he is always unequivocal in his attitude to Formula One. 'I think F1 needs to talk about sport and not arbitration' he says. 'You need to make sure that the sport is coming back.'

Of course, he was speaking as someone whose smaller team would benefit if the playing field were levelled and Ferrari's domination undermined. But the Italian entrepreneur clearly loves sport – his special guests on race weekends are usually sporting icons: swimmers Michael Klim and Massimiliano Rossolino, with seven Olympic medals between them; yachtswoman Ellen McArthur and several European footballers.

Flavio was also one of the first team bosses to hire a dedicated physical trainer for his drivers in the form of ex-SAS hard-man Bernie Shrosbree. Cycling camps, cross-country skiing and endurance runs were doled out to Jenson Button, Jarno Trulli and then test driver Fernando Alonso. Flavio wanted self-disciplined athletes, not over-paid chauffeurs, and the successes of Renault in 2003 proved him right. Nevertheless, the debate still rages as to whether racing drivers are really sportsmen.

My own sorry experience in an F1 car left me in no doubt that drivers undergo severe physical discomfort behind the wheel – but is it really comparable with the pain endured by other sportspeople? We never see a racing driver grimace like Steve Redgrave slumped over his oars after a race or Paula Ratcliffe crossing the line in a marathon.

F1 drivers grow accustomed to high speed through practice and experience: the vibrations, the g-force, the high temperatures. The average body-weight loss in fluid during a race is now 1–2 kilograms, which is far less than a few years ago – thanks to an electronic pump that allows drivers to press a button and drink in an instant. Previously, they had to suck on a pipette that only worked in straight lines, due to the centrifugal force of driving around corners. During a two-hour race, drivers regularly lost 4 kg (8.8 lb) and in the 1998 season, several drivers reported losses of between 2.7–4.5 kg (6–10 lb). Limiting dehydration enables them to concentrate for longer periods. The days of drivers collapsing on the podium from dehydration, as Nelson Piquet did in 1982, are long gone. In that same race in Jacarepagua the temperatures hit 50°C and Ricardo Patrese was forced to retire after spinning, becoming disoriented, and driving the wrong way down the track!

Drivers tend to be of average height – although the success this year of Mark Webber (6'2") and Justin Wilson (6'3") might signal a change – and are not especially muscular. In fact, they tend to be narrow-hipped, short-limbed and display few characteristics of a typical elite athlete – or Roman gladiator. Low body-fat percentages are important, however. Also, racing drivers would certainly excel at lifting weights with their necks. The stress of g-force on some circuit corners turns a driver's 14lb head and helmet into a 57lb lead weight – which needs to be held by the neck and shoulders. Drivers develop these vital muscles by doing head raises wearing helmets with weights attached or doing 'head press-ups' with weights over each ear.

Rubens Barrichello is one of several racing drivers who suffer from uneven muscle distribution due to the pressure of driving on clockwise circuits. But when the race lands in Brazil or Japan the strains can be even worse, as these anti-clockwise tracks pull the neck in the opposite direction. The twists and turns of Monaco alter the g-force from minute to minute, making heavy work for the neck and shoulders.

But it's the drivers' backs that take the biggest strain. During a two-hour race the spine receives a severe vertical pounding, compressing and decompressing the intervertebral discs (fibrous, elastic 'shock-absorbers' that work alongside the spinal muscles to counteract g-forces and actively maintain the driver's posture). Most drivers today and virtually all ex-drivers suffer from some sort of back and neck pain. Early arthritis and protruding discs are commonplace. Nowadays drivers have a dedicated team of physiologists, physiotherapists and chiropractors to keep their rattled skeletons in shape, so long-term damage is less likely. Plus they protect themselves from injury by maintaining greater fitness levels than their predecessors.

Twenty-first-century F1 drivers may be plastered in tobacco advertising, but none of them smoke (although Michael Schumacher has been spotted enjoying the odd cigar after winning a race). All of the teams now provide gym facilities for their drivers and most take their physical preparation very seriously. Mark Webber and Michael Schumacher are among those most committed to their training regimes. Mark admires the big names in cycling, rowing and swimming.

'You know,' he told me, 'real tough endurance sports.'

He is one of the few people in Formula One to admit that motor racing does not offer the same physical challenge as other disciplines – although the way some F1 insiders talk about the drivers, you'd think they were all Iron Man champions.

'Oh they are so strong!' one reporter told me. 'They're incredibly fit. They've got to be some of the best athletes in the world.'

Compared to most other sports, F1 drivers have it relatively easy. Few athletes can jet off to scuba-dive on the Great Barrier Reef after the opening competition of their season. But perhaps more than any other sport, F1 drivers must master their minds for sustained periods of time.

Psychologist David Hepworth has drawn up a list of attributes that would comprise the ultimate driver. They must be totally committed to their goals and the team and be prepared to try new approaches and admit their shortcomings. The ultimate driver must be able to concentrate for the entire duration of a race, judging speed, distance and reaction times, while maintaining technical control when attacking or pushing. They must remain committed to speed, even when rivals gain an advantage or they personally suffer a setback. And of course the very best drivers work closely with engineers to articulate mechanical problems and thereby develop the car. But today's drivers also have enormous off-track psychological pressures to deal with in the shape of sponsors, politics, public relations and the ever-present media.

Like Roman charioteers, F1 drivers are also 'slaves'. They are beholden to team orders, their sponsors and media commitments. Jacques Villeneuve is one of the few drivers to have a 'minimum promotional work' clause written into his contract. For most other drivers, satisfying the demands of sponsors and the desire of the teams to maximize media coverage falls firmly upon their shoulders. The business of Formula One has made PR as important as the racing, but for the drivers it is a frustrating distraction from competing in the sport they love.

Mark Webber's run-up to the Australian Grand Prix began the moment he stepped off the plane from London. Launching the new Jaguar XJ at a motor show was followed by a flight to Canberra and several phone interviews with local radio stations. The next day I arrived to spend the day filming him with his family. That evening he flew to Sydney for a question-and-answer session at a Jaguar cocktail party, but the late night was followed by an early morning as he appeared on a breakfast TV show at 7 a.m. An 11 a.m. press conference, photo-call, lunch at the Chamber of Commerce, a flight to Melbourne, a charity dinner and a late-night TV show appearance completed his commitments.

The next day involved an HSBC photo-call, an autograph session and a *Travel* magazine dinner. But even though first qualifying was just twenty-four hours away, he still had a corporate lunch to endure before the tyre meetings and team briefings began. Then, on the eve of first qualifying, Webber had to attend a Jaguar dealership drinks party, an HSBC cocktail party, a visit to the Mark Webber's Supporters Club party and a phone interview with the UK's Chiltern Radio and another with the journalist who writes his column for the *Daily Herald Sun*.

On Friday, after a day of paddock-club appearances, it was time to attend the Grand Prix ball. A flurry of cocktail parties might not sound especially exhausting, but no other sport would dream of placing such demands on its participants so close to competition.

'There are more demands on the time of a racing driver than in other sports,' says Mark. 'We just have to do what we can. I need about an hour before a race to get my head together. It's just a case of getting a balance.'

Mark's attitude is unusual. Most drivers despise the press intrusion and corporate responsibilities. Ralf Schumacher, in particular, bemoans the pressure (though he has been on the receiving end of some unwelcome and unfounded accusations in the German press about his sexual orientation). Most F1 teams feel they must prioritize grabbing column inches over driver preparation, because many of them (including Webber's Jaguar) never actually expect to win a race – a curious situation for any 'sport'!

This truth was brought home to me in Monaco when, following his defeat in the rowing world cup series, my husband James Cracknell flew out to the race. I knew he would be angry and disappointed. I knew to tread carefully and tactfully, but also that there was nothing I could say to appease him. James arrived at the restaurant where we were to dine with some people employed in Formula One.

They greeted him with warmth, but I was incredulous when they said: 'Oh dear! Third place...to a bunch of Italians!...Better get back in your boat mate!' and 'Did you bring your bronze, eh?' They kept on: 'It doesn't really matter though, does it? I mean, it's not the Olympics.'

These people who worked in a so-called professional 'sport' could not understand why James was so bothered by losing. His disappointment was a million miles from their own sporting ethos.

'What's the matter?' whispered one of them to me as James began to show his irritation. 'Was there prize money involved?'

Sport for sport's sake, winning for the sense of achievement and victory as its own reward, appeared to be concepts beyond their comprehension. They participate in Formula One for entire seasons without expecting a single podium finish. Often they don't even expect to complete the race. No other sport is founded on such defeatism and for this very reason the raw emotion that lies at the heart of any sport is a rarity in Formula One.

We've all seen the moment on TV: a race is in full swing, the camera cuts to a shot of the pit crew in the garage, arms folded, leaning back in their chairs, watching the cars on overhead monitors. One of their drivers suffers a mishap – slowing in a plume of smoke or spinning the car, perhaps colliding with another driver. Their race is over. Some of the pit crew throw up their hands, but most of them simply shrug and pick up their tools to mend the incoming vehicle.

Compared to any other sport – the football manager on the touchline, the athletics coach in the crowd or the boxing trainer in the corner – there is so little passion in Formula One. The fans in the grandstand or watching TV feel the pain of failure as their favourite driver under-performs, but the people actually in the 'sport' are usually worrying about the expectations of their corporate sponsors. The disappointed driver slouching back to the garage is of little consequence. They have to dust themselves down and prepare for the next round of glad-handing in the hospitality suite.

At the Nürburgring the corporate engine was all fired up for McLaren Mercedes. This was the home Grand Prix for the team's engine supplier. Their young Finn Kimi Raikkonen was only three points behind the leader Michael Schumacher in the drivers' standings and the team sat just eight points behind Ferrari in the constructor's table. There were sponsors to wine, dine and impress.

But it was also a big day for Schumacher – he had accumulated 999 F1 points in his career to date and was eyeing-up Senna's record 65 pole positions with his own total of 54. Coming off the back of Monaco and Montreal, the Nürburgring is a pretty soulless place. The average speed is a relatively mundane 125 mph, but unlike some tracks this one allows for overtaking. Driving skill is important, because hitting the braking areas is critical during the 60 laps.

Mercedes were elated after Saturday's qualifying session when Raikkonen seized pole position, giving the backers every reason to enjoy their champagne. Vice-President of Mercedes Benz Motor Sport, Norbert Haug watched Raikkonen's performance from the pit wall as TV cameras zoomed in for Haug's reaction. The stocky German raised his hands, smiling, gritted his teeth and beat his fists on the surface in front. However, team-mate David Coulthard was in ninth and still struggling to excel at the new single-lap qualifying. Schumacher's Ferrari was just three one-hundredths behind Raikkonen, with Williams's Ralf

Schumacher and Juan Pablo Montoya tucked in behind. Antonio Pizzonia, desperately in need of a good race, was in lowly sixteenth position, five places behind team-mate Mark Webber.

Schumacher senior had nipped into the Mercedes garage after Raikkonen's lap to sneak a look at the weight of his car. He knew that to find out how much fuel his main rival had on board was not entirely sporting, but it is this desire to gain an edge that makes Schumacher less of an F1 puppet and more of a sportsman. A sports psychologist would perhaps interpret this as the behaviour of a man preoccupied by the actions of his competitor (an uncontrollable factor) and a sign that Schumacher's confidence had been shaken.

The Mercedes executives could digest their paddock-club lunches with ease as Raikkonen led convincingly for the first twenty-five laps. However, Norbert Haug was in the doghouse. He admitted that team boss Ron Dennis had given him a 'bollocking' for publicly celebrating Raikkonen's pole position. There was no room for emotion with so much money at stake. Perhaps Dennis's expectations were higher – or at least that is what he wanted his investors to believe.

Speaking in an earlier interview, David Coulthard had shed some light on the behaviour of bosses: 'Some team bosses show great emotion and you can see them swearing if their driver goes off the circuit, but I'm not sure that's the right image when you are representing a major engine manufacturer and all the sponsors and partners who financially support the team. They have based their decision to support us on non-emotional factors and we need to respect their image as much as our own.'

In the grandstands, however, the emotion was tangible and the Schumacher faithful formed a deafening sea of red in the 27°C sunshine.

Ralf beat his brother off the starting line, but ahead of them Raikkonen extended his lead lap by lap. By the time he made his first pit stop on lap 16 he had a ten-second advantage. But on the twenty-sixth lap – with the Mercedes manufacturers looking proudly on – Raikkonen's engine blew up in a stream of oily smoke. The disappointed Finn pushed away a well-meaning marshal, sat by the track for a while, then hitched a lift back to the pits.

Meanwhile, Montoya was benefiting from new tyres and reeling in Michael Schumacher, until they were wheel-to-wheel on the run-down to Dunlop curve on lap 43. As he was overtaken, Schumacher ran up the inside kerb and the left-hand section of his Ferrari tagged Montoya's BMW as it moved up to second place. Montoya sped away as Schumacher found himself in a spin, finally sitting stranded, his wheels spinning comically in the gravel before three marshals and a crane driver pushed him back on to the track. But he was down to sixth place.

The BMW cars were running first and second on their engine-supplier's home turf. Barrichello was paddling up behind them, with Fernando Alonso battling McLaren's David Coulthard for fourth spot. They headed up to the chicane, Coulthard closing in too rapidly as Alonso's braking became dependent on his tyre wear. Coulthard had to take evasive action. He touched the kerb and launched himself into the gravel trap. There were just three laps remaining, but McLaren's hopes of a successful Grand Prix were over. Norbert Haug's celebrations now seemed a little premature.

Mark Webber kept his cool and strategically his long middle stint was a success. He brought his Jag home in the points with sixth place. Antonio Pizzonia, however, had been given the wrong tyres in his second pit stop, then incurred a speeding penalty in the pit lane. Jenson Button drove sensibly into seventh place, but team-mate Jacques Villeneuve had no one but himself to blame for a poor start, a 360 degree spin on lap 9 and the removal of his front wing by a chicane bollard. (Although ultimately his retirement was due to technical failure when his second gear broke on lap 51.) Williams sat back to watch their drivers bring home an impressive one-two, lifting them ahead of McLaren-Mercedes in the constructors' championship.

Juan Pablo's tussle with Schumacher's Ferrari grabbed all the headlines the next day. Opinion was divided as to whether it was skilful driving, irresponsible madness or ungentlemanly conduct. Distinguished Ferrari technical director Ross Brawn was fuming and described the move as 'crude' and lacking in 'class'.

Schumacher himself viewed the manoeuvre as a true sportsman should and refused to make excuses: 'It was a straightforward racing incident. He was faster than me and tried to pass, giving me just enough room to survive. I would have done the same thing.' As usual, the drivers see such events in terms of the contest and striving for optimum advantage, whereas their bosses are busy calculating the cost of a collision. But then again they have more issues to consider than the drivers.

Michael Schumacher's fifth place earned him his record as the first driver to exceed a total of 1,000 points in Formula One and Raikkonen's retirement left the German at the top of the table with a seven-point lead. Coulthard's call for Alonso to be penalized (for deliberately forcing him off the track in the closing stages) fell on deaf ears. Meanwhile, Raikkonen articulated the sort of frustrations only an F1 driver can understand: 'I'm disappointed because the race was mine. The car was feeling great and there was no indication that the engine was going to give way.'

Ralf Schumacher was enjoying the satisfaction of victory in front of the 120,000-strong crowd. In Montreal he had been criticized for failing to overtake his brother when several opportunities arose. In response to his detractors he sat back, shrugged and said, 'Even bad drivers can win.'

But often in Formula One, the best drivers can't.

7

Magny-Cours

After the concrete bleakness of the Nürburgring, the Magny-Cours Grand Prix bursts into life among winding roads and fields of sunflowers. It was the first weekend of July when the championship descended on the pastoral region of southern Burgundy in France. Over in Paris the 100th Tour de France was about to commence along the Champs-Elysées. The rainbow colours of the *peloton* were about to awe the fifteen million spectators who would line the roads over the next three weeks. The Tour and the Grand Prix jostled for position in the French newspapers, with the world's greatest cycling event a clear winner: would cancer-survivor Lance Armstrong claim a record fifth win?

Over on planet Formula One, few people were even aware that France's most cherished sporting event was about to begin. And even fewer knew that Formula One and the Tour had both originated in the French media.

The Tour de France was founded on a purely commercial basis. In the early twentieth-century, an intense rivalry existed between Pierre Giffard of the newspaper *Le Petit Journal* and Henri Desgrange, who worked for *L'Auto*. Giffard devised the infamous Paris-Brest-Paris (PBP) cycling event – a race from the capital to the coast and back – solely to generate more sales for his paper. In 1903 Desgrange went one step further, routing his race, the Tour de France, around the entire country – a total of 2,428 kilometres. Its success eclipsed that of the PBP and sales of *L'Auto* doubled as readers scrambled to follow the fortunes of the riders – which was lucky for the enterprising Desgrange, who could then recoup the money he had spent on the riders' accommodation.

The Tour de France continues to evolve, but in essence it remains Desgrange's brainchild – the high mountains, the individual time-trials, time bonuses for stage victories and the famous yellow jersey were all born in his imagination. Pierre Giffard might have been beaten by Desgrange in the battle of the bikes, but he could already boast that he had created Grand Prix motor racing.

While other countries banned cars from racing on roads, the French (never ones to let a little danger get in the way of fun) thought it a great idea. As early as 1887 the first organized event was planned by the publication *Le Vélocipède*. Unfortunately, it was cancelled because only one competitor turned up, but the French were undeterred and in 1894 twenty-one drivers raced from Paris to Rouen, a 126-kilometre journey, which in those days was more a test of a car's reliability than a race – especially as it included a civilized lunch break.

Naturally, Pierre Giffard's *Le Petit Journal* was behind the event. His Paris-Rouen race is generally regarded as the forerunner of modern Formula One, despite the fact that the first vehicle over the finish line in 1894 was a steam-driven tractor. Unfortunately the tractor was then disqualified because it wasn't a practical road vehicle – a fact the organizers might reasonably have been expected to have noticed at the start. Still, it showed a strict adherence to the rule book that Bernie Ecclestone would have admired.

Today's racing journalists continue to play a vital role in Formula One, though they are more likely to be found in the press centre or at a team dinner than at the cutting edge of developments in the sport. Modern Formula One keeps its accredited journalists on a very tight reign.

This amiable bunch of middle-aged men form part of the fixtures and fittings of Formula One, flying around the world to races, enjoying team hospitality and providing the daily newspapers back home with stories about Schumacher et al. Among the drivers they inevitably have a reputation as professional 'liggers' with generous expense accounts. One sportswriter is famously rumoured to have brought his curtains to a Grand Prix so that he could have them dry-cleaned at the hotel and charge it to his newspaper.

I once asked Eddie Irvine if he thought racing journalists had a hard life.

'They're taking the piss if they say they do,' he said. 'They swan over business class, they're lifted to the circuit by Jaguar or Mercedes or whoever and they go to the press room and copy the press releases. They don't even have to talk to you. And then they have a free lunch, free dinner and loads of bottles of wine for free. I know what I want to be when I give up racing.'

But *Daily Express* journalist Bob McKenzie told me that business-class flights are a rare luxury and Eddie's opinions should be taken with a pinch of salt: 'That's just him mouthing off . . . and he's very good at it.'

They might not have to sit in an office from nine-to-five, but the press-pack still suffer the vicissitudes of the F1 lifestyle. A Grand Prix journalist for five years, Tom Clarkson talks of being 'in the press room at midnight on a Sunday after the race, when you still have two hours of work to do. That's what F1 is to me.'

Kevin Garside, former F1 correspondent on the *Daily Mirror*, now on the *Telegraph*, told me that glamour is a rare visitor to the press corps. Arriving for the Austrian Grand Prix, he sought out his remote farmhouse accommodation to discover that it had been double-booked. The owner explained that she had found him a bed at her son's place nearby. He arrived to find it was simply a family home with a teenage daughter sulking because she had been forced to give her bed over to a strange Englishman.

'I was creeping along their hallway in the middle of the night to use the bathroom, with the daughter asleep on the settee downstairs, thinking "What the hell am I doing?"' he said.

Still, most racing journalists have been involved in the sport for more than decade, so it can't be all bad.

'We do have fun,' admitted Kevin Eason, motoring correspondent for *The Times*. 'We make fun, but you're away from home for so long it would get very tedious if we didn't. It's a marriage-threatening lifestyle where you have no real social life at home because we travel so often. This week is a classic example. I've been home for forty-eight hours this week and that will probably be the best forty-eight hours I have in June and July.'

Nevertheless, new journalists are a rare phenomenon in Formula One. Unfamiliar faces are always viewed with suspicion in this very private environment and strangers are harder to control: much better to dish out passes to those who already know the rules of the game.

'It's easier that way because everybody knows how the system works,' says Tom Clarkson. 'Nobody tries to push the boundaries.'

Each team's public-relations manager works hard to shape the team's image and to protect both drivers and bosses from adverse publicity. They are the bane of any journalist's life, but as Bob McKenzie explains the PRs also have a tough job: 'The PRs shit themselves about so many things. They have to dance to ten different tunes. The sponsors are saying "I've given you fifteen million quid, I don't want to be associated with that!"; the team owners say "Play this down and don't associate such-and-such with something-or-other." It's very hard because there are so many agendas.'

Another journalist who preferred to remain anonymous told me: 'F1 PR works on an invisible hierarchy. The more successful a team, the less they feel the need to work with you and it takes so much longer to get a "yes" or "no" to a question.' But the less successful teams are 'a dream to work with. If you wanted to dress a Minardi driver in a pink tutu and get him to sit in a bathtub full of baked beans, not only could you be almost certain you'd get a "yes", but they'd probably supply the beans too.'

The world of Formula One is fiercely protective of its image and tries hard to control the media. Such is the myth of Bernie Ecclestone's omnipotence, F1 insiders whisper in awe that he personally approves every F1 pass. However, for a man with a reputed worth of £2.4 billion, and one assumes, a very full diary, this rumour seems unlikely. Working for him on-site are Formula One Management (FOM) personnel, headed by Pasquale Lattanedu – Bernie's representative on earth, a rugged Sardinian with broad shoulders and a broad smile (though he keeps it in reserve for special occasions). It is Lattanedu who doles out TV and VIP accreditations. He has a reputation for being a strict disciplinarian, but he can also be charming. Lattanedu knows the media are vital to Formula One and doesn't go out of his way to upset them (though he still does on a fairly regular basis). The FIA rule the access granted to the press pack. They enforce the rules requiring journalists without 'permanent' passes to apply for accreditation at least three weeks before a race. That means no one can simply hop on a plane at the request of an editor when a big story breaks.

These accreditation swipe passes symbolize the power structures at work and dictate exactly who can enter the inner sanctum. They contribute to a sense of intimidation felt by members of the media: there

Not everybody loves Formula One: the SAPS campaign tent in Melbourne.

Mark Webber walked away unscathed from this crash in Brazil.

Interviewing Mark Webber before the 2002 race in Barcelona.

The master and the apprentice: Michael Schumacher douses Fernando Alonso on the podium in Barcelona.

Jaguar's Antonio Pizzonia feels the glare of the paddock in Barcelona. Fellow Brazilian Cristiano da Matta walks behind.

Fernando Alonso braves an interview with me at a teashop in Oxford.

Monaco attracts headline-seekers: interviewing boy-band Blue in the paddock.

Just another day in the office: Antonia Pizzonia, Mark Webber and Helena Christensen, wearing a £52 million pink diamond in Monaco.

The diamond party reconvenes for more corporate fun aboard the Princess Tanya.

Bubbly anyone? The on-board jacuzzi becomes a giant champagne cooler.

Wesley Snipes and friends at the Monaco Grand Prix.

Interviewing team boss Eddie Jordan on the grid in Magny-Cours.

Motor racing's unique angle on women in Formula One.

Another day, another PR stunt: Jenson Button takes a lawnmower for a spin in Silverstone.

Hosting the F1 Awards at Birmingham's NEC. From left to right: Cristiano da Matta, Ricardo Zonta, Olivier Panis, Justin Wilson, Giancarlo Fisichella, Mark Webber, Beverley Knight, me, Murray Walker and Antonia Pizzonia.

Demonstrator Cornelius Horan sprints towards the cars on Silverstone's Hangar straight.

always seemed to be a chance that our passes could be refused. Every journalist I spoke to recognized the possibility that someone might be banned from races for reporting something objectionable. But although I heard this rumour several times while working in Formula One, nobody I spoke to could actually identify any journalists it had happened to.

'It must have happened,' said Tom Clarkson, 'but I can't think of anyone.'

Bob McKenzie thought for a while, then said, 'Oh there must have been people, although I've been working in Formula One for thirteen years and I can't bring any to mind.' It's a curious situation: the fear of F1 management is quite real, but it appears to be based on nothing but rumour.

Bob McKenzie identifies 'a good deal of paranoia' in the sport, but attributes it to the claustrophobia of the F1 community. 'I think it's part of the whole deal that everyone lives and travels together.' 'There is so much insecurity and jealousy,' said another F1 insider. 'People are frightened that you're trying to muscle in.'

Even Bernie himself has jokingly contributed to the paranoia. When asked in 2001 by the *Sunday Telegraph* about his intimidating reputation, Ecclestone said: 'You cross me and sooner or later I'll get you. I may not get you beaten up or chopped up, but one day I'll level the score.'

He and his wife Slavica were mugged outside their Chelsea home in 1997 and Slavica's £600,000 ring was stolen. Speaking in the same interview, Bernie admitted to being 'so angry' about the police failing to find the criminals that he 'did some inquiries myself and found out who they were'. He had established the identity of the muggers by the afternoon of the following day and reported them to the police. 'They were wearing balaclavas. How could I identify them?' he said, when asked why he had declined to attend an identity parade.

Bob McKenzie recalled a 1993 interview in which Ecclestone had referred to drivers' deaths as a form of 'natural culling'. When the quote appeared in the *Daily Express* it caused enormous controversy and Ecclestone flatly denied using the phrase. 'All hell broke loose,' says McKenzie. 'Maurice Hamilton from the *Observer* called to say that he wanted to run a story about it and would I confirm that Bernie had said "culling". He warned me that there might be repercussions, but I said, "Yes," he had said that.' There were no repercussions.

But there have been several instances in which photographers have paid the price for disobeying the rules. At the opening race of 2003, a freelance photographer photographed the HANS safety device. In the background, behind a wire fence was the new parc ferme garage. Unaware that any rules had been breached, Sutton Motorsport syndicated the picture on their successful website. Nearly two months later, owner Keith Sutton was issued with a three-race ban from the FIA when the photo appeared as a small image in CAR magazine. Sutton reportedly argued that several photographers had taken shots of parc ferme – including the FIA themselves, through LAT photographic – but he was told that only his photograph had been published. After persuading the FIA that missing the races in Austria, Spain and Monaco would damage business, Sutton had his ban reduced to just Spain. But, while driving to the Austrian race, Sutton was telephoned by the FIA which had reconsidered his infringement and cancelled his pass. Many F1 photographers complain that the rules governing what they are and are not allowed to do are changed in the twelve-page booklet that appears at every race, without any other form of notification.

Such restrictions have resulted in the mass media being beholden to F1. But the system works, because there will always be someone younger, keener and more devoted to Formula One who is willing to step in and toe the party line. Bob McKenzie says that he receives 'lots of letters and telephone calls from people asking how to get in'. When Mach 1, the production company responsible for ITV's race coverage, recently advertised for a runner/researcher they had hundreds of applications and this bottom-rung TV job was eventually filled by a former management consultant. But as *Sun* columnist and F1 veteran of fifteen years Stan Piecha explained, job vacancies rarely come up.

'Once you get into this sport it really is a travelling circus. You really get attached to it and I can't think of anything else I'd want to do now.'

Another journalist told me: 'F1 is full of wankers and people just out to promote their own careers and climb whatever political or financial ladder they have their sights on. But I'm just happy to have the opportunity to follow and report on the sport I love.'

I was talking to these journalists on a glorious summer evening by the side of a football pitch in provincial Magny-Cours. The competitiveness of the French Grand Prix is rivalled every year by another sporting event: a football match between the British and German media. Magny-Cours is a fitting venue, because as well as the Tour de France, the Paris-Brest-Paris and the Grands Prix, the French also created the Jules Rimet trophy, which later became the football World Cup. There are no such standards of excellence here, though, as TV, radio and print reporters pant around the field, feeling the effects of years of F1 hospitality.

The Brits had assembled for their official photograph, hiding their intra-team competitiveness behind forced smiles. The Germans turned stereotypes on their head by bringing humour to the proceedings, posing for their photo with tins of sauerkraut. As the sun dipped behind the trees, sports journalism looked like the kind of job any man would love. The Germans won 6-1, ensuring the rivalry would fester for another twelve months. One member of the German team was Wolfgang Schattling, a ubiquitous and popular F1 figure who holds the important post of Head of Mercedes Media Communications. Later that weekend he helped to placate the losing team by hosting a media dinner at the circuit.

The Magny-Cours paddock is ideal for entertaining. It's smaller than other paddock areas, with the motorhomes parked around the edges of a square, giving it something of a courtyard feel or a village atmosphere, which is heightened by quaint wooden benches bedecked in heaps of trailing flowers. Mercedes arranged two long tables beneath an open-sided canopy to accommodate their media guests and attentive waitresses kept glasses filled to the brim with expensive local wines. The food matched the quality of any multi-starred Parisian restaurant.

Wolfgang had also organized a game of Beat the Commentator. A two-minute segment of race footage was played on a large plasma TV screen while pairs of reluctant 'commentators' holding microphones tried to describe the action. The comic attempts of the journalists only proved how skilful real TV commentators are. ITV's Martin Brundle and James Allen eventually showed us all how it should be done. It was a clever move on Schattling's part as Murray Walker's exit and questions surrounding his replacement had put pressure on rookie James Allen. He had been given a chance to prove his ability in front of the media and was no doubt grateful to Mercedes for the opportunity.

It also occurred to me that it would be difficult for any of Schattling's guests to sit at their laptops the following morning with complete journalistic detachment. Schattling laughed off the suggestion that such events are an exercise in back-scratching.

'That can't be the target,' he told me. 'We just want to get to know the people better and they want to get to know us...but it doesn't help writing better things about us.'

At the same time he suggested these events could be useful. 'You get to know the people much better having dinner with them, having some fun with them and when you want to approach somebody, you know how they will react, how their approach will be, so I think it is worthwhile doing.'

In other words, the communications guys work hard at knowing which journalists to trust and which of them will handle teams' stories in the desired way. Schattling is excellent at his job and an expert at the media game that underpins Formula One – a pure quid pro quo exchange.

The journalists have mortgages to pay, families to feed and a job that is perceived as glamorous and rewarding. There is little incentive for them to write anything that will jeopardize their place in this world. But the result is a sport that often goes unchallenged. Stories too often skim over unpalatable truths: the extent to which drivers are selected on the basis of their monetary value for instance or the fact that the car rather than the driver made the biggest difference to a race. That's not to say Formula One never receives bad press, it's just that those writers are rarely the ones given access to the drivers or the paddock.

David Coulthard joked that the British press have 'one major advantage over the other journalists...they're British! Other than that they're all cut from the same cloth.' However, he did acknowledge that they have a difficult job trying to find the truth in a sport so dogged by speculation and in which a legion of PR guys and communications executives seem to exist in a constant state of anxiety. 'We think we know what's happening on the inside,' said Coulthard, 'and the skill of their job is to try to find out what's happening with a bit of speculation. You know the members of the Press you can trust with a comment and you know the ones you wouldn't entertain.'

But the drivers have little to fear. Most journalists have an area of expertise, but they cover a variety of sports and events. The F1 media is overwhelmingly made up of F1 enthusiasts whose work is limited to F1. Several key figures were fans who sought out jobs by writing letters to *Autosport* and were soon filing track reports and the results of club events. In true F1 style these notable characters forged a 'brand' for themselves through their presence within the industry and were eventually writing for the British broadsheets.

The *Telegraph*'s Kevin Garside is unusual in that he 'came to the sport from a complete blank'. Although after five years he feels part of the community ('I'm now known – thank God!'), he admits to having felt like an outsider for some time: 'The weirdest thing for me was that on every other discipline I'd covered – football, cricket, tennis, whatever – you could talk about other sports, but in Formula One there's very little interest among the journalists about other sport. It had me wondering whether it really is a sport.'

And then there is the snobbery that is endemic to Formula One. Anyone who is not an aficionado is treated with contempt and newcomers are under enormous pressure to earn the right to walk on the hallowed tarmac.

Garside knows all about the prejudices of Formula One. 'People within the sport are incredibly territorial,' he says. 'If you're not an F1 fan, by extension you have no brain.'

There is a peculiar desperation among F1 media types to prove they possess a super-detailed knowledge of motor racing. Their conversations are littered with casual references to obscure drivers, pointless statistics and technological trivia. Garside speculates that this is because they will never be able to actually experience the phenomenon they are writing about. They overcompensate for knowledge that they will never have at first hand.

'It's very difficult for F1 journalists to intuit what is going on in the car,' he says, 'because we've never driven one at that speed. It's difficult to capture the emotional feel of what's going on.'

The racing journalist's job isn't made any easier by the powers that be. Most major sports today welcome the press with well-positioned seating areas and comfortable media centres from which to observe the action. Food and drink are normally provided. F1 journalists watch the race in a room on a silent TV screen – 'without so much as a kettle to make a cup of tea', adds Kevin. Following a seventy-lap race with multiple pit stops is hard enough with a good commentary, but without it, it is almost impossible.

'It's very difficult to decipher what's going on in the cars,' says Kevin, 'and after the race there are TV crews grabbing interviews and so on, so it's very difficult for us to get at the facts.'

The best explanation for this is that Formula One is so confident of its popularity it doesn't feel the need to better accommodate the media. But Kevin suspects it is more likely Formula One's habitual preoccupation with money.

'I can only think that it's a rights issue somewhere. Perhaps the promoter hasn't paid enough for an audio feed or something. It's bound to be quantifiable in that way.'

FOM representative Lynsey Parker explained that the silent TV unilateral feed is the same that is sent to the international broadcasters.

'The commentary would annoy everyone,' she says. 'What language would we put it in? Plus the journalists would just disagree with the commentary and the noise would distract them from their task.'

It was only in the seventies that the British media began to cover Formula One. The *Daily Express* was the first to take an interest, with the *Daily Mirror* following close behind in 1973. Ironically, the sport had to become commercialized before the press became involved: a reversal of today's relationship in which high-profile media attention attracts sponsors.

In 1968 Jim Clark took to the track in a Lotus 49 decorated with a sailor's head and the red, white and gold livery of (surprise, surprise) cigarette brand Gold Leaf. The FIA were outraged, considering it an unspoken rule that cars should race in their national colours: red for Italy, blue for France and silver for Germany. But Lotus boss Colin Chapman was determined, not least because he was enjoying a three-year £100,000 contract with Gold Leaf and the annual team running costs were about £90,000.

Track officials even tried to prevent the Lotus car from entering the track, but Chapman had picked the third round of the Lady Wigram Trophy Race in New Zealand to test out his new car colours, banking on the fact that the laid-back Kiwis would be more flexible than their snooty European counterparts. He was right and Clark and his sailor's head went on to win. But that summer the same car was entered in the non-championship Race of Champions at Brands Hatch, driven by Graham Hill. Unexpectedly, it wasn't Britain's Royal Automobile Club that complained, but a senior TV executive who telephoned Chapman during the practice session to say that unless his sailor's head logo was taped over, the race broadcast would be cancelled.

Ironically, the TV pictures were so poor in those days that the logo would have been unrecognizable to viewers anyway. Nevertheless, the tide had turned: the FIA and the international motoring organizations had to accept that their gentlemanly sport was about to become commercialized.

By the following spring of 1969, Gold Leaf Team Lotus (as it was then known) appeared on the grid in South Africa. The 1970 Spanish Grand Prix saw the arrival of another major sponsor: Yardley (the perfumery division of British American Tobacco) paid £50,000 over two years to see the cars of British Racing Motors (BRM) compete in its pink livery. Even the RAC, which owned the rights to the British Grand Prix, agreed to change the name to the John Player Grand Prix. In 1972 the American tobacco giant Philip Morris placed its Marlboro brand at the forefront of Formula One in a two-year deal with BRM worth more than £100,000, plus funding for marketing projects. All that was missing was the publicity.

Marlboro set the precedent by flying a hundred journalists – all expenses paid – to its European headquarters in Geneva. From there they took a chartered jet to the Circuit Paul Ricard in southern France and were granted a ringside view of the track as Englishman Peter Gethin burst forth from a giant replica Marlboro cigarette packet driving the new Marlboro-BRM car. The stunt had the desired effect: the image made the front pages of the motoring press all over Europe. By 1973 Marlboro were spending $3 million on such promotions and research showed that the brand recall of Marlboro was much greater than for companies spending larger amounts on more traditional advertising. Sponsorship meant more column inches, which meant more public awareness, more outside interest and ultimately more visitors to Grands Prix.

By 1977 the average gate figure at races was a record 84,411, despite the fact that Britain's major TV broadcasters, the BBC and ITV, refused to be used as a free marketing medium by broadcasting the commercial logos of the sponsors. But in 1976 the TV companies woke up to the increasing public demand that had been generated by the championship battle between the charismatic James Hunt and the enigmatic Niki Lauda.

Lauda's accident at the Nürburgring had left him in a critical condition with serious burns, but three races later he was back at the Italian Grand Prix. The championship came down to the final race in Suzuka and the BBC reluctantly agreed to give it some coverage: twenty minutes of edited highlights. It turned out to be no epic battle, as Lauda retired after two laps in a torrential downpour and Hunt came home fourth, gaining the four points he needed to clinch the title with 69 points against Lauda's 68. Nevertheless, the BBC accepted it must change its policy and in 1977 it treated its British audience to the first live coverage of F1 races.

Bernie Ecclestone was waiting in the wings. In October 1977 he described television as 'the big key' to Formula One's future and began prising the TV rights of races from organizers who had no idea of their potential worth. He went on to set up his own production company, FOCA TV. It developed quickly and by 1985 was broadcasting Formula One to more than ninety countries through the European Broadcasting Union (EBU), which set the fees for public-service broadcasters.

And then, in September 1987 – after being appointed vice-president of the FIA's promotional affairs – Ecclestone went on to hire Christian Vogt, an experienced media consultant who had been handling some of the TV rights for the football associations UEFA and FIFA and the IAAF in athletics. Vogt suggested that Formula One could bypass the restrictive EBU negotiations by approaching the new privately owned commercial TV companies that were emerging in the mid-eighties. This was much more time-consuming than doing a deal with the EBU, but it could also be more lucrative and, more importantly, it would allow Ecclestone to make demands of the new broadcasters that would benefit the sport.

Crucially, Ecclestone insisted that qualifying races be shown live and that there had to be post-race analysis. The significance of this move cannot be underestimated. Soon the public service broadcasters realized that their membership of the EBU did not aid their bargaining power and they began negotiating directly with FOCA TV. The EBU no longer had the monopoly on F1 TV rights and the airtime received by the sport was doubled.

Television has several potential problems with Formula One. The first is that, on paper, it shouldn't be a very exciting spectacle. Genuine sporting excellence – which in other sports is characterized by the clinically taken goal, the side-step and burst to the try line, the dogged century – is frequently hidden beneath the chassis of the racing car. Michael Schumacher may have moments of great judgement behind the steering wheel, but the difference between his car and, say, Montoya's is the multi-million-pound computing stuff under the bonnet, which was probably developed by a balding forty-six year old in Milton Keynes and is so technically complex as to be beyond the comprehension of most sports fans.

Second, the drivers can be difficult for TV viewers to distinguish and their emotions are entirely obscured by their helmets – viewers must content themselves with an occasional wave or shake of the head.

However, ITV Sport can turn a 74-lap procession into a thrilling duel of technical genius. Hiring people with a stupendously detailed knowledge of the sport helps and it takes genuine skill to talk for five laps about a change in engine sound before something more interesting happens. Even the most hardened F1 fan has confessed to a little mid-race nap, lulled by the soporific hum of the engines. But the TV coverage of motor racing has come a long way from the days when it was squeezed into BBC's *Grandstand* between gymnastics and the 3.30 at Kempton Park.

The BBC had been running Grands Prix for eighteen years when – according to racing commentator Murray Walker in his autobiography *Unless I'm Very Much Mistaken* – Bernie Ecclestone rang them to say: 'You've just lost the contract and we're making the announcement in half an hour's time.'

The stunned head of sport Jonathan Martin asked why he hadn't been given the chance to counter-bid.

'Unless you've been cheating me all these years,' said Ecclestone, 'there's no way you can pay what they're paying, so there's no point asking.'

ITV had offered a massive £60 million for five years, the promise of more airtime and a more sophisticated TV package. Unlike the BBC, which used its own in-house production team, ITV would employ an external company, MACH 1 (an amalgam of the 'Meridian, 'Anglia' and 'Chrysalis' production companies) to make the programme, using the technical and engineering facilities of BBC resources. MACH 1 would employ the behind-camera staff, but those on-screen would be employed by ITV Sport.

Murray Walker thought the scenario looked problematic. 'If ever I saw a recipe for politics, manoeuvring in the corridors, back-stabbing, deviousness, power struggles and double-dealing this is it,' he says in his autobiography, but he adds: 'Everyone got on extremely well, no one tried to do the other chap's job and the atmosphere was terrific.'

However, Murray Walker quite rightly identified the power struggles that would develop – only he was at the top of the pile and a big enough name to avoid the back-stabbing lower down the ranks. By the time he was ready to retire, his test driver James Allen was poised to jump into the cockpit. 'No one tried to do the other chap's job,' says Walker – a revealing comment, because people in Formula One seem to be extraordinarily territorial about their roles. It hints at an insecurity, an uncertainty that permeates every position in Formula One, from waitress to driver, engineer to commercial director, from long-standing journalist to novice reporter and TV presenter to work-experience runner.

My own foray into TV Formula One-style began with one senior television executive sitting me down to say, 'Look, I've been doing this programme one way for five years. We've won BAFTAs and now I'm being told to bring a pretty, female presenter on board...what do you think your role is?'

There were already seven people on-screen and before I had even covered my first race the wrangling had begun. I listened with amazement as I was warned to be wary of competition from the other female presenter, Louise Goodman. Several colleagues assumed, wrongly as it turned out, that I would be her eventual successor.

'They won't have two women working on F1,' said an on-screen colleague.

'Many people don't want you here,' warned another with refreshing honesty.

It took me a long time to understand the dynamics at play, but I eventually realized: Formula One is the only sport in the world in which your team-mate is your main rival.

That ideology has seeped through into every strata of F1. Journalist Kevin Eason has spoken of 'a tremendous streak of competitiveness' within the press pack: 'You can guarantee that every morning everybody goes through everybody else's story to see what they got that you haven't got or to laugh at other people when they got it wrong, so it's very, very competitive.'

The TV presenters watch their backs, just like David Coulthard aware of a newcomer breathing down his neck. After one Grand Prix I heard one commentator complaining to the head of ITV sport about another commentator's mistakes during the broadcast. There are no production meetings that engender camaraderie and the status quo is maintained, in my opinion, by a policy of divide and rule. Newcomers must find their own way, even at the expense of the quality of the TV coverage. Like Antonio Pizzonia, I became aware of the whispers and was hurt by the feeling that people wanted to see me fail. But I wasn't alone.

The MACH 1 conglomerate had been formed to pitch for the lucrative F1 contract, but I soon learned that the merger had proved problematic, with people from Chrysalis eventually outnumbering those from Meridian and Anglia. Although proclaimed as a merger, the new arrangement had all the hallmarks of a takeover and several producers and directors left to pursue other projects.

'It should have been the best job in TV,' one woman told me, 'but I can't cope with the people any more.' Another admitted: 'I wouldn't work for them if it wasn't such a long job. Ten-month contracts are hard to find in TV, so I just put up with it.'

To complicate matters further, Formula One is an arena in which many people have mutliple loyalties. Commentator Martin Brundle is perhaps the best sportsperson-turned-pundit on British TV. His 'grid-walks' are the most popular part of the broadcast and his relationship with drivers, team members and F1 management ensures good access and informative television. He is never afraid to speak his mind and doesn't pander to anybody. But Martin is also David Coulthard's manager, which inevitably raises questions about the extent to which he can remain an impartial interpreter of events. Similarly, race pundit Tony Jardine owns the PR company that promotes BAR.

But the truth is that almost every on-screen personality has allegiances to different teams: long-standing friendships that aren't worth sullying; a partner employed by a team; the chance to holiday on a team-owner's yacht; or simply the best lunches in the paddock. All of these factors, and many more besides, can put a gloss on stories that would otherwise be less flattering for Formula One.

The tight-knit community of race weekends and the longevity of the season mean that the risk of upsetting someone within the sport is generally not worth the hassle. F1 teams might be on-site rather than watching the ITV broadcast, but there is always someone monitoring the coverage, ready to report any unflattering comments to those at ground level. And they will always make their feelings known. It is unlikely to be as blatant as a face-to-face confrontation, but driver access might suddenly be restricted or a team mysteriously become less co-operative. If a team feels hard-done-by they might sulk for a while and favour one presenter or journalist over another, but they will recover with a promise of better coverage. On the whole this is rare, however, because the potentially damaging stories aren't often reported.

Damage limitation is part of the job of FOM, which implements a great list of rules to control TV coverage. Filming in Magny-Cours, I found myself in the garage during a practice session with award-winning photographer Clive Mason. We were shooting an item on the snappers whose job it is to capture the sport on camera. The producer and I had already gone through the ordeal of grovelling to FOM to gain access to the garage at this time, but we were then turned away from the photographers' room because of its appearance.

'It's not a very nice one here,' said the woman in charge of accreditation. 'If it was a new one, we'd let you film.'

I was also taking pictures, chatting to Clive about the necessary skills, etc., as the Jaguar drivers prepared for their weekend. I had my usual paddock pass, but no pit-lane pass that would let me in to the designated area that runs by the garages. As we talked, cameras rolling, my foot stepped onto the painted white line indicating the pit lane. The cars were in the garage and I was in no danger (other than exposing myself as a crap photographer), but when we got to the editing suite the producer reluctantly concluded that we couldn't use any shots showing my foot over the line because of FOM's insistence on the absolute rigidity of their rule.

It was beyond satire: one size-seven shoe steps onto a white line and a whole day's filming has to be reworked. Shortly after his crash in Monaco, Jenson Button appeared on Patrick Keilty's BBC television chat show and discussed the accident, but any footage of the event was conspicuously absent. The producers confirmed that FOM had refused to release any footage of the crash – at any price.

Ecclestone's fierce protection of Formula One may have helped to forge the sport's exclusive image, but in an increasingly competitive TV market it begins to look precious and short-sighted. By restricting access of the footage of F1, Ecclestone does the sport no favours at a time when TV audiences are falling and a new generation of fans may be hard to come by. In fact, Ecclestone's ability to judge the needs of a twenty-first-century F1 television audience has already been called into question by the recent digital fiasco.

As early as 1992 he began exploring the possibility of digital TV for Formula One. In 1995 he invested £36 million of his own money in his production company, FOCA TV, to create a multi-feed broadcast that allowed the viewer to control the television shots on pay-per-view broadcasts. It launched in 2002 and for £12.50 the armchair viewer could 'direct' his own programme, choosing from in-car footage, real-lap times, pit-lane activities and statistics. Even by Ecclestone's standards this was an expensive project and in 1996, he announced a £50 million deal with the German TV company Kirchgruppe, which was owned by Leo Kirch, then the sixth-richest man in Europe with an estimated personal fortune of £7.6 billion. Through one of their channels, DF1, the scheme would pilot these broadcasts in Germany, Austria and Switzerland. Soon afterwards Ecclestone made similar deals with the Paris-based Canal+ for French and Italian audiences.

FOCA TV became F1 Communications and was appropriately based at Biggin Hill – the former RAF wartime airfield in Kent. Ecclestone had bought the premises in 1997 as a handy place to keep his two executive Jets, while also acting as a base for his mobile TV production facility. Manned by a staff of 280, it required three 747 jumbo jets to transport the necessary equipment beyond Europe and 28 purpose-built articulated lorries within Europe. The production staff would be flown to every race in one of his BAe 146 jets replete with F1 livery.

But this time Ecclestone wasn't so infallible. The digital coverage was awful. The presenters and commentators were in a London studio trying to determine what was happening – when they weren't looking bored, humiliated or wryly amused. ITV was apparently none too worried by the competition, though any venture with Ecclestone's name on it should never be taken lightly. Nevertheless, the project collapsed after just one season. The Malaysian Grand Prix was the most popular, attracting 25,000 viewers, though some races drew only 9,000. In the same season ITV averaged three million viewers – considerably less than the seven million who tuned in when Damon Hill was competing.

Ecclestone and Max Mosley could not afford to let Formula One's TV viewing figures fall and if they couldn't control them by creating a rival on-screen package, they had to introduce new rules to reduce the predictability and increase the variables affecting the outcome. Like TV producers trying to make the next series of *Big Brother* more interesting, they had to come up with ways to alter the product itself. It might disappoint motor-racing purists, but it would help out the TV companies and the sponsors.

The failure of Ecclestone's digital TV exercise has ultimately benefited ITV, which now receives some of the more exhilarating 'on-board' camera shots that Bernie had been keeping for himself. However, the rest of his expensive TV hardware has been mothballed . . . for the time being.

Unfortunately, the better the TV coverage, the worse the race attendance figures. There were patches of empty seats at the Magny-Cours circuit. Crowd numbers at European venues have been low all season, with the last Nürburgring race down by 30,000 on the previous year.

I arrived at France's tiny Clermont-Ferrand airport on the Wednesday before the race. The weekend is known in the sport as 'Magny-Bore', because of its rural location and traditionally unexciting races, but I love its provincial charm and the incongruity of having a cutting-edge racetrack among silent pastures.

We stayed in a twenty-two-room country-house hotel straight out of a Joanne Harris novel. The rooms were low-ceilinged and wooden beams cut through swathes of pink flowers, which covered not only the walls, the carpet, the curtains, the bedspread and the cushions, but also the bathroom, crawling up behind the pink suite and swirling overhead. At the end of a long day it is a welcome contrast to the minimalism and austere chrome of the F1 paddock. Not everyone was treated to such quaint luxury, however. The journalists were holed up in a hotel with an outside loo and communal showers. One TV producer revealed that his bathroom was so small he had to sit sideways on the toilet.

This time last year Formula One was heavy with the weight of Michael Schumacher's success. It was here that he clinched his fifth world title, while the media looked down the barrel and wondered how on earth to keep people interested for the rest of the season. But 2003 was playing out with welcome unpredictability. Schumacher senior was just seven points ahead of Raikkonen, with Ralf Schumacher only eight points behind him. Williams went into Magny-Cours off the back of an impressive one-two at the Nürburgring and all the signs were that they would excel here too.

It seemed that tyres were taking on a greater significance with every race and in France it was generally accepted that the Michelin runners would once again claim a distinct advantage. Ferrari and Bridgestone were pretty much resigned to watching in vain as Williams and Renault threatened to head off into the distance. And they were right.

Ralf and Montoya cruised to P1 and P2 respectively for Williams. Michael Schumacher tucked in behind, with Raikkonen and Coulthard lining up behind the red Ferrari. Renault were hoping for an impressive result at their home Grand Prix and with nine races of reliable running behind them they anticipated no problems.

In TV terms, this race turned out to be somewhat challenging. Ralf led from start to finish and the seventy laps were almost totally free of overtaking. It was enough to make my preview piece about race photographers look like Emmy Award-winning TV gold. The only engaging moment of the race came as Coulthard erroneously received the signal to leave his pit stop. The instruction was slightly premature, as his hose man (nicknamed 'Forklift') was about to discover. The mechanic was dragged to the ground and the commentators suddenly found a reason to get excited. The confusion cost Coulthard seventeen seconds and relegated him from third to fifth.

McLaren's misfortune also extended to Kimi Raikkonen, whose rear-brake disc exploded three laps from the end. Fernando Alonso and Jarno Trulli suffered the embarrassment of engine failure in front of Renault's day-tripping employees, while running sixth and seventh. BAR had had a tumultuous weekend with bailiffs locking their cars away on Friday morning over unpaid sponsorship commission – a uniquely F1 scenario. But the drivers did make it to the track on Sunday with Jacques Villeneuve managing ninth position and Jenson Button failing to finish due to a refuelling failure.

'I thought the car was going really well,' said Button afterwards. 'Hardly surprising when there was next to nothing in the tank!'

Michael Schumacher earned the remaining podium spot, despite his inferior tyres. 'Third place was probably the best I could have done,' he concluded afterwards.

The following day's newspapers were keen to trumpet Williams's consecutive one-two finish and hailed Ralf as a genuine title contender. The headlines screamed of an exciting season and journalists were relieved that at last Michael Schumacher was back among the pack. They were finally able to justify their column inches to impatient editors prioritizing more 'popular' sports. While the TV viewing figures demonstrated a consumer demand, the papers had no choice but to follow the season through to its denouement. However, Kevin Eason of *The Times* was honest enough to describe the race as 'a dull affair' and pointed out that the French grandstands were far from full.

The Tour de France was a completely different affair. Every day brought more twists and turns than the road up the Alpe d'Huez. The race was receiving more global press coverage than ever before and UK TV audiences were tuning in to ITV's coverage in unprecedented numbers. The Tour de France is the ultimate team sport, an event in which riders push themselves to their mental and physical limits for the sake of their team leader. Individual personal glory is sacrificed for the sake of the team and the fortunes of one chosen man. This noble ethos filters through to the media teams working behind the scenes: nations share footage, reporters swap information and newcomers are judged on their enthusiasm and skill, rather than their ability to recall race results from twenty years ago.

Lance Armstrong went on to win his fifth consecutive title and was hailed a hero – even by those inside the sport.

8

Silverstone

It was April 2000 and the crowds were making their way to the British Grand Prix. The roads around the Silverstone circuit became one enormous traffic jam as furious spectators dumped their cars and set off on foot to the circuit.

It was 1.45 p.m. One first-time Grand Prix visitor recalls that as he was running to the entrance he spotted a German man sitting on a bench, his head in his hands, his flag draped over his shoulders.

'I knew I could make the mile or so in the remaining fifteen minutes,' he says, 'but this poor guy clearly couldn't. He must have come all the way across Europe and there he was, realizing that he was about to miss the start of the race. It was a nightmare.'

Three years later, the Silverstone Grand Prix was still on probation. Images of traffic chaos and hundreds of cars doing wheelspins in muddy fields across Northamptonshire has been extremely damaging to the event organizers and the reputation of the British as hosts of a major sporting championship. Articles in the continental press accused Bernie Ecclestone and Max Mosley of favouritism: if other host nations had been responsible for such a fiasco, they said, the race would have been snatched from them. In their eyes the UK was receiving special treatment.

But Ecclestone was quick to apportion blame and in the run-up to this, the fifty-third British Grand Prix, he was still publicly attacking the circuit's owners, the British Racing Drivers' Club (BRDC), for failing to improve the venue. The BRDC receives £5 million a year in rent from Octagon, which owns the rights to promote the British Grand Prix. Hours before the 2002 race, Ecclestone dismissed it as 'a country fair masquerading as a world-class event' and on the eve of the 2003 race he told an Indian magazine that Hyderabad is in the running for its very own Grand Prix.

Bernie was turning up the temperature on Silverstone and the man feeling the heat most was BRDC president Sir Jackie Stewart. He had a busy week thinking up sound bites for every publication and broadcaster that was interested.

'If we don't keep the British Grand Prix,' he told reporters, 'we'll lose the industry. Without the race you don't motivate young drivers or young engineers and there's no grassroots enthusiasm.'

Such altruism is so rare in Formula One that sympathy can quickly turn to cynicism. Losing the British Grand Prix would be hugely damaging to the BRDC members, not least Jackie Stewart himself and the Jaguar team he works for. And besides, it's hard to say how many wannabe drivers are lured to the sport by the fields of Silverstone, rather than the chicanes of Monaco. But as always in times of trouble, the people behind Formula One scatter financial projections like confetti.

The knighted ex-driver wants £40 million of government money to turn Silverstone into a flagship venue for the UK motor sport industry, which he says generates '£5 billion for the UK economy'. One local councillor anxiously claimed that the race is worth '£43 million to the area each year', though he also boasted they had spent 'more than £40 million on roads, car parks and the new paddock' and the use of a thousand police officers cost an extra £330,000.

Ecclestone and FIA president Max Mosley claim that 50,000 British people are employed in Formula One. However, there is some dispute about what it means to work in F1. Terry Lovell, author of *Bernie's Game*, regards that figure of 50,000 as 'something of an exaggeration. The number of jobs quoted included the entire motor industry, right down to the production of specialist flameproof overalls. The figure for Formula One was actually nearer 8,000.'

But the lobbying must have been persuasive, because in the build-up to Silverstone the government pledged £16 million to help nourish the roots of British motor racing. It isn't nearly enough as far as the BRDC is concerned, but even £16 million seems hard to justify when teams like McLaren and Williams operate on budgets of more than £200 million and are based less than an hour from the circuit. If ever a sport looks able to help itself, it is this one.

It struck me as very 'Formula One' to hear people arguing that public funds should benefit their business, which – in real terms – affects very few people indeed. It's hardly surprising that a sport which projects an image of financial largesse inspires very little public sympathy when it goes cap in hand to the taxpayer for help. The government funding of Wembley Arena made little logical business sense, but the decision to rejuvenate the site was largely sentimental – a feeling that is noticeably missing in Formula One.

It would undoubtedly be a shame if Britain – as the beating heart of world motor sport – could not host its own Grand Prix, but Stewart and his fellow members are in an interesting predicament: Bernie Ecclestone threw £12 million of his own money into the pot to revamp Silverstone, but still charges the BRDC £10 million a year for the rights to host the Grand Prix on their 850-acre site. However, the BRDC have somehow managed to find enough money to improve their impressive headquarters.

'What really gets up my nose,' said Ecclestone, with typical candour, 'is that we have these bloody lousy facilities, but they managed to spend three million on their own clubhouse.' The BRDC subsequently issued a statement insisting that the expenditure had not been 'to the benefit of the club and its members'.

Despite complaints about the circuit conditions, Ecclestone is less concerned about empty grandstand seats than the quality of the TV coverage, which nets hundreds of millions of pounds annually.

'Bernie would say the television audience is more important than gate receipts,' said Frank Williams as the topic gained momentum. Speaking at the Goodwood festival a few days later, Jackie Stewart said, 'The financial structure of the World Championship is completely unbalanced. Mr Ecclestone's group of companies (FOM) removes the television money, the circuit advertising, the corporate hospitality, even the title sponsorship of the Grand Prix support races. The only money left for the promoter or circuit owner is from the ticket prices.'

The BRDC have invested a total of £40 million themselves, but the only revenue they earn from the weekend is in gate receipts. Hence the high ticket prices.

A grandstand seat on race day will set you back £190. So a family of four is faced with a choice: an early start, traffic jams, shivering on a metal seat wearing ear-plugs, restricted viewing and an inaudible PA system, a hamburger and tea in a polystyrene cup ... or a week in Florida. Faced with such a dilemma, most people would chose Florida, but – fascinatingly – not everyone. F1 fans are a curious breed.

To some people the lure of Formula One is not the drivers or even the hedonistic lifestyle they represent. It is the cars – those noisy, unfeeling, carbon-shelled engines-on-wheels that arouse some people like a bonobo chimp at a tea party. Soon after I began working in motor racing, an F1 magazine gave away a CD called *Grand Prix Sounds*: '69 minutes of GP action'. I stared at it for a while, trying to imagine the audio delights therein. The track titles were no help at all: 'V10 in Action', 'V10 Spinning for Fun', 'Hairpins and Full-throttle', 'V10 Laps', 'On Board with a V10'. Intrigued, I paid £3.60 and played my new CD on the journey home.

At first I thought the CD-player wasn't working – then I realized a Ferrari had *not* just pulled up beside me. I had bought more than an hour of engine noises. Just engine noises. No race commentary, no driver interviews, no music that would spoil the enjoyment, just the revving of ten-valve engines negotiating bends in roads. All I could think was 'Who?' and 'Why?' At what point in life does this become entertainment?

Perhaps devoted F1 fans lie in darkened rooms imagining engine pistons jerking in and out. Perhaps they host dinner parties, extracting themselves from conversations in order to play their favourite engine noises.

'Is that the V12 at 17,500 rpm?' asks an envious guest ...

I honestly do not know why anyone would listen to such a CD, but I will continue on my quest to find out.

For some fans, the romantic journey to F1 devotion begins with their first car – perhaps an old banger that requires a little tinkering, until engines, exhausts and fuses start to fascinate. Or there's the seventeen year old who soups up his Capri and spends his lunchtimes reading car magazines, while enviously eyeing-up his mate's Ford Escort GTi. For these 'engine-fiddlers' it is a small step to fully blown hero-worship: eyes moistening in front of the TV as machines at the zenith of technological advancement whip around bends and screech along the straights.

For other people, however, the sport is less about mechanical intricacies and more about speed – it's as simple as that. These 'speed-freak' fans are attracted to anything that goes fast: motorbikes, cars, boats – anything with an engine that says 'I have horsepower, saddle up and ride me.' There are many hundreds of thousands of people who follow Formula One purely because they like to see cars going very fast indeed. And as every fan resigned to never being a racing driver knows: if you can't join 'em – watch 'em. If speed really is the wind beneath your carbon-fibre wings, there is no better place than Formula One to vicariously satisfy your craving.

And then there are the die-hard, petrol-sniffing, F1 fanatics who can be identified by their branded baseball caps and their ability to drop phrases like 'beryllium-aluminium alloy' and 'stability-management systems' into casual conversation. Petrol heads can witter on for hours about the beauty of Formula One and will often cite the fascinating combination of technical excellence, team-manager strategy and driver talent as the sport's defining qualities.

They are horrified at the thought of recording a late-night Grand Prix broadcast and prefer to set their alarms for 4 a.m. to watch the ninety-minute build-up, the race and the analysis before going back to sleep, waking only to catch the repeat at 2 p.m. They are utterly at one with the sport's complex rules and regulations, eager to dissect them at a moment's notice and always ready with a fistful of reasons why Formula One is neither predictable nor monotonous.

However, this almost religious devotion to one topic of conversation can leave one painfully ill-prepared for others. I've witnessed men who can discuss the finer points of F1 with an impressive eloquence struck dumb by any conversational gambit unrelated to motor racing. Chatting about the weather, for insance, is strictly off-limits – unless, of course, you're talking tyre-types, in which case you'd better sit down, because this could take some time. Nevertheless, passion is a wonderful thing and it ought to be encouraged (just check your table plan carefully if you ever attend an F1 do).

A fascinating trend emerges on closer inspection of these F1 types. The further you go from casual observer to hard-core fan, the less likely it is they will be able to name their favourite team or even driver. In other sports, football for example, a team's fanbase is most often made up of locals. Allegiances are formed on the basis of geography, a pride in local identity: you are shouting from the terraces not just for your players, but for your home and thus a little bit for yourself.

Then there's the inheritance of family loyalties: 'My dad supported Bury Football Club, I do, and so shall you, my son.' And there is also that memorable first time, that special trip to deflower a youngster of impartiality or ambivalence for ever – the inaugural trip to the ground with your dad. These are the moments in which football fans are made and tribal loyalties are cemented.

It doesn't always follow this pattern, of course, especially with Manchester United. Travel to the smallest African village and you'll find a prized red devil's shirt worn by a wide-eyed child who knows nothing of Salford's terraced houses and whose English extends solely to Fergie's current squad.

An attachment to Formula One can also have its roots in national pride – as shown by the Italian *Tifosi* or the religious fervour inspired by Barrichello in Brazil and McLaren's following in the UK, but Formula One is far more complicated than that.

Many F1 fans have never been to a Grand Prix and they were almost certainly never taken to one by their parents. In fact it's not a very child-friendly sport. I've seen tearful children in the stands look at their parents as if to say 'Why are you doing this to me?' in response to the sheer noise and volume of passing cars. Perhaps a minority of parents will take their new-born Michael, Ayrton or Enzo from the hospital, dressed in a red Ferrari Babygro, and place them in a motor-racing-themed nursery, playing *Grand Prix Sounds* through the baby monitor – but they are not the norm. Unlike football, passing on the love of one team or one driver is often much less important than engendering a love of the sport itself.

The 'engine-fiddler' and the 'speed-freak' are likely to cite one or two favourite individuals – the ones known for their impetuosity, like Montoya or Villeneuve; alongside the one who is simply the fastest, like Michael Schumacher. A team like Ferrari has a history, too, but most of all it's sexy: it's a red-hot prancing horse with a steamy Italian temperament. Their cars are very quick and very expensive. When you say you like Ferrari you are admitting to a sophistication of taste that isn't associated with Toyota, Renault or Minardi, which are just not as cool.

Jaguar returned to Formula One because it wanted to perpetuate its image, whispering sweet nothings from within a leather-and-walnut interior. If Jaguar's sleek cat says long legs in ten-denier stockings unfurling from the passenger seat, then Renault says mother-of-three loading the shopping in the boot. Jaguar hoped their iconic brand association would earn them a strong F1 fanbase, who would then buy even more Jaguar cars. As it transpires, their fanbase in these early days is predominantly female, drawn to the sport by Mark Webber's good looks. Thanks also to his impressive driving, it now looks as if Jaguar might not have to cut their losses and return to sepia ad campaigns. The point is, however, that some teams will always earn a loyal following because of their image alone.

On the other hand, the statistic-studying, baseball-cap-wearing, letter-to-the-editor-writing zealot is hard-pushed to state his allegiance and will often avoid the question as if it was an ill-timed enquiry into his genital health. They shuffle around the issue uncomfortably, answering obliquely that they enjoy 'the spectacle...the whole thing...it's not about one team...or driver...'

Formula One also attracts a following of people concerned only with 'elite' motor racing. They watch Formula One because it is the best in the world. Just as Premier League football is more popular than division three, Formula One has a greater following than touring cars, Formula Ford or Formula 3000. One motor racing fan described F1 to me as 'the aristocratic wanker of motor sport,' yet even he had to admit he would rather watch Schumacher at the Nürburgring than a nineteen year old from Essex bombing round Donnington.

In Silverstone, however, I found an altogether different type of fan: the 'camper'. It's debatable whether these people are really F1 enthusiasts. They look rather like groups of mates who enjoy leaving their wives and girlfriends, putting up a tent and lighting a barbeque – but who need a good excuse to do so.

I got the chance to investigate these campers during the race weekend of 2001, as the sun began to set behind the rolling hills that formed the temporary campsites. Each group had marked out its territory with strategically parked cars and purposefully pitched tents, while the truly well organized had even used yellow scene-of-crime-tape to secure their patch. Folding chairs and sturdy cool-boxes formed seats around camping stoves and mini-barbeques.

One group described themselves proudly as the Five-Star Campers. Corn on the cob simmered gently in the pan as they sipped at bottles of Stella Artois.

'I've been coming since 1988,' said Lee. 'There's nothing else like it ... You're very close to the circuit here, so you can get to and from really easy. We all work really hard during the week, but it's just nice to get back to basics, living out in the wild, really.'

They all agreed that the German fans are always the noisiest and the toilets are always appalling.

'They [the site owners] just dig a hole in the ground and build some wood round it ... You try to bung yourself up,' he said, smiling broadly, 'you don't want to have a Silverstone poo, basically.'

It was fascinating. Not just the poo stories, of course, but the culture, the rituals, the British, mustn't-grumble simplicity of it all. The mood was one of conviviality and joy in a shared experience. It didn't matter if your tent-mate's McLaren pyjamas clashed with your Ferrari ones – team loyalty did not spill over into animosity. Each camping group displayed flags from several different teams.

Thirty-something Martin showed me round his twenty-two-year-old VW campervan, a bright green and white tribute to quality engineering with a seventies' orange interior.

'I came all the way up the motorway at 50 mph,' he said. 'I've got everything I need: Pot Noodles, beer and Kettle Chips. I'm here to see the F1 and party with the boys.'

It was British stoicism at its outdoor best: a timeless delight in life's simple pleasures.

'I think we have a greater passion than a lot of nations,' said Martin. 'We find something we like, we go for it, we want to stick with it ... If you've got the sunshine, you'll basically be OK.'

Another group of eleven men, who varied in age from twenty to sixty, joked that they were from the Birmingham Gay Pride Club. It was a self-conscious admission that their organizing talents were atypical for a group of straight men on a weekend break.

They had three stripy gazebos erected above a trestle table covered in a blue and yellow flowered plastic tablecloth. In the 'kitchen' area, an enormous gas barbeque was cooking chicken breasts and thick burgers. The men all had their designated jobs, some opening wine, some laying out servers, some bearing bowls of salad and coleslaw. They had been coming to Silverstone for twelve years. In their adjoining caravan, two men were preparing cuts of meat and bread rolls. It was a slick operation.

I asked how much time they actually spent at the racetrack.

'Oh, at least an hour, wasn't it, today?' said one guy dryly, uncorking a bottle of wine and looking off into the distance. 'Unfortunately we have to go back again tomorrow.'

Were they never put off by the conditions? The rain?

'We have no alternative. The weather's like that in England, so we have to make do with it.'

They admitted that they weren't the most devoted F1 fans in the world.

'It is amazing considering how expensive it is to come. Spending £150 – it is incredible. It's not even fun is it, really?...It costs £55 for qualifying, £95 for the race tomorrow and £23 per head just to come into this field!' He was setting down elegant red wine glasses now and precisely laid silver cutlery. 'It's just a weekend away for the boys and, of course, because it's in July you always assume the weather will get better – but it never does of course.'

Across the field another group was enjoying the late afternoon ambience in less refined – but no less comfortable – surroundings. One side of their enormous blue and white striped tent was folded back to let in the sunshine, revealing five well-spaced camp beds occupied by languorous bare-chested young men in jeans. Near them was a turtle-shaped paddling pool filled with cold water and cans of beer. They only stopped laughing long enough to take sips from the cans in their hands.

'This is just wonderful,' said one, 'absolutely brilliant, spot-on, couldn't be better.'

The worst thing about the weekend for them was 'the *Tifosi*... crashing into your tent in the middle of the night. But it's all in good spirit.'

And it was. In a nation renowned for its rioting football mobs, it was quite a sight to see thousands of peaceful sport fans coexisting side by side in their colourful tents in the English countryside. The air was filled only with the whiff of smoking burgers and the sound of laughter.

*

The Northampton Hilton always greets you with a lobby full of cheap cover versions. This year it was a pan-pipe rendition of 'Wonderwall' by Oasis, followed by a saxophone obliteration of Abba's 'Dancing Queen'.

Close to Silverstone, it's a motorway-junction stop-over with aspirations to be Las Vegas. On Thursday morning only a few people were distracted by Murray Walker helping himself to cornflakes from the breakfast buffet. As for me, I had an important appointment in a muddy field. It was the start of the British Grand Prix weekend, so naturally I was off lawnmower racing.

As you might suspect, this was the brainchild of those PR people who keep Formula One in the newspapers. This time it was the BAR team, in association with their engine supplier Honda, who had organized the event to guarantee extensive coverage in the build-up to the weekend. Plus, of course, they had one of the four British drivers in Jenson Button and the tabloids were keen to whip up some patriotic fervour.

When I arrived everybody was huddled into an increasingly steamy awning that extended from one side of the Honda motorhome. Fleece-lined, waterproof overcoats jostled together as journalists and photographers helped themselves to tea and coffee from the flasks in the corner. As always in F1 hospitality there were bowls of fruit and glass jars of sherbet lemons. Some twenty snappers were already crouched around the huge BAR-branded four-wheel-drive lawnmower that awaited Button's arrival. On the side of the motorhome a large whiteboard listed the teams due to take part, comprising members of the media and corporate representatives.

Outside, bails of hay marked out a circular track. They were wrapped around with Honda-branded plastic tape, secured to three-foot-high metal poles. A commentary box was set up, its tall speakers broadcasting with a quality that Silverstone itself would do well to emulate. Garden trellises and gnomes completed the bizarre scene. In the distance three more fields were already housing the first of the weekend's campers. One group could be seen battling the ceaseless rain and strong winds as they attempted to erect a large tent. The green fabric billowed stubbornly as their jeans soaked up the rain.

Button arrived half an hour late, looking as though he had just got out of bed. ('I have,' he confided.) We were one of three TV crews and needed not only an interview with Button, but shots of him driving the lawnmower. It soon became clear that this was not going to be easy. There were three people presiding over whether Button would take the wheel: his personal manager, the organizer of the event and the BAR PR rep. Predictably, they all insisted that no, he would not be driving the lawnmower under any circumstances. It was too cold outside. Button would give a short interview inside the tented area. Celebrities the world over employ people to refuse things on their behalf – normally without even asking their permission.

I took Button's arm, told him he had no choice and we both laughed as he mounted the mighty four-wheeled lawnmower. He even challenged ITV reporter Ted Kravitz to a lap of the makeshift track. Yellow-coated marshals dived out of the way as the competitors went off-piste, turning over hay bails and knocking down gnomes.

Of course, Button won. His 'representatives' rubbed their cold hands with glee, delighted at their idea of making him race. Some disgruntled journalists were heard to remark that it was the only thing BAR would win all year, but the surreal event had its desired effect – the following day's newspapers ran full-page photos of Button trundling round the field, accompanied by headlines that made you proud to be British: BUTTON CAN MOW DOWN THE FIELD, JENSON: I WILL BE A CUT ABOVE and finally, JENSON WANTS TO BURY THE HATCHET, a reference to his abating feud with Villeneuve. It was a great British tabloid page-filler: a rural English scene and a millionaire superstar getting his hands dirty. Plus it involved a race – and we Brits just love a race.

By Friday of the Grand Prix weekend, the tabloids were once again gearing up for pages of 'pit babes' and glamour models holding spanners. There were PR-placed stories of Button's prowess on a lawnmower, Ralph Firman's 'lucky sunglasses' and one fan's decision to name his newborn son 'McLaren'. There were also plans to launch Firman down Blackpool's Big One roller-coaster in his Jordan E13 car.

'It's the first time it's been attempted,' he said innocently. 'I'm sure it will comply with all safety standards.'

A couple of days after Silverstone they strapped his car to a carriage on the Big One and down he went.

'It was fun!' Ralph told me after the event. 'We got some great publicity!'

The 'craziness' of the nation's biggest motor-racing event was illustrated in every tabloid with a photo of Michael Schumacher wide-eyed and tongue protruding as Frankie Dettori throttled him. THE CHOKE'S ON YOU went the headline, and after posting the quickest lap of first qualifying, Schumacher certainly was smiling.

For the crowd, though, the session was a damp, tedious procession as the remaining drivers tried fruitlessly to match Schumacher's time. The biggest cheer of the day was reserved for a hare that wandered on to the main straight before making a sterling attempt to burrow into a gravel trap.

By Sunday there was much more to talk about. In second qualifying, Rubens Barrichello had snatched pole position with Renault's Jarno Trulli at P2. Raikkonen, hunting Schumacher in the drivers' championship, was in third position and Schumacher himself was at fifth spot, behind his brother Ralf. It was only the third British Grand Prix in history without a home driver in the top-ten grid places. Coulthard was in twelfth, while Silverstone rookies Ralph Firman and Justin Wilson were at seventeen and eighteen respectively. Jenson Button did better on the lawnmower than in his car: he broke his front suspension on a kerb and didn't complete a lap, thereby sentencing himself to the back of the grid.

The biggest revelation of the morning, however, was the ease with which traffic had swept into Silverstone on the widened roads and come to rest in the 18,000 new parking spaces. The Silverstone circuit could once again claim to have the busiest heliport in the world, with more than 4,000 helicopter arrivals and departures.

Everybody hoped the weather would stay warm and dry, except Eddie Jordan, for whom rain was his only chance of success.

'If it's dry, not a chance. We need rain,' he said recalling the meteoro-logical fluke that had brought him and Fisichella victory in Brazil.

I spent the morning rounding up famous faces for quick interviews. Vodafone had invited cricketers Michael Vaughan, Alec Stewart and James Anderson, as well as Frankie Dettori, Lawrence Dallaglio, Carol Vorderman and Phil Tufnell (who drank too much champagne and lost his pass). The cricketers had taken part in a photo-call with Michael Schumacher the day before. Lining up in the garage, the Englishmen stood by in regulation Vodafone caps as Schumacher tried his hand with a bat, sending a ball forcefully over the heads of the assembled photographers and almost destroying a monitor on the pit wall.

Everybody was all smiles until I approached Schumacher for a brief interview that had been OK'd by Vodafone's PR people. But Schumacher's press manager Sabine Kehm had other ideas and barked at us 'No interviews! We said no interviews!' before leading Schumacher away. The cricketers raised their eyebrows at the scene, shaking their heads at the precious nature of a 'sport' so different to their own.

'How do you think you'd do in a Formula One car?' I asked Alec Stewart.

'Oh, marvellously,' he replied. 'I'd be excellent...although I can say that because I'll never get to do it.'

Jaguar once again pulled off the promotional stunt of the weekend by entering into collaboration with the new Schwarzenegger movie *Terminator 3: Rise of the Machines*. The première was being held in Leicester Square the following evening, with Mark Webber and the same mock-F1 car used at Monaco's diamond party. But on race day itself the film's big star would make an appearance. Arnold Schwarzenegger strode out of the Jaguar motorhome to be met by a scrum that would have intimidated Lawrence Dallaglio (who was meanwhile signing autographs at the other end of the paddock). Dressed in a white shirt and white linen jacket, Arnie was taken on a tour of the garages before posing for photos with Bernie Ecclestone and Frankie Dettori, who proved extremely skilled at popping up at every photo-call throughout the weekend.

Yachtswoman Ellen McArthur was a guest of Renault and apologized every time she was dragged away by the team's PR people to give yet another interview.

Singer Danni Minogue ate lunch in the BAR motorhome, sparking rumours of a reconciliation with ex-fiancé Jacques Villeneuve. Danni was all set to do an interview with us when – embarrassingly – our camera didn't turn up and she had to walk off without promoting the team that had accommodated her.

BAR itself, however, was at the centre of a big story. Villeneuve and Button might have publicly ended their spat, but by the eve of the British Grand Prix, the Brit had outscored his team-mate by ten points to three. The fate of the Canadian would become big news in the remaining races if he didn't pull something out of the hat soon.

Silverstone's fate also remained under scrutiny as the weekend unfolded. Sir Jackie Stewart, a staunch royalist, brought sports fan Princess Anne along to demonstrate her support for the occasion. Naturally, she tactfully avoided the topic of whether the government should help fund the event. Her son Peter works for BMW Williams, liaising with sponsors and VIPs, and it's ironic that one of the least affected men in the paddock is actually in line to the throne.

Meanwhile, Bernie Ecclestone took a one-nil advantage over Stewart in his own inimitable style. Arriving by helicopter with the Duchess of Kent and a brace of royal children, Sir Jackie took great pleasure in issuing them with paddock passes. After politely letting the royals go through the turnstiles before him, Stewart stepped up to find that his pass was rejected. Mortified, he apologized, then tried again and eventually had to send someone running to the FOM office to clarify the 'mistake'.

Eddie Jordan also found himself at the mercy of Ecclestone's sense of humour when his pass was rejected on his fiftieth birthday. As Jordan shouted for someone to go and get Pasquale, the electronic display read: *Too old to come into the paddock.*

Silverstone started to come alive as the race neared. There were empty seats, but excitement filled the air as the fans became more rowdy. The problem with the British Grand Prix, according to the chief executive of race promoters Andrew Waller, is the lack of a good home driver.

'We need a hero,' he said. 'We need a British driver to start winning again. That would make all the difference. You only have to look back to the days when Nigel Mansell was winning. We would have more than

100,000 people in on Sunday alone; this weekend we will get that number over three days.'

Another F1 stalwart who remembered those days accosted me as I walked through the paddock. She had brown hair piled into a wispy nest on her head, a camera slung around her neck and held laminated sheets of her photographs. She had seen the photographer's feature on the previous show and wanted it known that I had not done a good job. Apparently, I should have got nearer to the track for close-ups of the cars at full speed. I tried to explain how a painted white line on a garage floor had been deemed dangerous enough, so getting up close and intimate with the tyre wall was unlikely. But she wasn't really buying my excuse. Her name was Maureen Magee and she explained that she was a big player in Formula One in the sixties.

'It's completely changed,' she said. 'Look, Michael Schumacher's wife is here. I would like to talk to her. Jacques Villeneuve's mother, she and I would stand for hours and hours chatting. There was no tabloid press then. Everybody used to stand out on the pit lane and chat and joke, you know, but now it's all: who can they find out about?'

One tabloid reporter did admit to me that on Silverstone weekend they get pressured by the news desks to dish the dirt on the drivers, but they refuse.

'If I walked into the garage and found David Coulthard shagging someone over the car,' he said, 'I wouldn't phone the paper, because that's not my job. There'd be no point.'

If Jackie Stewart is looking to attract young drivers, such a story might prove more effective than a new grandstand.

The race itself turned out to be a very good advert for Formula One, with plenty of overtaking to keep the crowds happy. Barrichello started from pole, but was third into the first corner as both Raikkonen and Trulli took an advantage. On lap 5 Coulthard had to throw a piece of his own head cushioning from the car after it came loose.

'I tried to hold on to it for a coupe of laps,' he said afterwards, 'but you just can't drive with one hand.'

The resulting debris caused the appearance of the safety car for the first time as Coulthard pitted and seemed to be out of contention yet again.

But Coulthard's misfortune was forgotten six laps later, when the figure of a man running down the Hangar Straight came into focus in the heat-haze. Terrorist threats were uppermost in people's minds as we had just ended a war with Iraq and no mass gathering was deemed safe from attacks. But this figure was wearing bright green knee-length socks, a caped green waistcoat, a short red skirt and a green beret. He would have looked comical had he not been running towards cars exiting a high-speed corner at 185 mph. He was carrying a white poster, but we couldn't read the message. I turned away, unable to watch. The safety car was employed again and eventually the protester received a body-slam from a furious-looking marshal.

The teams seized the opportunity for pit stops and all the cars hurtled in to refuel. In the ensuing mêlée, Schumacher found himself behind team-mate Barrichello and was demoted from fourth to fourteenth when they re-emerged. A bizarre reshuffling of position had occurred, leaving Toyota's Cristiano da Matta leading a race for the first time. When the safety car retreated on lap 18, the battle began.

Schumacher tore his way expertly through the field, salvaging fourth place to keep him ahead of Raikkonen in the championship race. Coulthard overtook two cars in the final nine laps, placing him fifth at the finish. But the day belonged to Rubens Barrichello, who reeled off a series of quickest laps half-way through the race and on lap 42 executed an overtaking move on Raikkonen that showed the young Finn how the big boys do it. McLaren's 'Iceman' then lost out to Montoya twelve laps from the end, when he lost control of the car's rear at Stowe and the Williams (with its new £30 million sponsor Budweiser) stole through for second place.

If proof were needed that F1 drivers have nerves of steel, this was it. I was still shaken by the idea of what could have happened out there in front of millions of people watching across the world, while the drivers merely saw it as a chance to gain the advantage on their competitors. Barrichello hadn't even seen the protester.

'I was so concentrated that I didn't notice anything else. Everyone is going to say that he was a Brazilian,' he joked, 'but I still didn't see him.'

Mark Webber came closest to hitting the little green man and confessed to thinking his time was up.

'It absolutely blew me away,' the Aussie said afterwards. 'For a moment

I thought it was the end for me. Drivers are conditioned for a lot of things, but not that.' Perhaps as a consequence he had a scrappier race than usual, eventually finishing fourteenth.

His team-mate Pizzonia was still in need of a good performance. The Brazilian's seat at Jaguar had recently been looking more secure with the team agreeing to give him more time, but Silverstone was another disaster. He qualified tenth despite a gearbox failure, but had to pit with a steering-wheel problem at the end of the first safety-car period. He battled with Webber for a while, but was hampered by a suspension problem and finally ended his race with engine failure.

Button and Villeneuve fought a personal battle on the track, with the young Briton rising from twenty to fifteen and ultimately finishing an impressive eighth. Jacques was less fortunate, starting at ninth, but spinning off on the penultimate lap and finishing a lowly tenth. The British audience had been able to watch all four home drivers complete the sixty laps, though the question on everybody's lips was: who on earth was that guy?

Walking back through the paddock, I bumped into Webber's parents. Alan and Diane were still coming to terms with the fact that, had a car hit the demonstrator, the driver could have been killed, and that Mark had narrowly swerved to avoid him. They were very shaken by the incident.

Wandering into the BAR motorhome, I met the head of the TV production company.

'I wonder who that guy was?' I asked.

'Oh, we know all about him,' he replied. 'Got pages and pages on him back at the office. He's been writing to us for weeks.'

The protester turned out to be Cornelius Horan, an Irish, 56-year-old ex-priest who believes it is his job to communicate the word of the Lord. His placard read: *Read the Bible. The Bible is always right.*

Given that Horan was a known nutter, preventing his entry – or merely tracking his movements – especially when he was dressed in a green skirt, should not have posed too great a challenge to the security on every turnstile. Horan's antics had made every driver look vulnerable, but in the untouchable world of Formula One this was not the issue on everyone's minds. Geoff Willis, the BAR technical director, reminded us that F1's obsession with presentation never lets up.

'You imagine how bad an image for F1 it would have been,' he said, 'to have had a pair of amputated legs in the middle of the track.'

Horan spent six weeks in prison for aggravated trespass, then walked free saying: 'It just so happened the British Grand Prix was on and the whole thing was done spur of the moment.'

Most people expected Bernie Ecclestone to use this episode as the excuse he needed to drop Silverstone from the calendar. But he defended the venue and the actions of the organizers.

'It means the security was not good,' he said, 'but you can't stop someone doing this sort of thing.'

In the end, the sheer drama of the race was the most powerful argument that Jackie Stewart and the BRDC could have hoped for. This was no Magny-Cours procession, but a bitterly fought, overtaking extravaganza that even had people talking about a return to 'the good old days'.

The Press hailed it as a resounding success and the underdog Barrichello was a popular winner among British fans. The campers packed up their vans and the cows were led back into the fields.

A week after Silverstone, Jaguar announced they would be letting Antonio Pizzonia go. It didn't matter that his car had fallen to pieces under him during the race, the Brazilian was heading home. Sheffield lad Justin Wilson would be taking his place.

Much of the paddock reconvened for a birthday party in a swanky London nightclub the following weekend and the topic was a conversational favourite. Jenson Button was just one of many people who sympathized.

'It's awful, poor guy. That's it now. He'll never be able to come back to F1. To have all of that and suddenly it's taken away. To be kicked out mid-season is the worst.'

Others had advice for Jaguar's PR guy Nav Sidhu.

'Change Justin's mobile number,' said Matt Franey, former deputy editor of *Autosport* and editor of *F1 Magazine*. 'Don't let anybody near him. Let him keep his head down and just do the job.'

A British driver was on his way up the F1 hierarchy. Maybe, just maybe, he would be the one to bring back the crowds. Then perhaps next year our lasting image of Silverstone won't be the green underpants of a man in a beret spread-eagled on a grass verge.

9

Budapest

After Silverstone the F1 community took a break from racing, then headed to Budapest on the penultimate weekend of August. The Hungarian capital lends itself to some atmospheric TV footage – provided you point the camera away from the graffiti. It's the first and so far the only former Eastern bloc state to host a Grand Prix, though its torturous circuit is used only once a year and is famous for its thick dust and lack of overtaking opportunities.

But three years ago, the Budapest Grand Prix offered more basic amenities. For one weekend only, the country provided race visitors with their very own open-air brothel in the wooded area between the Gold and Silver entrances. The white banner above the gate advertised *Erotik Camping*, but there were no tents, just twenty whitewashed booths each fitted with red carpet, a grey-blanketed bed and a neat stack of toilet rolls.

Perhaps more shocking than the venture itself is the fact that it didn't leave a more lasting stain on Formula One. Although it was one of those rare F1-related projects that did not in any way involve Bernie Ecclestone, the timing was hardly coincidental – Formula One was perceived as a prime market for prostitution. It's hard to imagine any other sport engendering such an obvious association, but then no other sport has such an outdated attitude towards women.

It was a hot, dry day at the Brazilian Grand Prix and I was chatting to friends in the makeshift paddock. Irish driver Eddie Irvine was sitting at an adjoining table and the conversation turned to a mutual friend of ours, a German TV presenter whose contract had recently been cancelled.

'Oh Eddie,' I said, 'do you know that Nova won't be at any more races this year?'

He paused, then slowly turned his head, eyes hidden behind his trademark mirrored sunglasses.

'Really?'

'Yeah, because of the Kirch collapse. Her Premier World channel have had to cut costs.'

'Oh, that's a shame,' he replied, 'It was good watching her ass walk down the paddock.'

'Hmm...' I said, assuming he was being sarcastic. 'I'll miss her conversation too.'

'No, I won't miss that,' he said quite seriously. 'She just looked good.'

'She didn't *just* look good!'

'Yeah, she did. She was there to be looked at. That's all any of you are here for, just to be looked at.'

There were eight other men sitting listening. Nobody said a word, except for Niki Lauda. He looked at me from beneath his baseball cap and shrugged.

'It's a man's world,' he said.

Of course, in my opinion, Edmund Irvine is a man of few redeeming personal qualitities, but he was being honest at least. In Formula One 'men do' and 'women adorn'. It is simply further proof that the sport is oblivious to the real outside world. Men like Irvine say such things because they can and nobody questions them. Image might be everything in Formula One, but where women are concerned it's more than everything: an attractive appearance is a prerequisite to gaining acceptance and the yardstick by which all women are judged. Walk through the paddock in anything other than a chador, and you're likely to receive a chorus of wolf whistles from the mechanics who are under the illusion they are paying you a compliment.

In Monza I watched as one young woman visiting the Grand Prix walked uneasily through the unfamiliar paddock. A group of mechanics by the Ferrari motorhome looked her up and down, then one of them shouted something inaudible and the others laughed. At first she stopped, but when she realized they were heckling her she quickly walked on, embarrassed, as people turned to see what all the commotion was about. And such behaviour is not confined to mechanics. Renault boss Flavio Briatore took my arm as I walked through the Silverstone paddock and said: 'You! You come have lunch with me today.' I extracted myself from his grip and politely explained that I was working.

In summer 2001 I was filming at the Budapest Grand Prix. The item culminated in a boat trip down the Danube. But this being Formula One, it was no ordinary outing. It was a champagne dinner-cruise organized by the McLaren Mercedes team, who had invited their important sponsors, VIP guests and, of course, the TV crews who would guarantee them publicity. Loosely translated that means a group of people who spend all evening looking at each other and chatting animatedly without hearing a word anybody actually says.

It was the middle of August and we sipped champagne as the balmy daylight faded and streetlights lit up the riverbanks. Irvine's favourite 'ass', Nova, was aboard with her crew and although she had been voted Germany's sexiest TV presenter, there was much more to this twenty-seven year old than long blonde hair and red stiletto boots. She was perspicacious and performed with enviable flair in front of the camera. Nova liked to punctuate her sentences with 'blah-blah-blah...you know...I mean' and was always ready with a smile and a well-timed compliment. The world of Formula One loved Nova. And she loved it.

I stood with my producer deciding upon our closing link, watching Nova chatter away to the camera on the upper deck. The filming light highlighted her cheekbones against the backdrop of the black river as she nodded to her German viewers and raised a glass of champagne to toast the beauty of Budapest. Her script was similar to mine and went something like: 'So that's Budapest: old, foreign, big. This is a posh boat trip. I'm here, you're not. Enjoy the race!' Then it was time for dinner.

One of the senior men from Mercedes asked Nova and me to join him at his table. It felt more like an order than a request, but not wishing to offend our hosts we accepted his invitation. Or rather, Nova had instantaneously replied 'Suuurre!' and I felt safer in her company.

The buffet adorned a circular table in the middle of the room. Fine gourmet meats lay alongside soft balls of white mozzarella and rich cherry tomatoes. Delicate salad leaves graced glass bowls, olives glistened in golden oil and succulent chicken breasts nestled beside cubes of Camembert. And there were incongruous trays of steaming sauerkraut and bratwurst: the unmistakable stamp of our German hosts.

Approaching the buffet was like playing chicken in fast traffic. Glancing one way, then the other, I'd take my chance, make for the food and keep my head down as I filled my plate. But with Ferrari-esque reliability, some lone male would always sidle up out of nowhere and press close by my side, allowing the whiskey fumes on his breath to make the initial introduction.

'Hello,' he'd say in various shades of English. 'I haven't seen you before.'

'Hi, yeah. I'm new here, haven't been in F1 long,' I'd reply, my tone carefully modulated to deter any further questions, but without being rude.

'I just saw you and thought "Wow, I must talk to her."'

I was a woman. He'd noticed. And now he was taking his chance.

I suppose you can't blame him – there were few of us around. Over by the desserts Nova was doing a fine job of batting away her suitors.

My dinner guests were two of the most influential men in McLaren Mercedes. One was a warm, engaging man wearing the skin of someone older than his forty-odd years and the smile of Raquel Welch. The other was quiet and watchful. He was short, squat, appeared to have no discernible neck and chewed slowly, like a gorilla: the ultimate alpha male.

Nova and I sat across from them, drinking just the right amount of wine and complimenting them on the night's event. I felt like a geisha. I wanted to stop myself from engaging in this centuries-old ritual, but I couldn't. We clearly had a role to play and we were putting in an Oscar-worthy performance.

'So, I get on the plane and my crew have put up the poster, the *FHM* one, you know? On the wall of the cabin!' said Nova, laughing. 'So I say "Guys whaddya doin"? Blah-blah-blah . . . and they are all like "Ahh, Nova, c'mon – iz funny!"'

She waved her fork, a mozzarella ball castrated on the end. We all threw our heads back, laughing. She was good. I was impressed.

It was clearly a night for non-controversial conversation, but I still faced an age-old British concern when seated at an all-German dinner table. What to discuss? At that stage, I knew very little about traction control, launch systems, down-force variables, pit-stop strategies or tyre dimensions. I felt like a *Big Brother* winner at the Oscars. Any minute now I'd be found out. Soon we were discussing drivers and how their talents compared.

'I was amazed by how small these guys are,' I said. 'I tower above them. I couldn't believe it.'

'Ja, they are not tall,' said the nice tanned German. 'But they are very strong and mentally very, er, very good.'

'I wonder if we'll ever see a female Formula One driver?' I asked, watching the lights of the Danube float by, a glass of wine resting comfortably on my lap.

'Ach ja!' came the enthusiastic response. 'Sure, they are very good. We have good drivers, very talented. The problem is, Beverley –' and he paused, searching for the right phrase – 'they are just not very, ah, very pretty.'

'What?' I said.

Even Nova balked.

'Ja. It is bad. They are fast, strong, very good indeed. But there is a big problem. They look not pretty. Not pretty at all. They are like man, really.'

'Have you looked at the male drivers?' I asked.

'But it is important,' he insisted.

'Why?' I was still smiling, but perhaps my shock showed. Alpha male was digesting his sauerkraut and nodding in agreement.

Nova rolled her eyes. 'Ah, c'mon,' she said. 'That's not right. The drivers are not all, like, beautiful men.'

'It is different,' he replied. 'Women must be more beautiful, more feminine. That is how it is.'

'That is so fucked up!' I said, somehow still managing to smile. 'How can women ever expect to be given a fair chance?'

'Formula One is about money,' he said, shrugging his shoulders and examining the bottom of his glass. Then, sensing our shock, he playfully raised his brown eyes.

'What we need, it is beautiful women. What about you two? Can you drive? Ha ha ha.'

We welcomed the chance to lighten the mood, but I remained dumbfounded. These intelligent, powerful men were incapable of seeing how prejudiced they were and how their Stone-Age values would eventually damage the sport. They weren't arguing that women couldn't drive F1 cars, they were saying that they could, provided they were beautiful.

I was at the Silverstone Ball in 2002 with a group of men who hold significant positions in F1. The Foster's Girls were in attendance, a troop of young women who appear at Grands Prix wearing blue micro-minis and tight Lycra tops. They are led around the circuit in a line, stopping from time to time to have their picture taken. On this particular night, they were handing out bottles of Foster's to men who were groping their bottoms.

'I can't believe that a global sport still has women like this on display,' I said to my dinner companion.

'I know,' he replied. 'They're pigs... You'd think they could find some attractive ones.'

Formula One stands alone in its use of women to promote the sport. Boxing still uses scantily clad girls to carry the cards between rounds, but they form a very small part of the event. Women don't feature in boxing's promotional activity and nowadays several clubs allow women to partake in the sport. Some American sports still have cheerleaders, but at least these girls actually do something. Shaking pom-poms might not qualify as an Olympic sport, but cheerleaders train long hours and many are gymnasts. Formula One sits its models on car bonnets and drapes them over drivers.

Of course women do work in Formula One, but none hold positions of real influence. *F1 Racing* magazine recently ran a feature on the 'Fifty Most Powerful People in Formula One' and not one was a woman, after fifty years of the sport. Right now the woman who wields most power is probably Sabine Kehm, Michael Schumacher's media manager, and her power comes from Schumacher.

'At the beginning you have to fight more to gain acceptance and for people to find out if you are competent,' she says on the subject of women in the sport, though she admits that feminine 'charm' can be a powerful negotiating tool in Formula One. Sabine is slim and blonde. She fits the F1 criteria perfectly. She is also good at her job.

Silvia Colombo works for Ferrari as a sponsor liaison handling the

Vodafone account. She also recognizes the old adage that women have to be twice as good as men in the same job.

'Because we are few, everybody expects that you are really good. You have to be really good and it is a bigger challenge sometimes,' she told me. Silvia is normally referred to by the men as 'that pretty one with brown hair and a fit body'.

Silvia and Sabine were among many people that I interviewed for a TV feature on 'Women Behind the Scenes in Formula One'. The teams seemed to have put forward their most attractive women to speak in public. But the most depressing part of the exercise was the disparity between what some of them were prepared say on-camera and what they confessed to me afterwards. They were naturally anxious not to criticize their own teams and with a shrug they all decided it wasn't worth challenging the system. Most of them accepted sexism as a necessary evil of Formula One and admitted to being on the receiving end on a regular basis.

'There is so much sexism,' said one woman who left her job in PR, 'but it's very subtle. It's not just about leggy blondes everywhere, it's much more hidden than that.'

But a few women said they didn't find Formula One chauvinistic at all. One of them worked as an IT engineer, setting up the pit-wall electronics, checking the telemetry was working and handling most of the computer-related emergencies. I asked her what characteristics she needed to do her job.

'You can't be too, erm, I think too girly, if that's the right phrase.'

She claimed never to have been the victim of sexism, but off-camera I got chatting with one of her colleagues, a well-respected member of a big team.

'She was great,' I said. 'Thanks for the interview. It's great to show a woman working on the technology side of things.'

'Yeah,' he agreed, 'but just think what we could do with her if she wasn't such a dog.'

I pointed out that the male colleague she worked alongside – the one whose beer belly was bursting out of his shirt – wasn't exactly an Armani model, but that was different, apparently. It was like going back in time thirty years. Without any shame, this man was admitting that the IT engineer would be treated differently and given more opportunities if she were prettier.

F1 bosses are quite happy to give the sponsor liaison and PR jobs to women, along with the waitressing, cleaning and being a brolly-dolly. This is surely the most demeaning job: wearing short, tight skirts, brolly-dollies stand on the grid at the start of a race, shielding each driver from the sun with an umbrella.

The Australian Grand Prix boasts the highest percentage of bare flesh per driver. Promotional models walk the circuit handing out leaflets and posing for photos with punters. They move around in groups, huddling together ever more closely as drunken men hug their bare shoulders and slobber kisses on their made-up cheeks. Occasionally one of the girls will push them away or totter towards a marquee for cover, her tiny bottom cowering in tight Lycra shorts.

As the weather grew colder they were given clear cellophane plastic macs: the must-have item for any girl who wants knee-length protection from the rain without the inconvenience of hiding her behind – or feeling any warmth whatsoever. By Sunday the girls were frozen and very short-tempered. That included nineteen-year-old Kelly.

'It started out OK,' she told me, 'but now my feet are killing me in these heels and I'm bloody freezing. Most men are OK, but some are total sleaze-bags.'

So why did she take the job in the first place?

'It's a good way to get into the Grand Prix and we get about $80 a day, but I still have to work while the race is on. I'm not that bothered anyway. It's a pretty boring sport.'

I know these girls are young and that they enjoy the sense of occasion, but as long as lipsticked pit-babes and brolly-dollies remain the female face of Formula One there will never be a woman team boss and, most importantly, there will never be a female driver.

The issue of female drivers isn't new: it rears its head from time to time, but is never taken seriously enough to warrant a thorough debate. So let's get a few things out of the way. The reason there are no female F1 drivers is not because the rear-view mirrors aren't big enough to check their make-up. It's not because there's nowhere for the baby seat. It isn't even due to the fact that they wouldn't be able to park for a pit stop. And it has nothing to do with how messy their hair would be on the podium when they take off their helmets.

Women have actually been involved in motor racing from its inception. Bizarrely it was the romantic novelist Barbara Cartland who acted as the force behind some of the earliest female racing drivers. She backed a team who made their mark at the English track, Brooklands, in the twenties. But the first woman to drive in Formula One was the Italian Maria Teresa de Filippis, who competed in four Grands Prix in 1958. She failed to reach the qualifying time for two other Grands Prix, including the 1958 Monaco race, though fourteen male drivers also failed to make the grade there – one of whom was a little chap called Bernie Ecclestone.

Then between 1975 and 1976, another Italian, Lella Lombardi, raced in twelve Grands Prix and became the only woman to score a world championship point by finishing sixth in Spain. Next came the Briton Davina Gallica, who drove between 1976 and 1978, but failed to qualify in any of the three races. (She also competed in four Winter Olympics as captain of the British ski team.) Between 1978 and 1981 the South African Desire Wilson also struggled to qualify in an underfunded, uncompetitive car, but made it into her home Grand Prix where she famously overtook Nigel Mansell only to spin out on the 51st lap. Most recently, the Italian Giovanni Amati and her male team-mate failed to qualify in a floundering Brabham in the early 1990s.

Admittedly, these results aren't exactly impressive, but these women all had one vital thing in common – they drove incomparably bad cars. It's impossible to compare their performances with male drivers in competitive machines.

One argument that I've heard repeatedly is that women aren't physically equipped to face the challenge of driving in Formula One. This theory is mainly based on F1's misguided belief that its drivers are as fit as marathon runners and as strong as the Incredible Hulk in a strop. They aren't.

Sport's psychologist Hugh Mantle coached the British Olympic canoeing team for eighteen years and has worked with rally drivers, athletes, golfers and F1 drivers. He describes the fitness of today's male drivers as 'certainly attainable by women'. Formula One is an endurance sport that demands good cardiovascular capacities and, of course, upper-body strength is important, but driving does not demand explosive power – the area in which women would certainly be at a physiological disadvantage to men.

Crucially, the drivers aren't actually competing against one another in a purely physical arena – they are competing individually against the stresses of the car. A woman – just like a man – could therefore train herself to handle the rigours imposed upon her. Many experts now accept that physiologically women are, in fact, better suited to F1 racing than men.

The tremendous heat that must be endured during a two-hour race in hot climates is often cited as the most gruelling physical factor facing today's drivers. Hugh Mantle explains why men are at a disadvantage: 'There is strong evidence that proves women survive better than men in extreme concentrations of temperature. Drop a man and a woman in the desert or the Antarctic and the woman will outlive the man. They excel where environment plays an important factor.'

So perhaps women are ill-equipped for the mental challenge? Not so, according to Professor Adrian Moran, Director of Psychology at Dublin University and psychologist to the Irish Olympic squad: 'Concentration under pressure, strong hand-eye co-ordination, effective peripheral vision, the ability to control anxiety, visualization skills and motivation' are not, he says, gender-related. 'There is no logical or scientific reason why women could not be as good, if not better, than men at motor racing. It is invalid and misleading to suggest that women are not as capable as men of being successful motor-racing drivers.'

With so much money at stake, however, F1 teams avoid taking any risk that might affect race results or the sport's public image. Women are seen as a risky option and their poor track record in Formula One doesn't help (overlooking the fact that their cars were uncompetitive). In the 1990s, as cars got quicker and therefore more dangerous, the prospect of putting a woman in the cockpit became even more remote.

Even though Formula One's safety record has improved, Bernie Ecclestone has admitted that women will probably never drive in the sport: 'In all likelihood they will never get the opportunity, because no one will take them seriously or sponsor them financially, therefore they're never ever going to get into a competitive car.'

The notion that women won't be taken 'seriously' is key to the problem. In sport there is a general perception that any event in which men and women can compete equally can't be very hard. Formula One, in particular, needs to be seen to be 'hard'. Its manufactured image is based on testosterone, aggression and the fighting instincts of those modern-day gladiators, the drivers. Put a woman alongside Schumacher on the grid today and that veneer of machismo would slip – despite the fact that female gladiators did fight in ancient Rome's arenas. And let's not forget that driving still holds a curiously significant place in the gender wars. Despite statistics to the contrary, the majority of men still claim superiority behind the wheel and most women know that to criticize a man's driving is to undermine his very masculinity.

Perhaps we are simply not ready to stomach the threat of injury or even death when it comes to female racing drivers. But in these days of female explorers, soldiers and war correspondents do we really still harbour the belief that the fairer sex needs protecting? Even if a woman has climbed into a racing car of her own volition, knowing and accepting the risks?

Ironically, the only major sport in which men and women compete against one another is also the most dangerous. Formula One's chief medical officer Professor Sid Watkins has seen first-hand the damage that elite motor racing can cause – yet he still regards equestrianism as far more dangerous. Three-day eventing and showjumping continue to pit man against woman without question. So the issue is surely about culture, not about human nature.

Driving to the Magny-Cours circuit in 2001 with commentator James Allen and reporter Louise Goodman, the issue of female drivers came up.

'Women aren't as good at driving as men,' said Louise, who competes in rally driving herself. 'There was a female driver once, but she was shit and you're either born with it or you're not.'

I suspect it's a little more complicated than this. Research suggests that the number of female drivers is largely determined by cultural pressures. In 1997 the RAC Motor Sports Association of Great Britain commissioned a study of female participation by the psychologist Dr Judy Eaton. Her results were never published, but her findings are supported by anecdotal evidence from today's female drivers. Dr Eaton discovered that in the eight to fourteen age group, 40 per cent of British kart licences are held by girls. Yet beyond karting, the number of female competitive licence-holders falls to only 2 per cent (32,000).

Four main reasons for this dramatic drop were identified: peer pressure, physical changes, over-scrutiny and financial support. Teenage female karters come under increasing pressure to give up what is seen as a 'boys' sport'. The onset of puberty can also leave some girls at a physical disadvantage in their early to mid-teens. This is not balanced out until they become stronger in their late teens, by which point many have given up. A number of young female karters have reported feeling 'over-scrutinized' and there have been several incidents in which girls who raced well were accused of cheating. But without a doubt the most influential factor in discouraging girls from continuing competitive driving was a lack of financial support. Parents consider motor sport too unlikely to bring financial rewards later in life. Given the cultural pressures at play, it's a miracle there are any women racing drivers at all.

Of course, they aren't as numerous as the men scrambling up the ranks, but they certainly exist. They just have to shout louder to get noticed. 2003 is the fortieth anniversary of the British Women Racing Drivers' Club and female motor-racing drivers are increasingly commonplace in the USA.

The twenty-nine-year-old Irish driver Sarah Kavanagh is one such contender eager for a seat in Formula One. She was already seventeen by the time she decided to take up karting competitively, after watching the twenty-four-hour Le Mans race. Despite her parents' outrage, she went on to become the first woman to compete in the Irish Formula Opel championship, British Formula Two and the Japanese Formula Nippon. Sarah has also set lap records at Brands Hatch and Mondello Park in Formula 3000 cars. My friends from the boat trip might also be reassured to know that she is very 'pretty'.

Sarah's website deliberately plays up her attractiveness – her dark eyes stare out from under a racing helmet with the caption *Expect the unexpected*. That particular image advertises TAGHeuer watches and usefully demonstrates her commercial potential to team bosses. It's a necessary evil that Sarah isn't entirely comfortable with.

'Marketing potential is not the most valiant of reasons for being accepted into Formula One,' she says, 'and as a racing purist it also leaves me cold, but if that's the only way the opportunity can be presented, what choice do women have?'

American driver Sarah Fisher clearly feels the same pressure to be judged on more than her driving ability. She appears on her website in moodily lit shots: head raised, lips parted, blonde hair skimming sculpted cheek-bones. The Ohio-born driver is only twenty-two, but is already in her fourth consecutive season of the Indy Racing League (IRL) Indy Car Series. In 1999 she became the youngest person – not just woman – to pass the IRL rookie test. In May 2000 she was the third woman and one of the youngest drivers to compete in the world-famous Indy 500. The following year she claimed second place at the inaugural Homestead Miami Speedway, the best result ever by a woman in Indy-style racing. In 2002 she was hired by the Dreyer & Reinbold team to replace an injured male driver at the Nazareth Speedway and finished fourth. This excellent result caused them to build a second team around her and in May 2002 she became the fastest woman ever to qualify for the Indianapolis 500 with a four-lap average speed of more than 229 mph.

Despite such obvious successes, Fisher's website seems desperate to convince potential sponsors and teams that she is still feminine. Her appearances in magazines such as *Cosmo Girl*, *Glamour* and *Teen People* are noted and her favourite hobby is 'renovating her home'. Also, she is superstitious about 'painting her toenails before a race weekend'.

The websites of Sarah Kavanagh and Sarah Fisher emphasize their femininity. Kavanagh calls her 300 or so financial contributors her 'sweethearts' – but imagine a male racing driver calling his backers 'sweethearts'! The male team bosses demand that their women drivers are not 'like men' and the women have no choice but to oblige.

Definitions of masculinity and femininity are clearly defined in Formula One. In order not to be seen as boyish freaks, these aspiring drivers amplify their femaleness. On the other hand, it's hard to imagine any male driver respecting a competitor who publicly admits to being superstitious about painting her toenails. The situation will change when a woman wins an F1 Grand Prix, but first, paradoxically, she must be taken seriously enough to be given a competitive car.

It's a no-win situation. But like the female employees in the paddock, women drivers know better than to complain about double standards.

'I am always asked if motor racing is sexist, male-dominated and particularly difficult for a woman to be taken seriously,' says Kavanagh. 'While the answer is yes, yes and yes, I don't like to sound like a moan.' She is now twenty-nine and time is running out, so I'm more than happy to have a moan on her behalf and for all the other women who have had their F1 aspirations dashed.

Most seasons the teams spin rumours that they are about to employ a female driver and set tongues wagging by inviting the women to be photographed in the motorhome. In 2001 Sarah Kavanagh was tested by McLaren, who pronounced her fit and strong enough to race in Formula One, but the offer of a race never materialized. In 2000 she was invited to the Jaguar motorhome to be photographed with Eddie Irvine, but never made it into the team. In my opinion these women are effectively publicity pawns. Nobody has any real intention of offering them a drive – although time will tell.

In January 2004, during Ferrari's press week at the Madonna di Campiglio ski resort, Michael Schumacher was asked why he believed there are no female F1 drivers. He said that the reasons are 'cultural'. There are, he said, 'too few women coming up the ranks', but he didn't accept that women are physically unable to drive an F1 car.

Before this PC response became the norm, some drivers spoke out against women competitors. In a 1997 television documentary '3·D', David Coulthard said that the absence of women in Formula One was 'nothing to do with their physical strength in handling high-powered cars. It's simply they don't possess the right attitude to succeed.'

Eddie Irvine once said that women couldn't drive in Formula One because 'they don't have the right brain make-up'. In 2004 Murray Walker said 'Motor racing is no place for women,' but admitted he may have been wrong when more than two thousand of them applied to take part in a televised women-only driving competition.

I can't imagine many drivers that I've met conceding that women are their equals and should therefore sit alongside them on the grid. Most of them have partners who have sacrificed their own careers to travel with them.

In 2003, Connie Montoya relinquished her studies to follow Juan Pablo around the world. 'This year,' she said, 'I'm just dedicated to him, actually.'

Many drivers' relationships develop along these lines. Independent women with strong characters gradually become subsumed by the careers of their famous and wealthy partners. Eighteen months after I filmed with David Coulthard's girlfriend in Brazil, she was no longer working.

'She's doing up our place in Switzerland,' David cheerily told an F1 magazine. 'But apart from that she dedicates herself to our relationship, which is wonderful.'

Lost in a world that time forgot, Formula One keeps alive those stereotypes that most damage the sport. Market research recently showed that F1's audience losses were mainly from women and young men. With spectators and viewers dwindling, it's time for Formula One to stop ignoring one half of the human race and to face the fact that using women as sexual objects holds no appeal for a younger generation who see it as cheap, old-fashioned and unoriginal. F1 websites and competitions urging us to pick our 'favourite pit babe' only alienate women fans and undermine the sport's claims to be 'cutting-edge'.

A female driver in a competitive car would revolutionize Formula One's image, re-energize the competition and attract a new fan base. Her team would receive an unprecedented amount of global media exposure as the most enlightened and forward-looking brand on the grid. Jackie Stewart is one high-profile figure who backs such a scenario, seeing it as a means of broadening the sport's commercial appeal.

For now, however, it seems that in Formula One, sexism can even defeat the forces of capitalism.

*

The Budapest Grand Prix was once again a hot, sweaty affair. However, the only groans to be heard this year came from the grid girls, sweltering in red PVC trousers and clinging tops, and not from the *Erotik Camping* booths.

This year's race visitors had to look a bit harder for their sexual kicks. The sex-camp idea had been dropped after the Hungarian press criticized the venture and some of the European media took an amused swipe at it.

The mayor realized his plan threatened to link the town of Mogyorod with prostitution forever and there were protests from the predominantly Catholic population. The F1 authorities hadn't exactly come out in opposition to the brothel, but they were probably relieved it had been scrapped. Although prostitution is legal in Hungary's designated 'tolerance zones', setting up a supermarket-style experience was probably taking things a little too far, even for the F1 community.

The teams felt refreshed after their break and the Hungarian Grand Prix meant the final leg of the season was now under way. The most exciting championship for years would be concluded within four races. Just nine points separated the top three: Michael Schumacher, Juan Pablo Montoya and Kimi Raikkonen. The constructors' championship was still led by Ferrari, but Williams were breathing down their neck after an impressive season from Montoya and Ralf Schumacher.

Conversation in the paddock was all about the dusty track and its effect on the cars. Budapest is notoriously gritty, because of the warm wind blowing across the arid Hungarian countryside. This year, the problem was exacerbated by recent building work to improve the track. After Friday morning testing, Pat Symonds, executive director of engineering at Flavio Briatore's Renault, said: 'The circuit conditions were appalling this morning. We appreciate that this is an extremely dusty area, but it still seems remarkable that the owners cannot have the track cleaned better than this.'

The problem was worse on the right side of the circuit, where sand lay ready to hinder the grip of the tyres at the all-important start. Qualifying isn't just about aiming for the top of the grid, but hoping to get the fastest side.

All of the title-contenders fared badly at Saturday's qualifying session, with Michael Schumacher achieving eighth spot – his worst grid position of the season. Montoya was content with his P4, saying that he hadn't taken any unnecessary risks on such a potentially treacherous track, while Raikkonen down in seventh drew consolation from starting on the cleaner, left side of the track.

The big surprise of the day came from the little man in Renault's baby blue. Fernando Alonso had bagged the second pole position of his fledgling career. If Alonso could win Sunday's race he would make history as not only the first Spaniard, but the youngest ever Grand Prix victor. As usual, the Oxford resident with a knack for card tricks was keeping his cool.

Alonso was the last driver to climb into his car on a burning 47°C track. Unusually, Michael Schumacher was one of the first. Several drivers wore towels soaked in cold water around their necks. The grid girls held aloft the placards denoting the grid positions: P1 down to P20. Their costumes revealed as much flesh as was permissible on Sunday afternoon TV. Hundreds of people buzz around the cars on the grid before a race, but the girls are never spoken to.

The Hungarian ladies looked straight ahead, occasionally raising a hand to wipe sand from their lip-gloss. They were surrounded by photographers in regulation khaki waistcoats snapping close-up body shots. The vacuum-packed, shiny red bottoms of the grid girls provided a great visual for the TV cameras to pan back from.

Bernie Ecclestone was out on the grid with a man whose importance was evident from his black sunglasses, confident posture and open-necked shirt. Ecclestone introduced him to Martin Brundle as he completed his live TV 'grid walk', quickly whispering to the commentator that this was the Hungarian prime minister. The PM was delighted that a Hungarian driver was racing. The man in question was twenty-two-year-old Zsolt Baumgartner.

During Saturday's warm-up, Jordan driver Ralph Firman had learnt what it feels like when your rear-wing falls off at 160 mph. He slammed into the tyre barrier sideways, incurring the lash of 46 g-force – the biggest impact in Formula One this year. Although unconscious at the scene, he was released from hospital on Sunday morning with nothing more serious than a badly bruised ankle, a stiff neck and a pair of crutches.

Professor Sid Watkins credited the HANS device for saving the Brit from further injuries and Firman retained his usual imperturbable manner.

'This is the sixth mechanical failure I have had this year that has resulted in an accident,' he said, 'but I still have faith in the mechanics.'

This from a man who agreed to be sent down a roller-coaster in his yellow racing car.

The Jordan Team contacted Baumgartner. The Hungarian had spent the year racing in Formula 3000, in which all the cars are the same, so – unlike Formula One – driver proficiency completely determines the results. In 2001 Baumgartner failed to score any points. The following year he finished fifteenth out of twenty-four competitors and in 2003 he finished fourteenth out of seventeen. The highlight of his F3000 career was in 2003 – fifth in Monaco – in a race littered with crashes.

Yet Zsolt had generous backers waiting in the wings, including the Hungarian government. Three months before Firman's crash in Budapest, Eddie Jordan had met Gyorgy Janosi, the Hungarian Minister of Children, Youth and Sports.

Despite his poor record, Baumgartner was appointed as a Jordan test driver and was due to participate in the team's private Friday testing sessions at the German and Hungarian Grands Prix. Firman's accident had been a happy coincidence for the publicity-hungry team, for whom sponsorship is an ongoing concern. Eddie Jordan himself has a reputed personal fortune of £60 million, with the obligatory yacht and several homes.

Zsolt Baumgartner sat on the penultimate spot on the grid, which reflected his meagre experience. But as the red lights went out all eyes were on the front. Alonso's Renault went off like a rocket and the other cars never stood a chance. The horns in the crowd drowned out the sound of the Ferrari team banging their heads against the wall as Schumacher failed to keep pace. But worse was to come.

On lap 20 Rubens Barrichello felt the snap of his left-rear suspension and he speared into the safety barrier as his wheel bounced dangerously away from him. Once again, the Brazilian emerged unscathed, but it made his victory in Silverstone seem a long time ago.

Eight laps from the end, Alonso, still leading the pack, completed a manoeuvre that brought a cheer from all those in Formula One who delight in Ferrari's misfortunes. Schumacher spotted him in his mirrors and courteously moved over to let the Spaniard lap him in front of a global audience. Alonso later described the event as an 'important moment' (though he knew better than to gloat at a world champion). As he took the chequered flag, his team climbed on to the pit wall, cheering him home. Alonso raised a gloved finger, saluting his Number One position and waving to his mechanics.

His boss and mentor Flavio Briatore helped him from his car in front of a scrum of photographers as Raikkonen and Montoya pulled up behind in second and third places respectively. The crowd ran down the track to watch the podium ceremony, a surging vision of red, blue and yellow – only this time the red flags moved a little more slowly than usual.

Alonso stood on the podium, smiling and bouncing excitedly from foot to foot, his brown hair long and messy, a small nick of a beard under his lower lip and long sideburns running along the imprints left by his helmet. Montoya looked as cool as always, but the heat had brought a pink tinge to Raikkonen's pale, Finnish cheeks. Alonso's father watched proudly from the crowd as his son put down his trophy to clap his rivals.

It was Renault's first victory in twenty years. But Fernando Alonso's win also symbolized the beginning of a new era. Perhaps more than any other driver, the Spaniard represents the future: a young, professional, athletic sportsman from a country that has yet to get hooked on Formula One. The young drivers were moving forwards, but the question was, did those in power recognize the need to move on into a new era?

Michael Schumacher came in eighth, sneaking the last point on offer. Rumour had it that he might have blown the championship. Non-Ferrari fans could barely conceal their excitement at such a prospect. As one journalist wryly observed: 'If Michael had driven that race as he has done in the past, they would have decried the day as boring. This time with the tables turned, they thought the race was a classic.'

Schumacher still led the championship, but only by one point: 72 to Montoya's 71 and Raikkonen's 70. In the constructers' championship, Williams were now sitting ahead of Ferrari by seven points and Renault had leapt up to fourth place.

The Renault marque and the name of Fernando Alonso were splashed across newspapers worldwide the following morning. Zsolt Baumgartner retired on lap 34 with engine failure. But the Hungarian's F1 career didn't end there. He competed for Jordan at the next race in Monza, making a name for himself as the man who held up Montoya as he tried to lap the rookie while chasing Schumacher. Baumgartner finished eleventh, two laps behind the winner, but seven cars retired with mechanical failures.

Ralph Firman recovered from his injuries in time for the last two races of the season, but Jordan still offered a driver's contract Baumgartner for 2004. Zsolt said: 'I am extremely flattered and I hope we will be able to meet the requirements.' All he had to do was find sponsors with $13.8m to back him. In December 2003 the Hungarian government pledged $4 million to help their driver buy a seat in Formula One. Baumgartner also had $2.8 million from other sponsors, including oil group MOL. But shortly before Christmas, it was Minardi, rather than Jordan, that confirmed Baumgartner as their driver for 2004. MOL withdrew its backing, stating that it 'heard of the latest developments and rumours through the press and didn't wish to take any financial risk with weaker performances' from the Minardi team.

The state-funding of an F1 driver caused controversy in Hungary. The Budapest *Sun* newspaper ran an editorial entitled 'A grand waste', in which journalist Robin Marshall said: 'There are far more important things for the Government to spend its money on (like fuel for the emergency services, for example) than Baumgartner's near-certain failure to shine in an underfunded, underpowered car.'

Marshall, who considers himself 'a fan of F1', speculated that the government was banking on 'the tourist dollar that the Grand Prix attracts' and that 'a successful home-grown driver will boost that by raising interest in the country'. The outcry caused the Hungarian government to reduce its input to $300,000. Zsolt's management set up the 'Baumgartner Club' to accept donations from fans.

F1 Racing magazine called Baumgartner 'rubbish' and without 'a shred of pedigree'. BBC Sport denounced him as proof that in F1, 'talent is inversely proportional to wallet size'. But the Hungarian still found himself behind the wheel of an F1 car – which is more than any female driver can currently hope for.

10

Monza, America and Japan

Monza, 12 September 2001. Twenty-four hours earlier I packed my suitcase as news of the World Trade Center attacks unravelled on TV. I waited for confirmation that the race had been cancelled. Every other major sporting event around the world had been postponed as a mark of respect. There was an unspoken global consensus that this was no time for the frivolity of sport. Besides, there was too much uncertainty about who or what would be targeted next. Large public gatherings and international travel were deemed to be high-risk. But the call never came and I soon found myself in the pine-scented paddock of the Italian Grand Prix.

The F1 community had boarded their planes as usual. In Monza, Ecclestone called a meeting with the team bosses. Flavio Briatore emerged to tell a press conference that it was 'business as usual'.

Several teams and drivers were unhappy about the decision. Waiting to go through security at Heathrow, one of the Jaguar representatives told me that their sponsors, HSBC and Credit Suisse, had offices in the World Trade Center and had suffered major casualties.

ITV anchorman Jim Rosenthal opened the programme by expressing his discomfort at broadcasting under such circumstances and before the race Michael Schumacher urged the drivers to observe restraint on the first two corners.

'After things that have happened in the United States and with one driver in hospital badly hurt,' he said, 'we have to question whether we should be racing.'

By mentioning the terrorist attacks in the same breath as ex-F1 driver Alex Zanardi – who lost both legs in a CART accident – Schumacher hoped to broaden F1's outlook beyond the sport itself. The FIA did not back his plan to start the race under yellow warning flags and Schumacher had to approach each driver individually to gain a consensus. The Ferraris were fitted with black nose cones and drove without sponsorship branding. But not everyone seemed to feel the gravity of the situation. Fifteen minutes before the start, Schumacher was still pacing the grid, urging his competitors to be cautious: 'It was decided that after the start there would be no overtaking on the first two chicanes,' he said later. 'One driver did not agree.'

'All I know is I'm a professional racer,' Jacques Villeneuve told *Autosport* journalist Adam Cooper. 'I registered to drive a race car when I signed a contract.'

When asked if the other drivers were simply trying to capture the mood of the world that weekend, he replied: 'I really don't know. If that's the case, then that would be very political and I'm not into getting into these things.'

More unsettling were some of the reactions in the paddock: bizarre comparisons to 'Africans' who 'starve every day and we don't stop racing for them do we?' For others it was as if Formula One transcended terrorism and was unaffected by global events. And they looked to one man to confirm this impression.

'It wasn't a hard decision,' said Bernie Ecclestone. 'You cannot bow to terrorism.'

The next race was due to take place at Indianapolis. 'It's a bad joke intending to race in the United States,' said Ralf Schumacher. 'I don't think it's safe and I will for sure not take family and friends.' David Coulthard said, 'We are all nervous at the prospect of going over there but if the championship is there, then I will be there, though I'll be going at the last possible moment.'

By Monza 2003, with three races to go in three different continents, Formula One's far-flung ambitions were being played out both on and off the track. Strolling through Melbourne's Albert Park circuit at the start of the year, I had come across an enormous, elevated revolving globe at the paddock entrance. It was a hollow, chrome structure showing the countries of the world. But it was not instantly familiar as planet Earth. Beneath was an inscription, *The World According to Formula One*, and as I squinted through the sunlight it dawned on me that the globe showed only those nations that host a Grand Prix.

The world according to Formula One is set to be redefined, with Ecclestone intent on adding many more nations to his revolving silver ball: Dubai, Turkey and India are among those waiting in line like wannabe queens at the prom. In Monza, however, Formula One once again found itself on familiar ground: Italy, like Britain, is the only other country to have held a place on the F1 calendar since 1950.

The inaugural F1 race was held at Silverstone, but Monza is the spiritual home of Formula One. The final round of the first championship was held there in 1950, with the first three drivers from Italy driving for their home team, Alfa Romeo. But for almost half a century Ferrari's position as the Italian motor-industry leaders has been unchallenged, its supremacy in modern Formula One commonplace.

The prancing horse of Ferrari's marque is one of the most successful European brands. In 2003 Ferrari team manager Stefano Domenicali was asked if any sponsor and any amount of money could cause them to change their livery. He replied that under no conditions would Ferrari abandon their trademark red.

That's certainly good news for most of the 65,000 fans at Italy's Autodromo Nazionale. Replacing all those red T-shirts, baseball caps and flags would be expensive. Monza is Formula One at its most 'European', a quality that helps Bernie Ecclestone sell his product all over the world.

'What we have is something that appeals to people that want European things,' he says, 'someone who wants to buy an Armani suit.'

'Europeanness' is a concept with its roots in the Roman Empire and its present identity in the metropolitan cities of the European Union.

Spectators at the Melbourne Grand Prix explained to me that more than any other sport, Formula One allows them to indulge in their loyalty to a heartfelt European ancestry. 'I have some German blood in me,' explained one visitor, 'so I like to support Schumacher, but my girlfriend's grandparents were Scottish, so she shouts for Coulthard.'

To many Australians – and other non-European fans – Formula One is a little piece of Europe in their own backyard for four days of the year and they love the association. To some Australians, admitting a love of the sport distinguishes them from fans of Aussie rules football, who clearly do not share a similar appreciation of European sport and culture.

Veteran Australian F1 journalist John Hamilton described the ambience of the paddock in the *Herald Sun* newspaper: there were 'reporters gabbling in French, German, Italian, Spanish. This is Albert Park, but you could be on the Champs d'Elysées [*sic*] in Paris or the Via Condotti in Rome.'

Melbourne in particular has many European immigrants, including the largest Greek population outside Greece (although because of the absence of a Greek driver or Greek team in the history of Formula One, Greece isn't exactly a major player). But the principle remains: Australian – and increasingly Asian – fans see Formula One as the epitome of a pan-European sport that carries its culture across the world: from the *Gauloises*-smoking team bosses to the Italian wines and espresso machines, German sausages and British tea bags. And if Formula One is a European religion, Monza is its Mecca.

Archbishop Dionigi Tettamanzi of Milan passed through the paddock on qualifying Friday, causing some less-than-holy types to scuttle into their motorhomes. The only praying to be done was for the sport itself as a tyre controversy threatened to burst F1's remaining vestiges of credibility.

After one of their most disastrous races in recent memory in Budapest, Ferrari had lodged a protest against teams using Michelin tyres (principally McLaren, Williams and Renault) on the basis that their measurements contravened Article 77c of the FIA regulations. Williams and McLaren were both in spitting distance of snatching the world championship crown and for a moment it looked as if the red barons were prepared to try anything to win it back.

Ferrari technical director Ross Brawn had seen a photograph taken by a Japanese photographer in which he claimed the Michelin tyres appeared 'irregular'. The debate revolved around the 'contact patch' of a tyre: the bumps between the grooves that are in constant contact with the tarmac and must be no more than 270 mm wide.

All season the Michelin tyres had provided great speed in the first few laps, then tailed off, but then suddenly found their speed again: a 'graining process'. Michelin argued that their tyres had been legal all season, but Ferrari countered that the FIA had measured the rubber before a race rather than after, when the contact patches had widened and that therefore the Michelin tyres should be banned. Ross Brawn said, 'I hope Michelin realize that they have enjoyed an unfair advantage for too long.' The FIA agreed with the Ferrari claim and all the Michelin teams were sent letters informing them that there would now be strict post-race checks.

With all ten Michelin cars liable for disqualification in Monza, a new tyre had to be developed in three weeks. This caused considerable disruption and team bosses muttered that once again Ferrari had been given preferential treatment by the FIA. Max Mosley defended his positon: 'It was only after Hungary that we realized our previous method of tyre measurement might need to be reviewed. An illegal tyre is illegal so it's not something we allow if we know it's happening.' Ferrari had effectively exploited a loophole in the regulations. Once the new tyre was produced the FIA issued a statement saying, 'the matter is now closed and the championship can now continue with all teams on an equal footing.' It could have overturned the whole season, but in Monza the *Tifosi* couldn't care less.

They were simply there to scream for their team and Michael Schumacher acknowledged their importance.

'Even though we will not be able to celebrate winning the title with them – unlike in the past couple of years – we need their support even more.'

Ten miles outside Milan, 'La Pista Magica' (The Magical Track) possesses some of the world's most famous twists and turns: the 'Curva Parabolica', the 'Curva del Vialone', the 'Lesmo' corner and the 'Ascari' chicane make up an evocative circuit that runs through miles of luscious woodland. Schumacher smacked home a resolute qualifying lap, securing his fifty-fifth pole position and the best view of the 3.6-mile track. Montoya sneaked in behind, with the red of Barrichello's car in third. Raikkonen's grey McLaren sat snarling at P4.

It was a perfect late summer afternoon with thousands of bare arms waving against a sapphire sky. Schumacher flew off the start so fast he almost missed the first chicane. Approaching the second, Montoya's navy Williams sat right on Schumacher's rear wing and as the German edged slightly to the left, Montoya plunged down the outside, braking at exactly the same moment. Montoya had the choice of hitting Schumacher or staying wide. He played it safe, watching as the Ferrari took a breath and headed off into the sun. To all intents and purposes the race finished there. Schumacher's metronomic lapping began, the rhythm so familiar in recent years, though it had been noticeably lacking this season.

The only drama of the race occurred at the back of the grid as the starting lights went out. Hungarian race winner Fernando Alonso had quickly fallen from grace with a spin in qualifying and started from the back row. Justin Wilson was trying hard not to become the new Pizzonia as he settled into the Brazilian's seat. But he also seemed jinxed as his engine died at the start, while team-mate Mark Webber zoomed off from P11 to eventually finish seventh.

Jos Verstappen's Minardi swerved to avoid Wilson and sped into the path of Fernando's Renault. The mêlée at the back contrasted with the decorum at the front as the top four drivers swept around the track, ultimately finishing in the exact order of qualifying. Montoya might have had a better shot at Schumacher had he not been stuck in traffic while lapping Sauber's Heinz-Harald Frentzen and Jordan's new Hungarian boy – referred to later by Montoya as 'Baum – what's-his-name? That new guy at Jordan.'

'This is the greatest day in my career,' said a delighted Schumacher afterwards. 'We made a big push over the summer break with everyone in the team giving more than 100 per cent. To everyone in the team who was so motivated and worked so hard, from the engineers, the mechanics and even the tea lady, I have to say a big thank you. I'm so in love with all those guys.' The Italian spirit seemed to have rubbed off on the man renowned for his cool Germanic exterior.

The *Tifosi* had not only watched their hero win at the team's home race, but had also witnessed the fastest Grand Prix in history. At an average of 154 mph, Schumacher had exceeded the record set by Britain's Peter Gethin at the same track in 1971.

BMW still led the constructors' championship on 141 points, but Ferrari was on its tail with 137 and McLaren was still in the running on 120. Schumacher had extended his lead over Montoya from one point to three and Raikkonen had slipped seven points. At Indianapolis there would still be everything to play for. It was time to go transatlantic.

*

Americans regard Formula One with a mixture of confusion and curiosity. During qualifying the stands were empty, but it's unlikely that American sports fans would flock to watch a time-trial. They also have no concept of a draw in sport and to most of them motor racing without ramming is like a trip to McDonald's without a burger. The country's most popular motor sport is NASCAR, in which ordinary-looking stock cars race side-by-side in circles, scraping wings and bumping rear ends to muscle their way in front.

The 2002 F1 race had done nothing to help Americans grasp the peculiar beauty of this foreign sport. After leading for the majority of the race, Schumacher slowed down to enact a dead heat with his team-mate in a gesture that referenced earlier events in Austria, when team orders pulled Barrichello back to let Schumacher pass. But a dead heat at 150 mph is tricky and Barrichello was awarded victory by 0.01 seconds.

'American racing fans who still aren't quite sure what to make of Europe's elite Formula One series didn't get much help from the head-scratching finish to Sunday's US Grand Prix,' reported USA Today.

Schumacher had taken the title two months before and gave the victory to Barrichello because 'he deserves it'. This was the fourth consecutive race in which Ferrari had finished one-two. With the title sewn-up part-way through the season, viewers were switching off and USA Today was not alone in calling Formula One 'monotonous'. Ferrari orchestrating the result was the last thing the sport needed.

Cracking the North American market is a high priority for Formula One, but the gap in sporting cultures might prove too wide to bridge. This was the fourth race back in Indianapolis after an eight-year hiatus. Michael Schumacher took a break in Las Vegas on his way over and delighted in the fact that nobody there recognized him. Europeans might consider Formula One to be 'the world's greatest sporting spectacle', but Americans tend to think it's rather dull. Ironically, the first Indianapolis F1 Grand Prix in 1950 was deemed so irrelevant by the European teams that not one of them bothered to race at the famous oval track. Today, however, America is one of the few countries in which Formula One is not a major sport.

Broadcasting for National Public Radio, reporter Jason Paur tried to explain Formula One for an American audience.

'The cars look similar to the ones used in the Indianapolis 500, but they are far more sophisticated,' he revealed. 'Mr Michael Schumacher's annual salary is more than the combined budgets of all the teams who usually race at Indy.'

The *Washington Post* clarified further: 'In F1, exotic needle-nose jets scream around twisting road and street courses, rarely making contact and seldom passing (known as overtaking). Its appeal revolves around the genius of engineers and what is possible when money and technology have no limits.'

But Jason Paur went on to highlight why Formula One wants to infiltrate America: 'While most Americans probably don't know who Michael Schumacher is, they do know the companies involved in sponsoring Formula One.'

'America is very important to Formula One,' confirmed Jackie Stewart, 'because most of the big companies that are involved in it either have their world headquarters here or it is their biggest market, or at least their second-largest market. So Formula One, I think, will be good for America. And America will be good for Formula One.'

But motor sport in the US has a typically blue-collar fan base and it remains to be seen whether Americans will embrace the Formula One jet-set.

The desperation with which F1 wants to be loved by the US was illustrated in 2004 by an unprecedented Thursday morning 'walkabout'. Formula One normally exists in a cocoon of paranoia: laminated passes, tinted motorhome windows and rules about white lines on floors that must never be crossed. So it was revolutionary when 20,000 'outsiders' were invited to stroll through the pits twenty-four hours before first qualifying – joined by the likes of Schumacher and Montoya signing autographs. Video cameras were even allowed and no one was charged for the footage!

As the F1 veterans put it, it was like the 'good old days' of the fifties and sixties, when entrance to the world of Formula One was bought with a reasonably priced paddock pass. But Bernie Ecclestone realized Formula One's success depended on an illusion of exclusivity, élitism and privilege: access had to be denied to make people appreciate it more and the drivers had to become more elusive. That tactic worked well with Europeans raised on a diet of royal families and strict class hierarchies, but Americans were unimpressed. The American Dream is about access for all and if it's denied – as in Formula One – they will simply look elsewhere.

According to a recent report on US attitudes towards sports, 96.3 per cent of the American population plays, watches or reads articles about sport frequently or identifies with particular teams or players. Nearly 70 per cent follow sport every day and 42 per cent participate on a daily basis. There simply isn't enough time in the day to waste on a motor-racing championship that appears unjustifiably 'precious'. Ecclestone's walkabout was a shrewd move.

But it would take more than some handshakes to fill the stands. The Indy 500 attracts a 400,000 strong crowd to the Indianapolis Motor Speedway, whereas F1 race day saw 135,000. Most of them had come from Colombia: their red, yellow & blue flags denoted their support for Montoya. They were speed junkies who enjoy watching the cars on the longest full-throttle section of any F1 circuit: twenty-two seconds flat-out on a track where there's a 160 mph difference between the fastest and slowest sections. Americans are used to watching complex sports but most have yet to master the full technical intricacies of Formula One. Opening ITV's coverage in the rain, reporter Ted Kravitz announced without a hint of irony: 'You do need an anorak down here.'

Qualifying had thrown up an unpredictable grid: Raikkonen was eyeing up Schumacher's lead in the championship and he had produced a flawless lap to take pole. Barrichello was at P2 and with their best qualifying slot to date Toyota sat at P3: Frenchman Olivier Panis felt the full weight of Japanese expectations. Montoya was just three points behind Schumacher in the championship, but now found himself three places ahead of him on the grid: at P4 compared to Schumacher down in a disappointing seventh.

The statisticians were busy calculating that Schumacher could win the world title if he won here and Montoya was lower than fifth and Raikkonen was lower than second or if Schumacher came second and Montoya was lower than seventh and Raikkonen lower than third, but if Schumacher finished third or lower it would all be decided in Japan.

I reached for my anorak.

Overnight, the track had been soaked with more than an inch of rain.

The race-day temperature was a chilly 13°C and twenty minutes before the start there was a hailstorm. In Monza, Ecclestone had marked the teams on the calibre of their celebrity guests and concluded: *Must try harder*. He sent out official instructions to invite 'bigger names'. In response, Indianapolis played host to aged rocker Johnny 'Rotten' Lydon, a surfer named Sunny Garcia and the bald bloke in *ER*.

The opening lap saw Schumacher sprint up from seventh to an incredible third place. Montoya found himself languishing back in seventh. Raikkonen kept a confident lead, but by lap 5 the rain began to dictate events.

Schumacher, on his inferior Bridgestone tyres, was casually picked off by Coulthard and the Renaults. Montoya had hit the back of Barrichello's slowing Ferrari on lap 3, but while the Brazilian's race was over, the Williams driver managed to stay out, pitting only on lap 17. One commentator explained that the race was now all about 'the Bridgestone Inter versus the Michelin Wet...no contest' – but I had thought it was about driver versus driver. A tyre competition didn't have quite the same allure.

Apparently, the Michelin dry tyres, in light rain, had been much better than the Bridgestones, but their 'shallow-groove' wets or 'intermediates' were just as poor when the rain fell more heavily. So rubber variations meant Raikkonen was back in the pack with Jenson Button and Heinz-Harald Frentzen in the rain, but he broke free as the track began to dry. Raikkonen was quicker than Schumacher in the closing stages, but by then the Ferrari driver was twenty-two seconds ahead. Montoya had been given a controversial drive-through penalty for nudging Barrichello at the start and was also held up during his first pit stop thanks to a faulty fuel nozzle. The disappointed Colombian fans took their *Formula Juan* flags and used them as raincoats.

Button led the race for fifteen laps before being overtaken by Schumacher, but as the Brit headed for his first-ever podium finish his Honda engine blew up. The lowly Sauber team made the podium for the first time that season as veteran Heinz-Harald Frentzen finished third.

'We changed Heinz to wet tyres at just the right moment,' said owner Peter Sauber.

Toyota didn't manage to capitalize on their grid position and brought Panis in for wets too early, changed them again when the rain didn't materialize and changed them back when it finally did. By that point, however, both cars were a lap behind. Panis eventually spun out and Da Matta finished ninth. Justin Wilson was relieved to claim his first championship point in eighth and his Jaguar team were now level-pegging with BAR going into the final round.

After crossing the finish line, Schumacher jumped excitedly from his car and banged his gloved hands on his helmet. This may have been his seventieth win and his sixth this year, but his hunger for victory was clearly unabated. He leapt into the air on the podium, shaking his fists in celebration as a cold, damp crowd spread out under the presentation area.

The Americans turned on the glitz, raising the three cars ceremoniously on slow-moving platforms as the national anthems played. Schumacher took great delight in showering the blue suit of his friend Heinz-Harald with champagne. But Raikkonen stood quietly to one side, half-heartedly shaking his own bottle and doing the maths in his head: he could still take the title in Japan – if Schumacher failed to win a single point.

That seemed a remote prospect. Schumacher had already had five victories at Suzuka.

*

Formula One arrived in Japan in 1976, but the first Grand Prix was held at Mount Fuji. It wasn't until 1987 that the race came to Suzuka, the track it now calls home. It's a challenging figure-of-eight circuit originally built as the centrepiece of a motorbike-themed fun park.

In its sixteen-race history, Suzuka has settled the championship nine times and thus holds special memories for almost everybody in Formula One. But the sport's relationship with Japan is based on more than sentimental ties: it places Asia on Ecclestone's tailor-made globe and that brings backers flocking.

FOM figures imply that F1 is more popular globally than soccer and claim that in the 1990s, 831,234,186 people watched Formula One on

TV in the Western Europe and Mediterranean region. In Central Asia it was 1,374,277,629 – more than 1.3 billion. FOM's calculations use a method that includes any people who might have seen *any* reference to Formula One on TV, from a full two-hour race to a mere ten-second clip on the news. Such figures are used to entice sponsors into F1. FIFA also use this technique to calculate worldwide audiences for the World Cup, but the International Olympic Committee adopted a different standard after the 1996 Atlantic Olympics.

On 11 September 2003 it was announced that China would host a Formula One race in 2004. It's an effective indicator of the direction China is taking. A week after FIA president Max Mosley visited Shanghai in October 2003, Bernie Ecclestone signed a deal with mayor Chen Liangyu securing Grands Prix from 2004 to 2010.

This was more than a decade after China first began pitching for a Grand Prix. Over nine years a circuit was developed in the southern city of Zuhai and was scheduled to join the F1 calendar in 1998. But it failed to meet FIA standards and five years later the $240 million, 200,000-seat Shanghai track was chosen instead.

'We've had many, many offers for us to hold Formula One racing in different parts of China,' said Bernie Ecclestone in October 2003, 'and I'm very, very pleased that we decided to wait for Shanghai.'

The city is home to the first commercial train using magnetic levitation technology and is adding the world's tallest Ferris wheel to its ultra-modern skyline. The Formula One administration and F1's sponsors are hoping to widen their market to China's 1.3 billion people. The population of Shanghai alone is 16 million.

China too is hoping to boost its international profile by hosting the ATP tennis masters and the 2008 Beijing Olympics. But its association with Formula One is the greatest statement of its economic prosperity.

F1 is not only a product of capitalism, it is capitalism: the embodiment of conspicuous consumption and the cult of personality. Formula One is capitalism on wheels. By hosting its first race in 1986, the Hungarian government were symbolically declaring that Communism was dead. Similarly, India wants to convince FOM and the FIA that the city of Hyderabad, in the state of Andhra Pradesh, should host a Grand Prix. An Indian government delegation held two rounds of talks with F1 representatives before being invited to Italy in March 2003, where they made a presentation to Ecclestone outlining their circuit and facilities. The state chief minister, Chandrababu Naidu told reporters that the Grand Prix would give a tremendous boost to Hyderabad's infrastructure and tourism.

Motor racing, economics and governmental politics are inextricably intertwined. Poor countries do not host motor-racing events and developed nations such as Germany and Italy use Formula One as a benchmark for their economic prowess. If F1 teams bemoan a lack of sponsorship it usually reflects a downturn in the global economy. Modern Britain's three main recessions occurred in 1973–6, 1980–82 and 1990–92. The BRM F1 team pulled out in 1977; Lotus in 1994; Pacific and Simtek only survived from 1994–5. The most telling team history, however, is that of Max Mosley's March, which existed from 1970–77, 1981–3 and 1987–92. They disappeared after every recession only to resurface before leaving at the next recession. Of course, the major financial challenge facing several F1 teams today is not a global recession, but the loss of tobacco advertising. This also means finding new race venues.

Bernie Ecclestone is tapping into developing markets at a ferocious rate. India, Turkey and Libya are among those lining up for confirmation that they have been granted a Grand Prix. But as far as I can see the desire to truly globalize Formula One is nothing to do with embracing multiculturalism.

In November 1995 British American Tobacco (BAT) revealed that profits for the first nine months of the year rose by 22 per cent and the *Guardian* newspaper reported: 'The growth in international brand sales has come mainly from exports to Asia and eastern Europe.' In 1996 BAT launched 'Project Battalion', the code name for a corporate strategy to target Asia. In 1997 Imperial Tobacco announced that it was aiming to seize the Far-East market in China and Korea to offset declining European sales. In August 1997 figures showed that 320 million Chinese smokers consume 1.7 trillion cigarettes – a third of the global total. Lord Swaythling, the chairman of Rothmans, said in 1993, 'We are not encouraging the Chinese to smoke. They all smoke like chimneys anyway. We just want them to smoke our brands.' According to the anti-smoking group ASH, 700,000 of them die annually, a figure that is due to increase this century to 3 million.

'Thinking about Chinese smoking statistics is like trying to think about the limits of space,' mused Rothmans' regional public affairs manager.

'We must demand,' said the director general of the WHO at the tenth World Conference of Smoking and Health in Peking, 'that the large multinational tobacco companies that experience controls in their home countries are not free to expand in other countries.'

But the transnational tobacco companies are targeting low- and middle-income countries in Eastern Europe, South America and India.

'Until recently,' said Mike Pavitt, public affairs manager of Rothmans, in 1992, 'perhaps 40 per cent of the world's smokers were locked behind ideological walls. We've been itching to get at them . . . That's where our growth will come from.'

In that same year, Philip Morris's annual report stated: 'Our world-wide tobacco business has greater opportunities now than ever before. Our strong bases in the US and Western Europe, our expansion in Eastern Europe and the former Soviet Union and our growing businesses in Latin America and the Asia/Pacific region position us well to meet the challenges of increasingly linked and prosperous world markets.'

BAT are also looking to fully exploit India's desire to be modern, by equating smoking with Western individualism.

'While Europe's market arteries are becoming clogged with old age,' says a document in BAR's Guildford depository, 'India's are young and free-flowing. It is sometimes hard for a visitor to India to appreciate this point, that this huge and growing population is an asset, but such are the economics of the marketplace. A young population buys consumer products such as cigarettes much more keenly than does an old one, because as Mr Chugh [India Tobacco's chairman] says, such products have to do with living life to the full.'

The transnational tobacco companies (TTCs) who fund Formula One are desperate to enter new markets such as India in order to snare customers before they establish tobacco-control measures. So far they have been pretty successful. The per capita consumption of cigarettes in high-income countries has fallen by 10 per cent since 1970, but in low-

and middle-income countries (LMICs) such as Poland, Thailand and Malaysia consumption rose by 67 per cent in the same period.

The TTCs really need the publicity and the credibility that Formula One gives them. They are currently killing their best customers at a rate of three million a year, with a million of them in LMICs, but if the rates continue unabated, a total of 10 million a year will die from smoking, with seven million of them in LMICs.

Oil-rich Bahrain, which hosts its first Grand Prix in 2004, might not qualify as a developing country, but one statistic makes it ever so appealing to TTCs: Arab men are 30 per cent more likely to smoke than men in North America or Western Europe.

Formula One's eagerness to tap into such virgin territories makes financial sense – and that's all that matters. None of the proposed nations has grass-roots motor sport – many don't even have a circuit. Unlike Monza, Indianapolis and Suzuka, the new venues have no motor-racing history and it could take decades to establish a following.

For a sport that prides itself on its heritage, it looks to me as though Formula One is sprinting towards a vacuous future that might look pretty on TV (if we pan away from the empty grandstands), but possesses little cultural resonance: replacing Montreal, Spa-Francorchamps and Silverstone with countries more amenable to tobacco advertising such as Bahrain, China, Turkey and India will change the face of Formula One for ever.

Ironically, in the long term the American fans might prove the most loyal. The franchising of their sports teams has been going on for decades and the movement of a team's base from one state to another happens without much sentimentality. In the US a city pays for a team to move there and it goes. It can be hard on the fans, but new allegiances are formed and the stadiums are still packed. Filling a stadium in Delhi, where there is no significant motor-racing fan base, will be a much tougher task – no matter how aesthetically satisfying the venue.

In the UK we have just seen a glimpse of this trend with Wimbledon Football Club, which moved its base from West London to Milton Keynes. The fans were outraged and boycotted games, but it's hard to imagine F1 fans going to similar lengths. When Silverstone was threatened in the summer there wasn't so much as a hint of a mass protest beyond the odd letter in *Autosport* magazine.

But it is Bernie Ecclestone's description of the ideal female racing driver that most confirms Formula One's global ambitions: 'Perhaps a black girl, with super looks, preferably Jewish or Muslim, who speaks Spanish.'

It was a joke, I think, but it speaks volumes.

*

Back in Suzuka the BAR team were embroiled in a situation that illustrated Formula One's eagerness to tap into Asian markets. After two weeks of rumours, the 1997 world champion Jacques Villeneuve had left BAR when it was confirmed he would be replaced in 2004 by Japanese driver Takuma Sato. Villeneuve was due to leave at the end of the season, but refused to partake in the final race. He had watched his home circuit, Montreal, wiped off the F1 calendar due to tobacco-advertising laws and now he had fallen prey to international commercial interests.

BAR had originally been the brainchild of Villeneuve and his agent Craig Pollock. Arriving in 1999, it was funded by British American Tobacco to the tune of $25 million a year, with Honda supplying the engines. As both Villeneuve's agent and boss, Pollock effectively negotiated his client's salary with himself, hence Villeneuve's massive $18 million a year. But in December 2001 Pollock was dismissed, having amassed debts of more than $150 million.

The management brought in David Richards and Villeneuve was robbed of his closest ally. When Villeneuve's contract expired at the end of 2003, Richards decided it was time to bring in some new blood.

'If an organization doesn't live up to its expectations,' he said, 'you have to change things and it was the end of Jacques's contract. It was the opportunity to make that change.'

Takuma Sato was the answer. The twenty-six year old began karting in 1996 and a year later entered Honda's Suzuka Racing School. He graduated top of his class and with backing from Honda moved to Europe to race in Formula Vauxhall Junior, then Formula Opel. In 2000 he competed in Formula Three, taking third place in the British championship, and in 2001 he won the title. That same year he was contracted to Honda and soon became the BAR Honda test driver.

In 2002 Sato joined Jordan Honda and quickly gained a reputation as a liability after he became the first rookie to crash in Melbourne; ran into team-mate Fisichella in Malaysia; spun off in Barcelona; was hit by Nick Heidfeld in Austria; crashed into Raikkonen in Monza; spun off in Monte Carlo; retired with a blown-up engine at Silverstone; and spun off in Magny-Cours. In the final race of the season in Japan he came a surprising fifth.

Eddie Jordan counted the cost of Sato's accidents, but said publicly that he wanted to keep the Japanese driver. Honda terminated their agreement with Jordan to focus solely on providing engines to BAR and once again Sato found himself appointed as the BAR Honda test driver. When Villeneuve refuse to drive at Suzuka, Honda found themselves in an ideal situation: here was a Japanese driver making his 2003 debut in Japan.

A year that started with Villeneuve publicly deriding team-mate Jenson ended with Button promoted to team leader and Villeneuve leaving under a cloud of anger and resentment. In the fifteen races that they had both driven, Jenson out-qualified Villeneuve eight times to seven and the Brit finished the season in ninth place with seventeen points, while the Canadian finished sixteenth with six points. However, Villeneuve retired with mechanical failures in eight races.

Nevertheless, F1 magazines and websites were inundated with people mourning Villeneuve's unceremonious exit.

'Jacques will be sorely missed,' wrote a fan in *Autosport* magazine. 'His irreverent, non-PC style was a treat and his ability, skill and courage marked him out as one of the best of the current generation of drivers.'

However, I couldn't help noticing that the vast majority of comments, from inside and outside the sport, lamented the loss of Villeneuve's 'personality', rather than his driving skills. It was an ignominious end to his F1 career.

Fresh-faced Sato was immediately paraded in front of the global media.

'I'm just so excited I can't believe it,' he said. 'Obviously I haven't racing since Suzuka last year – twelve months – but, erm, I'm totally confident in the car and do decent job, I hope.' He seemed utterly unaware that his appointment was so controversial.

On Friday morning Button's engine blew up in practice and although there wasn't a shred of evidence to support it, the whispers began immediately that it had been a deliberate attempt by the engine manufacturers to make Sato look good.

'That was handy for Honda, wasn't it?' observed one journalist.

Shuhei Nakamoto, Honda's engineering director, issued the following statement: 'We are sorry that Jenson couldn't show his true potential due to lack of running-time this morning, caused by an engine failure. Takuma did a good job under the pressure of his first attempt at one-lap qualifying, which is exactly what we expected, having worked closely with him over the last few years.'

Nevertheless, in Saturday qualifying Button took ninth spot with Sato 0.4 seconds behind in thirteenth.

Michael Schumacher has started on pole in Suzuka every year since 1998, but in 2003 the grid positions were ultimately decided by the weather. Rubens Barrichello enjoyed the tail end of the drier conditions, conscientiously securing pole before the last six drivers began to suffer in the rain.

Jarno Trulli was hoping to match his team-mate Alonso's win in Hungary and after running fastest on Friday was hopeful of starting at the front. But as he came out last on Saturday his hopes were washed away by a downpour that convinced him to abandon any qualifying attempt and start the race from the pits.

Schumacher and Raikkonen both did their flying laps in the wet, but Ferrari's Bridgestone tyres coped less admirably with the conditions, placing Schumacher in an unprecedented P14. Title-contender Raikkonen managed eighth.

'It could have been worse,' smiled Schumacher afterwards. 'Kimi might have got a dry run.'

His main concern now was getting away safely from among the less-experienced drivers near the back. All he had to do was finish eighth for his one point, but if he didn't, the title would still be his as long as Raikkonen didn't win. Barrichello was given team orders to go out and beat the 'Iceman'.

This was it. The final race of the year, in which Schumacher could either take a record sixth world title or hand the baton on to the pale-faced Finn who talks without moving his lips. Sato was elbowed into the path of Martin Brundle, who was doing his usual grid-walk. From beneath a wide-brimmed baseball cap, the youngster smiled: 'I want a happy race.'

They all got away cleanly under an ominous grey sky, watched by a 155,000 sell-out crowd waving their new BAR and *Taku* flags. Villeneuve was already a fading memory.

Schumacher gained two places and Montoya got the better of Rubens part-way round the first lap, leaving the Brazilian to fend off the aggressive Renault of Alonso. Schumacher was playing it safe, watching as Sato picked off Justin Wilson.

The Ferrari's every move was scrutinized for possible slip-ups. Schumacher overtook Wilson on lap 4 and two laps later took a peek down the inside of Sato. He made a half-hearted attempt at overtaking, but his reticence cost him his nosecone as he snagged the BAR gearbox. He limped into the pits.

Spoiling Schumacher's party would have made Sato public enemy number one, but Michael was soon out again, hunting down the eighth place that was currently forty seconds away from him with forty-two laps to go.

Montoya started to coast and eventually dropped out with a hydraulics problem. Barrichello moved back to first, but Alonso was breathing down his neck, knowing that he also had one less pit stop to complete and 'sensing a win', as he explained later. But as this thought crossed his mind his engine failed and he had to pull onto the grass verge. Alonso climbed over the safety rail and repeatedly thumped his gloved fist on the corrugated iron. It was an image that confirmed the Spaniard as a future world champion. Meanwhile, Schumacher was calmly picking his way through the field.

After his third and final pit stop he rejoined the track and had a strong out-lap before squeezing in front of his brother as Ralf exited from his final stop. Ferrari breathed a sigh of relief: their prodigal son was finally in eighth position.

The Schumachers sat behind Da Matta's Toyota, but Ralf was twitching to overtake. Three quarters of the way down the pit Ralf made his move, but Michael squeezed him towards the wall at 180 mph and the younger brother was forced to concede. Ralf was now determined not to cut Michael any slack – regardless of what was at stake. Michael was watching Ralf in his mirrors when Da Matta braked slightly early, triggering Michael into a wheel lock and a quick shift to the left. Ralf responded, his wheels also locked and the pair ran off the circuit in tandem. Michael rejoined behind Da Matta and Ralf sloped off for a new nose.

Michael was in eighth and Raikkonen was a distant second behind Barrichello. But Ferrari couldn't relax just yet. If the rain that was forecast decided to make an appearance, Raikkonen could catch Barrichello by three seconds per lap and Schumacher could slip dangerously backwards.

David Coulthard played by his team's rules and stayed behind Raikkonen, despite setting a lap record a full second faster than his team-mate.

Jenson Button endured a long battle with Jarno Trulli, but held him off to take an excellent fourth place. Button's new team-mate Sato, who spent his formative years training at the Suzuka Racing School, was at home on the Japanese track and managed sixth place to give BAR a double dose of points that earned them fifth place in the constructors' championship – the 'best of the rest' prize. The home crowd went wild for their Taku. I wondered if Villeneuve was watching at home.

Barrichello's victory, Raikkonen's second place and Schumacher's eighth led a jubilant Ferrari team to lean over the pit wall, waving and giving the thumbs-up to their all-conquering hero. For everyone else, it was something of an anticlimax, as Schumacher freely admitted.

'Usually I have won my title by winning my race,' he said, 'and here I am having finished eighth.'

Unbelievably, he wasn't invited onto the podium and was nowhere to be seen when Barrichello, Raikkonen and Coulthard received their trophies. An elated, exhausted, victorious Schumacher was the final image the whole world wanted to see. Sport is defined by such moments: the tears, the exultation and the relief that are shared by the onlookers. But F1 fans were deprived of this sight. Television broadcasts across the world went to commercial breaks. The official presentation ceremony took place in Monaco two months later in front of 700 people – corporate sponsors, FIA and F1 officials. Fans would never see this untelevised event.

Despite all of the rule changes aimed at undermining the dominance of Schumacher and Ferrari, despite all the ill-will towards the team that had made Formula One 'boring' and despite huge advances by Williams and McLaren, 2003 was once again Michael Schumacher's year. He summed it up himself at the press conference.

'How many people wrote us off?' he asked. 'How many people wrote things about us, outspoken things, and here we are. We're back. And we never give up. We are always there. We always fight. It's just a huge big family and we are all proud to be part of it.'

11

Conclusion

Schumacher's victory was not a popular one. Team directors issued the usual congratulatory statements. 'This has been a fitting end to a great season,' announced Renault's Pat Symonds. 'Well done to Michael and Ferrari,' stated Williams's Patrick Head; and Norbert Haug from Mercedes said, 'At least he can't say we made it easy for him.' But team-mate Barrichello was the only driver to be heard congratulating Schumacher on his sixth world title. 'What Michael has done today,' he said, 'is a fantastic achievement.'

The F1 community has a long, merciless memory and Schumacher's misdemeanours in the early years have not been forgotten: his 1994 crash with Damon Hill, which took them both out of the race and handed Schumacher the championship; the 'arrogance' of his manner in 1995; his disqualification from the 1997 standings for driving Jacques Villeneuve off the track; and the audacity of finishing every 2002 race on the podium.

It seems that Ferrari, winning their fifth consecutive constructors' title, had also committed offences deemed unforgivable by other teams: the controversial tactics of Austria 2002 – giving an orchestrated victory to Schumacher at the expense of Barrichello – had handed their rivals a stick with which they were still happy to beat them a year later. And, of course, they hadn't been forgiven for achieving nine one-two finishes the previous year, with an impudent 87.7 per cent reliability record in 2002.

There was little recognition of the fact that Schumacher had spent the season clawing his way back from behind, against a seriously improved opposition. Resentment and jealousy, sponsorship pressure and paranoia had settled on his victory like a corroding dust. Another Schumacher win wouldn't help Formula One shed its 'predictable' image.

'Schumacher's record sixth title is a good story,' said Jackie Stewart, 'but there's a feeling of "been there, done that".'

McLaren boss Ron Dennis chose to highlight Schumacher's 'moments of indiscretion' and announced: 'I want him to race until 2006 or beyond, so that we can beat him.'

Four times world champion Frenchman Alain Prost joined the debate about Schumacher's possible retirement. 'To get a seventh [title] will take him a lot of motivation,' he said. 'I don't believe in Michael winning another title.'

This was the thirty-four-year-old German's thirteenth year in Formula One, but few beyond his own team were queuing up to shake his hand.

At least fans, teams, drivers, journalists and commentators were unanimous about one thing: the rule changes, however artificial, had resulted in the most exciting championship showdown for perhaps twenty years.

The TV audience numbers had climbed back up; although ITV's highest-ever viewing figure – recorded during the Brazilian Grand Prix – was largely due to the broadcast running over and *Coronation Street* fans switching on, only to find aquaplaning cars in São Paulo. McLaren's Ron Dennis and Frank Williams had both expressed fears that the rule changes could 'seriously diminish [Formula One] as a spectacle', but they were happy to eat their words – a rare occurrence indeed.

F1 aficionados applauded this 'classic season'. *Autocourse* annual called it 'One of the best seasons in recent memory, which happily was reflected by revived fan interest and steadily rising viewing figures'.

A combination of luck, weather and tactics had resulted in a close contest that might just keep people interested and would therefore be more appealing to big corporations, tobacco sponsors and advertisers with deep pockets. 2003 will also be remembered as the year in which Formula One took steps to launch itself onto an even bigger global stage.

The European Union's tobacco-advertising ban was a brave and costly move that signposted a new resolve. Since 1990, when the EU proposed a Europe-wide ban on tobacco sponsorship, the WHO (which described F1 as a 'non-stop commercial' for cigarettes) have been battling against the tobacco companies – who claim not to encourage people to start smoking, but to persuade them to change brands. The EU's ban on tobacco advertising will come into effect in July 2005. The precise value of F1's tobacco sponsorship is difficult to ascertain, but is believed to be $300 million a year. Meanwhile, seventy countries have signed up to the WHO's Anti-Tobacco Treaty to establish 'a comprehensive ban of all tobacco advertising, promotion and sponsorship', although only two have ratified the deal. The agreement will come into force as soon as 40 of the selected 192 countries have ratified the deal. This will take some time and a worldwide ban may not come into effect until 2015 or even 2020.

At the end of 2003 the British government introduced a new law targeting anybody 'carrying on business' related to the promotion of tobacco in the UK. BAR, Jordan, McLaren and Williams all have offices in England and would therefore be liable for prosecution. Team principals could face two years in prison. Some members of the British press reacted unsympathetically, with columnist Patrick Collins hoping that Formula One would 'vanish in a puff of smoke'. 'Some of us,' he went on 'would raise a glass if they all decided to decamp, taking their garish, clamorous, polluting apology for a sport with them.'

F1 management have reacted to tobacco restrictions by removing Grands Prix affected by the legislation from the championship, thereby holding European nations to ransom, rather than look for ways round the predicament. For the sport to lose the evocative Spa-Francorchamps race was a shame, but a victory for the anti-smoking lobby. However, by the end of the 2003 season, it had been reinstated. A new Belgian government reneged on the deal to lead the EU in the fight against cigarettes and passed legislation that authorized tobacco advertising in events of 'world importance'. The F1 crowd was let back in to play.

After 1 October 2006 Australia will no longer permit Formula One tobacco sponsorship and it remains to be seen whether Melbourne will be erased from the World According to Formula One. Canada reacted swiftly to its removal from the season, with both the federal and Quebec governments stumping up $6 million each as part of a $23 million deal to keep the Montreal race. Every team receives $2 million compensation, regardless of whether they have tobacco sponsors or not. Many

Canadians are furious about footing the bill through their taxes and increased ticket prices.

Such anti-smoking measures have caused Formula One to tap in to virgin motor-sport territories and drive the tobacco brands into new towns. 2004 would see the arrival of China and Dubai, but shortly after announcing confirmation of the Chinese Grand Prix, the Shanghai press reported that the race had yet to be given clearance to run with tobacco branding. China's 1994 advertising law states: 'The setting up of tobacco advertisements in public places, including all kinds of waiting rooms, cinemas and theatres, meeting rooms and halls, sports stadiums, etc., is banned.' However, the Chinese have made exceptions for tobacco advertising in football and volleyball; and the deputy general manager of the Shanghai International Circuit, Yu Zhifei, is seeking a government 'franchise' to permit the legal appearance of tobacco brands. However, China is poised to ratify the WHO's Anti-Tobacco Treaty in 2004 and might not make an exception for Formula One. But in a defiant tone that suggests he'll fit right in with the F1 crowd, Yu Zhifei retorted: 'Chinese people are wise enough to deal with such matters and we will achieve our goal.'

Meanwhile in the Middle East, while Bernie Eccleston has been glad-handing billionaires keen to host a Grand Prix, Arab governments have begun to adopt stringent new rules to limit and discourage smoking. Despite the fact that many of these governments earn vast profits from tobacco monopolies, they are facing up to the fact that tobacco kills and have implemented more sophisticated means of data collection to quantify the scale of the problem. They also appear to have the backing of the public: because although Arab men are more likely to smoke than their European brothers, an overwhelming 96 per cent of the Dubai population supports a ban on smoking in public places, according to a study by the PR section at Dubai municipality. Nevertheless, a news story that emerged during the off-season suggests that Ecclestone has the right people on his side.

Wearing his trademark Harry Potter specs and holding aloft a hooded falcon, Ecclestone gave a rare smile for the cameras as he announced that he had been awarded the Bahrain Medal of the First Degree. This is the highest personal honour of the Bahrain kingdom and is reserved for heads of state or 'people who perform outstanding services or achievements'. It is awarded at the sole discretion of His Majesty the King Sheikh Hamad bin Isa Al Khalifa. The love-fest continued.

'Bahrain International Circuit will be one of the best in the world,' Ecclestone declared. 'The standard is so high, it's raised the bar so much...If I wasn't directly involved in F1 myself I'd be buying a ticket before they sell out!'

Without government pressures, cigarettes and Formula One could have a long future together. The absurdity of associating a physical sport with tobacco only further undermines its claims to be a bona fide sport. I spent much of my time in Formula One looking for 'sport', but found very little.

I might catch a glimpse of it in a tired Mark Webber, fuelling himself up with a plate of chicken and pasta on a Saturday evening; or Fernando Alonso, beating his fists as his car broke down once again; or Kimi Raikkonen muttering that second place meant nothing to him; Ralf Schumacher's aggressive duel with his brother in the final race of the season; Justin Wilson's talent for eating up cars in front of him at every start; Jenson Button's frustration at not being allowed to race in Monaco; and the cheers from the crowd at every driver's parade lap. These were small, temporary glimpses of something I recognized as a sport.

It is the fans and the drivers themselves who embody the last vestiges of sporting passion, ambition and accomplishment in Formula One. The desire to improve that Ayrton Senna felt in his go-kart lives on as a gleam in the eyes of Fernando Alonso. Emerson Fittipaldi's pride in representing his nation beats away in the heart of Rubens Barrichello. But more often that not, I saw the sport of F1 devoured by business.

Today's drivers are marginally less likely to have wealthy parents, but they must still bring considerable financial backing. As a result, Formula One is perilously close to a point at which it will no longer be able to claim its drivers are the best in the world. British competitor Ralph Firman waited for Jordan to confirm their drivers for 2004 and had to read that he had lost his seat on a website. By that time, most other options were closed to him. He admits that F1 without the world's best drivers is a 'real possibility', but hopes – perhaps naively – that 'if the world economy picks up, then maybe they won't have to pay for drivers.'

Bjorn Wirdheim is a talented Swedish competitor who dominated this year's F3000 championship, but was unable to find the requisite backing to buy him an F1 seat. Less than two months before the start of the 2004 season, however, Wirdheim benefited from a new FIA ruling insisting that F1 test drivers must have driven in no more than six Grands Prix in the last two seasons. He therefore qualified for the position at Jaguar. It is rumoured he will bring sponsorship from the telecommunications company Ericsson.

Justin Wilson, having traded his body on the stock exchange, eventually followed in the footsteps of Antonio Pizzonia and was replaced by Christian Klien, a twenty-year-old Austrian who just happens to bring with him £12 million from his personal sponsor, Red Bull. In fact, so keen were the Austrian drinks manufacturers to find young Klien a seat that they repeatedly upped their offer from an original £6 million.

'I certainly don't remember him from lower formula,' observed Ralph Firman of Klien. 'I don't know anything about him.'

In 2002 Klien was the German Formula Renault Champion and in 2003 he finished second in EuroF3. But he lacks experience, and youthful exuberance can be costly in Formula One. The best that his predecessor Wilson can now hope for is a drive in an American league, while searching for new backers.

'It's disappointing that I won't be driving for Jaguar,' he admitted, 'but I expected it, as there was nothing I could do about it. It's not as if it is about someone being quicker. There is nothing you can do unless you have got a huge company behind you willing to pump millions into your career.'

Of course, Jaguar's managing director David Pitchforth insists that the unknown Klien was hired solely on account of his 'talent' and 'potential': 'The fact that Christian brings sponsorship is a win-win situation,' he declared, although maybe not for the sport itself – and per-haps not for Klien, who is going onto a track where life-and-death decisions are taken at 200 mph.

In the continued search for competitors from within F1's 'virgin terri-tories', Minardi have established an agreement with the Algerian driver Nassim Sidi Said to assist Arab racing drivers. Promising newcomers will then work with Minardi's commercial development department to secure new Arab partners.

Russia, home to a new breed of entrepreneurial millionaire, is also an attractive prospect to Formula One and in the run-up to the 2004 season, Jordan were rumoured to be courting Russian driver Vitaly Petrov – a valuable commodity to leverage Russian backing. This new band of East European capitalists is looking for interesting ventures, and linking Petrov to the Jordan team pricked the ears of Chelsea Football Club's new owner Roman Abramovich. It was reported that he offered £150 million to Jordan after holding secret meetings with Eddie Jordan and hosting the Irishman in the director's box at Stamford Bridge during a game.

But after enjoying the extra publicity, the deal failed to materialize and Jordan was the last team to announce their 2004 driver line-up. Dutchman Jos Verstappen with $10 million of backing was considered, but eventually Italian Giorgio Pantani and the twenty-seven-year-old German driver Nick Heidfeld were appointed. The financial support they brought to the team has not been disclosed, but given Verstappen's sponsorship package it is likely to be considerable.

Meanwhile BMW Williams appointed the twenty-one-year-old unknown Ho Pinhg Tung as their new test driver. He won the 2003 Formula BMW Asia championship, but in Williams's pre-season testing at Jerez he was six seconds off the pace. The sponsorship potential in his homeland of China is gigantic, a fact that Frank Williams freely admits: 'I believe his engagement with the BMW Williams F1 team will stimulate valuable interest in one of the sport's few remaining virgin territories.'

So, don't be fooled into thinking Formula One showcases the twenty best drivers in the world – it doesn't. It offers a stage to those lucky enough to carry the logos of ambitious multinational corporations.

The avaricious manner in which drivers are selected only goes to show how the drivers themselves have been marginalized in the sport. Technology is normally cited as the main threat to an F1 driver's relevance, but that is increasingly matched by the undermining power of commercial politics. And during a race a 'safe second' is becoming increasingly preferable to a 'risky first'. The motor-racing ethos is now more business-oriented than ever before, which inevitably affects the way drivers drive. In fact, I was often surprised at how little power the drivers have in Formula One. They aren't even allowed grandstand tickets for their families on race day. They can lunch them as guests of the team, but they must watch the race on a silent screen in the motorhome. After the 2003 season, Kimi Raikkonen told journalist Bill Borrows, 'I love to drive, but I hate all that other shit that goes with it. There is so much bullshit around Formula One.'

More and more shackled by media and sponsorship obligations, hired and fired on funds rather than ability, the drivers are discovering that loyalty means nothing in Formula One. Before he was finally ousted from BAR, Jacques Villeneuve had to deal with one final moment of F1 madness. Inspired by Jenson Button's girlfriend Louise's appearance on BBC TV's *Fame Academy*, BAR boss David Richards suggested a televised 'shoot-out': a time-trial to determine the team's other driver for next season. The idea was discussed quite seriously, with eight drivers proposed for the winter event. Villeneuve was appalled as the last remnants of F1's credibility slipped away.

'Formula One is supposed to be a sport,' he reminded the world through the Press Association.

There is only one place where the drivers feel truly relaxed and only one time when they can talk to each other away from the eyes and ears of the paddock: the driver's 'parade lap' before a race.

'You'd be surprised,' explains Michael Schumacher, 'that's the area where we all talk to each other... and even amongst drivers where there appears to be no understanding, you take advantage of that moment and you try to clarify things. It's probably the best moment to try to qualify any accident or any moment you had in the previous Grand Prix.'

It's a moving oasis on the back of a truck where the politics doesn't count and the drivers feel more like sportsmen than pawns in someone else's financial game. The noisy crowd, the flapping flags, the adulation and respect – the sporting arena a million miles from the boardroom.

At least the drivers can now say their sport is safer than ever before. In 2003 there were several high-speed crashes, but no driver suffered lasting physical injuries. Testing, rather than racing, threw up the most serious incidents, with Montoya, Ralf Schumacher and Ralph Firman all getting intimate with tyre walls. Max Mosley's 1994 policy of 'zero mortality' has been achieved – for now at least.

'Zero morality' should perhaps be their new cause for concern.

F1 fans have not only been turned off by Ferrari's domination of the last few seasons, they have begun to sense that they are being cheated by a self-policing business that claims to be the 'greatest sports event in the world', but is in fact a made-for-TV, 90-minute advert for car and tobacco companies.

After three years in Formula One I do now enjoy watching the races. I'm not enamoured enough to set the alarm for 4 a.m., but I doggedly avoid the results until watching the recorded event. Knowing the drivers, seeing them battle against every hurdle and unjust decision off the track, empathizing with their anxious families, I have come to see the humanity of Formula One that is all too often hidden behind the technology, commercial interests and masculine swagger. But I am under no illusion about the animal I am watching every other Sunday afternoon between March and October.

Sport plays a vital role in expressing and illustrating our values. Fair play and sportsmanship are learned on the rounders pitch, the running track, the football field and the netball court. Does Formula One embody social values of which we should be proud? I have to conclude that it does not.

Ironically, a sport that is based on ruthless competition and self-serving ambition isn't all about coming first. The motto of more than half of the teams could easily be 'it's not the winning but the taking part that counts'. Except in this instance, perhaps, 'it's not the winning but the headline-grabbing, money-making that counts' is more apt. They aren't in it to win it, which is why Formula One is a business and not a sport.

F1 is not short of competitive instincts, but it is very much a self-contained world, existing only for itself and for the sponsors and hosts who create the events every fortnight. If we plucked Formula One off the planet, the impact would be pretty minimal. It doesn't offer the sort of 'way-out-of-the-ghetto' routes that we find in boxing, football or American basketball. There are no free college scholarships, no community purpose and very little charitable contribution. Formula

One is to sport as cosmetic surgery is to general practice: it doesn't affect anyone apart from those who are prepared to pay for it.

At the end of the season the drivers headed off for luxury holidays before recommencing testing, promotional activity and visits to the new tracks. In November Michael Schumacher took part in a 'karting-on-ice' charity event organized by Ferrari's parent company Fiat. The man who earned more than $60 million in 2003 donated $1 million to UNESCO. His manager Willi Weber presented the cheque at a ceremony in Germany.

Mark Webber used his time and growing fame to launch his own charity. The inaugural Mark Webber Challenge involved a gruelling ten days of kayaking, cycling and trekking through the Tasmanian jungle in aid of two children's causes.

But perhaps the most surprising development was announced on Jordan's website. They were going to use part of their car to 'promote a number of diverse international, humanitarian, charitable and cultural messages'. The move was initiated by His Highness the Crown Prince Sheikh Salman bin Hamad bin Isa Al Khaifa of Bahrain, who had paid handsomely to use the space in that way.

'I'm proud that Bahrain is associated with this fresh and inspired way of communicating sensitive yet significant issues,' he announced. The first race of the new season in Melbourne would see the yellow cars sporting a small dove of peace.

While the rest of the paddock partied the night away in the karaoke bar, the journalists were filing their last race copy of the season from Japan. A willingness to report on the sport – and the freedom to do so – is hugely important to Formula One. Bernie Ecclestone bought *F1* magazine in 2003. But former employees have complained that although this is the 'official' F1 magazine, they were denied access to drivers and were 'kept out of the loop'.

'The only time we'd ever hear what Bernie was saying or where he was visiting,' said one, 'was via a website which would always quote Bernie from a "statement". We were never given the statements. Ever!'

Ecclestone initially appointed Matt Franey, a well-liked motor-sport editor who resigned after six months. *F1* magazine then began to resemble an in-flight brochure in which many articles contained a barely concealed business agenda. The first issue of 2004 contained a ghostwritten piece by 'Jenson Button' about his visit to the Bahrain track. It contained clumsy plugs for the construction company Tilke GmbH among reassurances that the sand won't cause the teams any problems ('Tilke's men have worked endlessly on trying to produce the grippiest track surface in the world') and desperate appeals to potential ticket buyers: 'I expect there to be a similar atmosphere to the Monaco Grand Prix' (which is hard to imagine, as Bahrain is in the middle of the desert).

Consumers thought they were buying a colourful storybook of the latest F1 news, but they were actually shelling out £3.70 for a series of press releases and advertisements and sales fell. Seven months after Franey left, Ecclestone informed his staff that the magazine was closing with immediate effect. Along with Ecclestone's FOCA TV venture, it was a rare business failure.

*

Image is everything in Formula One. The manufactured glamour of the sport and its associations make it attractive not only to sponsors, but to corporate moneymen who spend thousands of pounds in the hope that some of the high life rubs off on them.

It is the ultimate male fantasist's sport: fast cars, expensive kit, global jet-setting and beautiful women with spray-on smiles. It's a seventeen-stage ego stroke, and there will always be men keen to buy into it. But celebrities beware. You never know what people are saying behind your back.

Sitting in the bar of Coulthard's Columbus Hotel at this year's Monaco Grand Prix, three integral figures from Formula One were enjoying a drink while recounting the day's activities.

'That Nick Rhodes guy,' said one. 'What a wanker.'

'Yeah, I know. He may have been in Duran Duran, but never in all my time have I had to deal with such a pretentious twat,' laughed another.

'No. He looks like Snow White with a dick!'

'He's the scruffiest bastard I've ever seen on a yacht.'

At that moment they heard a slow handclap – as Nick Rhodes leant around from the adjoining booth.

Back-stabbing is not uncommon in Formula One and its television arm is no exception. After being warned, 'they're not going to have two women working on Formula One,' I'm glad to say that they did find room for both of us, although the assumption that we were somehow in competition never really went away.

When I left, a fellow presenter admitted: 'We felt you didn't deserve to be there, because you weren't an F1 fan.'

Several team members and journalists have since divulged that I was a 'victim of a dirty tricks campaign'.

'Some of your colleagues didn't want you there,' said one, 'so they didn't exactly encourage the teams' PR people to accommodate you.'

Formula One is a purveyor of chauvinistic values. It's the only place I've been where men still apologize if they swear in front of a woman. Bizarrely, they think it is polite to say 'Oops, sorry, ladies present,' but it always feels patronizing. For as long as the men continue to think like that, there will never be a female driver in Formula One.

In March 2004 Jaguar Racing announced that they had invited Sarah Kavanagh to become a member of their extended driver squad, alongside Webber, Klien and test driver Wirdheim. Jaguar operations director Sir John Allison stated that Sarah would 'be under contract for both driving and promotional activities'. The conditions stipulated that she must drive in Formula Three and 'at the end of the season', said Allison, 'assuming her performance and progress so justified, we would give her an extended F1 test, with the real prospect of taking her on as one of our F1 drivers.' Sarah was also invited to bring £1 million to the team. However, once Jaguar had enjoyed the extra publicity surrounding the story, the deal fell through.

While Louise competed in *Fame Academy*, Button's team-mates added a new sign to his car: *Louise's Boyfriend*, just like the badges worn by the proud families in the TV studio. They were gently poking fun, but the joke worked because it's so rare for a driver to be upstaged by his partner. Few people at BAR expected 'Jenson's Girlfriend' to pursue her own career. At the end of the 2003 season, Louise found a week in her busy schedule and they jetted off to Barbados. The lad from Frome got down on one knee and presented her with a diamond ring. Soon after this romantic episode, it was also announced that Renault boss Flavio

Briatore was to become a father with his girlfriend the German lingerie model Heidi Klum, twenty-three years his junior.

By anyone's standards Flavio had had a good year. Sleeping with Heidi Klum and finding time to nurture his prodigal sons Fernando Alonso and Jarno Trulli into fourth position in the constructors' championship is impressive and commands wide respect in Formula One. Flavio is one of the names most often cited as integral to the running of Formula One once Bernie Ecclestone retires. Ecclestone and the Italian playboy who helped to establish the Benetton clothing brand in 1977 have a great deal of mutual respect.

The future of a sport so closely controlled by one man is forever in question and Ecclestone once joked that he has been able to hold the whip for so long because he has made all of the team bosses into multi-millionaires. And though many would hate to admit it, it is probably true.

The Concorde Agreement determines the division of F1 revenue and details the financial arrangement between the teams and the FIA. The particulars are closely guarded and asking about it only elicits frosty stares. The Agreement was devised in 1981 during a thirteen-hour meeting at the FIA headquarters and states the financial arrangement between the teams and the FOA, headed by Ecclestone. Each circuit's promoter pays Ecclestone more than $10 million a year and he guarantees them every team and driver at their race. The teams receive a cut of this money in prize funds, as well as a percentage of TV-rights revenue. The Concorde Agreement expires in 2008 and during the last few seasons Formula One had been threatened by a breakaway world championship.

The Grand Prix World Championship (GPWC) company is comprised of a group of leading manufacturers – including Ferrari, Ford, BMW, Daimler Chrysler and Renault – who want more control over the sport. However, two months after the end of the 2003 season, *Autosport* magazine announced that an agreement had been reached which effectively ended the GPWC threat.

The new deal would add $12 million in revenue to each of the ten teams by distributing a bigger share of the TV income. They currently receive 43 per cent of the TV-rights money (30 per cent to the FIA and

23 per cent to FOM), which equates to 25 per cent of the total commercial income. But vitally, the new deal means that three directors on the board of the F1 holding company SLEC (JP Morgan, Lehman Brothers and Bayerische Landesbank) will be from the GPWC, thereby giving the manufacturers more influence over the sport's long-term future.

This reconciliation offers a secure future for Formula One (until 2015), but it also guarantees the survival of small, independent teams like Minardi and Jordan. The sport needs these whipping boys to come last. Without them, Jaguar or Toyota might finish at the back in every race. No major manufacturer wants to back the team that comes last.

The new contract (which includes an extension of the Concorde Agreement) states that Mr B. Ecclestone remains in charge of the sport's commercial-right's holder, Formula One Administration. This means that Ecclestone has bought the lease (from the FIA) giving him the right to sell Formula One through TV and radio deals, images, videos, computer games and all associated 'F1' or 'Formula One' equivalents for the next 100 years. He is attempting to trademark 'F1' and 'Grand Prix', but has so far been unsuccessful.

Some may say that this new agreement signals a more 'inclusive' power structure in Formula One, but if history is any guide, Ecclestone looks set to stay firmly at the helm of the phenomenon he has created. This induces anxiety among those who feel powerless to counter Ecclestone's absolute rule and there are many who would like to see him toppled from power. His critics call for him to devolve more of his power to the teams and to distribute the TV revenue more generously – which he now appears to be doing. But the big question remains – who on earth would replace him? There isn't a clear line of succession and it's unlikely he will ever retire. Ecclestone has two daughters, but one can hardly imagine him handing F1 over to a woman.

I had lunch with his nineteen-year-old daughter before starting work on this book. Tamara is strikingly pretty – slim with long, golden hair and a shy smile. She wore baggy, hipster trousers like any fashion-savvy teenager and seemed typically self-conscious, timid even. Then I saw a black tattoo snaking up her lower back and suspected there was probably more to her than met the eye.

She was enjoying working at *F1* magazine, but had to leave to attend a make-up course she had previously signed up to. She would have preferred to continue at the magazine, but the course had cost a few hundred pounds and her dad wasn't going to let her waste money like that. But mostly I remember her chain-smoking all the way through lunch – lighting up whether others were eating or not. Despite his success at selling cigarettes all over the world, Ecclestone despises smoking.

'God, Bernie absolutely hates smoking,' one of his former employees told me. 'He goes mad about Tamara smoking so much.'

Some people in Formula One find Ecclestone's close relationship with FIA president Max Mosley problematic. As one long-time F1 enthusiast and pundit explained: 'When the president of the international governing body is in league with the competitors' organization it is inevitably a bit worrying.' But having mingled in the F1 world, I cannot see how the sport can be governed any other way. There are so many people with so many different interests that one person must rule the roost. Trying to agree on anything – from qualifying rules to the type of biscuit offered to dignitaries – would be a complete nightmare. Mosley agrees.

'I would hate to see it all go down the drain,' he said, 'because it was badly managed. If all the teams owned it they would destroy it. They can't agree on anything.'

Talking to the *Independent* newspaper in July 2003, Mosley summed up the current situation: 'My term of office ends in 2005. One should never stay too long and I am very sensitive to that. As for Bernie, he could stop working tomorrow; he has trousered a significant amount of money. He doesn't do it for the money and neither do I. So why does he still do it? Because he derives pleasure from it, and he will continue until such point as he prefers to sit on his boat. He may even go on for as long as the old boy Ferrari did, into his nineties. There is an argument that it keeps you alive. So Bernie may be there for a very long time, but I may not be there for much longer.'

There is effectively nothing to stop somebody else building a series of racing circuits and convincing teams, drivers and officials to become involved in a new championship – a political revolution of sorts. The lesson that history teaches us, however, is that after revolutions those who take charge reveal the same flaws as those who were overthrown – and often surpass them.

At the end of 2003, Formula One is secure. The arrival of a new team would, however, be the most persuasive sign that its future is safe. It is rumoured this might just happen in either 2005 or 2006, but that is probably just a PR story.

At present, the system is designed to make newcomers extremely unlikely. A $48 million deposit paid to the FIA is the first requirement. Secondly, any new team would have to survive three years without the financial benefits of the Concorde Agreement. Only then would they be allowed to join the existing ten teams – up to a maximum of twelve teams. It really is the strictest private members' club in the world.

But why is it made so difficult? The team bosses would like to limit the number of competitors to ten. That way, they earn a greater share of F1's income. And, as we've seen, Formula One isn't predisposed to welcome new people. A new team might upset the already delicate status quo. So with bare-minimum annual costs of $30 million, on top of $48 million to the FIA, the potential takers are pretty limited.

However, in February 2004 Bernie Ecclestone told an Australian newspaper that reducing costs to the teams was vital.

'The amount that teams spend is vastly different,' he said. 'It is impossible for the Jordans of the world to compete with teams such as McLaren.' Though he also admitted that the richest teams had no intention of increasing the comparative strength of the competition.

Silverstone's inclusion on the 2004 F1 calendar did not bring an end to the tension between Ecclestone and the circuit's owners, the British Racing Drivers' Club. Ecclestone said that he still didn't see a future for the race in Formula One and Jackie Stewart responded by calling for government backing. This was vital, he said because of 'the massive financial power and draw of those countries trying to get into the Formula One calendar'. Ticket prices for the British race remained high – from £99 to £229 for adults to watch just the race (£95–£109 for children) – but in an attempt to sell tickets early, fans were encouraged to buy before 1 March and get all three days for between £219–269 – still the price of a package holiday.

'I want a British Grand Prix,' said Bernie Ecclestone, 'but I want it to be the best. We are supposed to be the best in this country and this should be the best Grand Prix in the world.' Competition for that title now seems almost as important as the championship itself.

At the start of 2004 Bahrain appears to be leading the pack. However, it almost stumbled not long after the calendar was announced, when the Foreign Office warned that the race could be a target for a terrorist attack. Ecclestone shrugged off the threat.

'Many of us live in London,' he said, 'which is constantly under threat from terrorists, but it doesn't stop us going around the place every day.'

A major change to the diary is that Brazil rather than Japan is now the final race of the season. The community grumbles that São Paulo won't be as much fun for last-night parties, but Ecclestone wants to recreate the Sunday afternoon 'tea-time' slot that brought in thirteen million viewers. I guess nobody told him about *Coronation Street*.

At times, the 2003 season came dangerously close to being a mere platform for tyre manufacturers. The Michelin teams – McLaren, Williams and Renault – were at a distinct advantage, while Bridgestone struggled to satisfy their users, including Ferrari and BAR. Michelin's Pierre Dupasquier blamed his rival's prioritizing of Ferrari above their other teams.

'The mistake Bridgestone have made is putting all their efforts into trying to ensure Ferrari stay world champions,' he said. 'When the competition gets closer, you have to know whether it's the tyre or the car that's good or bad. We give equal treatment to all the teams we supply, so when four or five cars are all getting good results we can evaluate things.'

Jenson Button summed up this rather depressing situation: 'You can spend as much money as you want on a car or an engine, but if you bolt on a set of tyres that don't work, that's it.'

The problem is, handing a trophy to a tyre and spraying it with champagne wouldn't look quite so good on TV.

I have made some good friends in the world of Formula One. As *Telegraph* journalist Kevin Garside admits, once one is no longer treated with suspicion, people began to reveal their true natures.

'I got to know their personalities and actually got to like them,' he says. Garside now enjoys working in Formula One, viewing its more frustrating attributes as idiosyncrasies that must be endured.

I will never be a 'petrol head'. Believe me – I have tried.

I've watched cars fly by in dangerous proximity, I've had my eardrums battered by the scream of super-powered engines and I've tried to understand what motivates someone to speed over tarmac at 200 mph in a carbon-fibre shell. But I still need convincing.

Critics of competition in sport object to the institutionalizing of negative attitudes – namely the primary goal of defeating an opponent. They argue that competition is either inherently immoral or reinforces socially undesirable attitudes. But they are in a minority – and thank God for that!

I love sport. Competition is healthy, natural and at the root of even the friendliest kick-about in the park. But the F1 playing field struck me as too imbalanced, impure and dishonest (to itself and its fans) to produce anything other than an empty commercial spectacle.

I understand the passion with which people devote their lives to shaving milliseconds off their performance. But Formula One has driven further and further away from being a true sport. I found myself feeling sorry for the drivers (and I never thought I'd say that about twenty-something millionaires). They grew up wanting to be world champions and found themselves at the mercy of company directors.

Ancient artefacts depicting sporting scenes speak of a deep-seated desire to push ourselves to the edge of physical and psychological endurance. The last forty years have seen technology advance at a rate that divides both commentators and fans. There are those for whom technology is at the heart of Formula One, the very thing that defines elite motor racing – and there are those purists who see it as downplaying driver skill, as well as closing the door to drivers with a bit of backing and a lot of courage.

I wanted to love Formula One, but my reservations only deepened until I had no choice but to walk away. A blind passion for F1 helps most people survive inside the sport, from the exhausted waitresses to the stressed-out team bosses. And at the top of the pile is the awesome power of the Formula One brand and Formula One Administration.

The Save Albert Park Society in Melbourne never stood a chance. They are just one example of the smaller voices drowned out by the omnipresent din of money. They have a strong case against the Grand Prix being held in Albert Park, but in F1 David never beats Goliath. He can't even get close enough to take aim.

Formula One has come a long way from being a minority sport in the fifties – a sport populated by middle-class public-school boys and journalists who shared lifts with the competitors. Thanks to Bernie Ecclestone's vision and determination, it is now a TV spectacular and a global business enterprise that has also remained, essentially, a small, private community.

Its protagonists are few compared to other sports, which is perhaps why they are so extremely protective of their position. Paranoia and secrecy arise from fear. It doesn't matter if the intrigue, gossip, accusations and backbiting are unpleasant defining characteristics of Formula One or just an inevitable by-product of it. Either way, F1 is no fun to be around. My only regret is that I never did find out who listens to an engine noise CD.

*

Michael Schumacher began his winter training in earnest. Talk of retirement was laughed off as he set about his usual round of promotional events and physical preparation.

His win seemed not to have earned him any more friends in Formula One or, it appears, at home in Germany. The Germans voted for a cyclist as their annual Sports Personality of the Year – a guy called Jan Ullrich who had come back from a drugs ban to race in this year's Tour de France. Part-way up a mountain, Lance Armstrong fell off his bike and Ullrich stopped to wait for him. This small gesture of humanity won the hearts of his home fans.

The most enduring image I have of Michael Schumacher is in the Italian paddock one sunny afternoon. As always, he had to walk quickly, politely but firmly declining requests for photos, autographs or those who just wanted to chat. Beneath his baseball cap his eyes were focused on making it to his motorhome before being mobbed.

Then he caught sight of his wife. Corinna was chatting casually to a friend, seemingly unaware that her husband was around. Schumacher's face took on an expression the cameras never see. It was as if the turmoil and commotion around him had simply melted away. He walked purposefully over to Corinna, took her face in his hands and kissed her as though powerless to stop himself. He said nothing, but smiled at her and was gone. She resumed chatting as if nothing had happened – though she was smiling more broadly than before – and the paddock hustle and bustle struck up again.

All those people clamouring for a piece of Michael Schumacher had been left in no doubt as to who really owned him.

And I was glad to see it wasn't a sponsor.